INTERGROUP RELATIONS
AND LEADERSHIP

INTERGROUP
RELATIONS

Approaches and Research

JOHN WILEY AND SONS, INC.

New York   London

AND LEADERSHIP

in Industrial, Ethnic, Cultural,

and Political Areas

A PUBLICATION OF THE
INSTITUTE OF GROUP RELATIONS
THE UNIVERSITY OF OKLAHOMA

MUZAFER SHERIF, *Editor*

Library of Congress Catalog Card Number: 62–17470.
Printed in the United States of America.

THE AUTHORS

(The authors are listed according to the sequence of the chapters.)

MUZAFER SHERIF, Director, Institute of Group Relations, and Research Professor of Psychology, The University of Oklahoma.

ROBERT E. L. FARIS, Professor and Chairman, Department of Sociology, University of Washington.

RALPH M. STOGDILL, Professor and Research Associate, Bureau of Business Research, The Ohio State University.

ROBERT DUBIN, Research Professor of Sociology, University of Oregon.

ROBERT R. BLAKE, Professor of Psychology, The University of Texas.

JANE S. MOUTON, Assistant Professor of Psychology, The University of Texas.

LEWIS M. KILLIAN, Professor of Sociology, Florida State University.

S. STANSFELD SARGENT, Clinical Psychologist, Veterans Administration, Phoenix, Arizona.

OTTO KLINEBERG, Professor and Chairman, Department of Social Psychology, Columbia University.

ROBERT C. NORTH, Director, Studies of International Conflict and Integration, and Associate Professor of Political Science, Stanford University.

JAMES A. ROBINSON, Assistant Professor of Political Science, Northwestern University.

RAYMOND E. CRIST, Research Professor of Geography, The University of Florida.

DAVID H. FRENCH, Professor of Anthropology, Reed College.

ALAN R. BEALS, Assistant Professor of Anthropology, Stanford University.

NORMAN A. CHANCE, Assistant Professor of Anthropology, The University of Oklahoma.

THIS VOLUME IS DEDICATED TO

CORTEZ A. M. EWING (1896–1962)

RESEARCH PROFESSOR OF GOVERNMENT

AT THE UNIVERSITY OF OKLAHOMA, SCHOLAR

IN THE GREAT JEFFERSONIAN TRADITION,

WHO, AS CHAIRMAN OF THE SYMPOSIUM

AT WHICH THE ORIGINAL VERSIONS

OF THESE CHAPTERS WERE PRESENTED,

MADE IT A MEMORABLE EVENT FOR US.

PREFACE

The chapters of this book, devoted to one of the most crucial problem areas of our times, are the outcome of the fourth interdisciplinary lecture series in social psychology at The University of Oklahoma. The original papers, with one exception, were delivered by their authors and discussed by participants in the symposium, and were subsequently revised by the authors to constitute the chapters of this volume. Chapter 10, by David H. French, was written after the symposium was held in April, 1961.

The problem area is intergroup relations and leadership. The ramifications of this general problem area in specific spheres of living are revealed in the various chapters. It may not be too far off the mark to state that the various social science disciplines—and their respective preoccupations with particular aspects of intergroup relations—have developed more or less insulated pictures. In view of this predicament, the objective of the symposium was primarily interdisciplinary stocktaking and exchange of notes on theory, research, and possible practical implications in this complex problem area by active researchers from several social science disciplines.

An attempt is made in this volume, starting with Chapter 1, to conceive of the various specific problems encountered in relations between particular groups and their leaders as part processes of the intergroup system in question. Perhaps this attempt may prove to be a distinctive feature of the present volume.

Sincere thanks are due to my colleagues, Henry Angelino, Norman R. Jackman, Roger E. Nebergall, Nicholas Pollis, and Carolyn W. Sherif, for both taking the responsibilities of organizing and conducting the symposium, as members of the arrangements committee, and also for invaluable contributions to the discussions. Cortez A. M. Ewing, Research Professor of Government and a great supporter of the development of social psychology at the University, was chairman of the committee, coordinating the arrangements in such an effective manner that all participants could not help feeling grateful throughout the three days of fruitful give-and-take in the sessions and informal discussions that continued through late hours. Our work at this production stage of the book is saddened by his untimely death in March, 1962. We sorely miss his counsel.

The following colleagues contributed as chairmen of the various sessions of the symposium: N. Henry Pronko of the University of Wichita, Noel P. Gist of the University of Missouri, W. R. Hood of Texas College of Arts and Industries, Saul B. Sells of Texas Christian University, Robert W. Scofield of the State University of Oklahoma, and our colleagues in social science at the University of Oklahoma—Alfred E. Glixman, William E. Bittle, Norman R. Jackman, Roger E. Nebergall, and Jack E. Dodson. We are particularly indebted to Professor Noel P. Gist for contributing so significantly to a session at which the speaker could not participate due to sudden illness.

The alert cooperation of Mrs. Betty Frensley in typing and retyping the manuscripts and in other chores related to the preparation of the symposium and this volume is greatly appreciated. Thanks are extended to Lee O. Thayer, who helped in proofreading most of the chapters and preparing the subject index, and also to Mark MacNeil, George Sarkis, John Reich, Luther Elliott, and Richard Vallejo for help in various tasks.

Grateful acknowledgment is extended to the Group Psychology Branch, Office of Naval Research, for making this project possible through a grant for that purpose.

As in all the successive episodes of the developing program of the Institute of Group Relations for initiating and conducting research and for communication of theory and results, the symposium and present volume had the good fortune of support from President George L. Cross, whose policy of encouraging development in all aspects of human relations study is basic to these efforts. We are also appreciative of Dr. Pete Kyle McCarter's interest in the symposium, which went beyond administrative facilitation. Dr. Lloyd E. Swearingen again has our gratitude for his patient and effective hand, as in all such undertakings for over a decade.

It is with warm feeling that we extend our thanks to the authors of the various chapters, both for making the symposium a period of intellectual fermentation for all participants and for relieving the editor from most of the vexing problems which often are met in preparing a collaborative volume. Whatever lasting merit the volume may have is, of course, theirs, since a minimum of editorial prerogative was exercised in the final versions of their contributions.

From the inception of the project, Dr. Carolyn Wood Sherif, my wife, went with me through the chores of voluminous correspondence with contributors that are necessarily involved in an interdisciplinary venture of this sort, through writing Chapter 1, and through the arduous task of writing the editorial introductions to each chapter, articulating the high points of each and relating them to common threads. Crediting Chapter 1, as well as the editorial introductions, to my name alone reflects a bureaucratic tradition in our intellectual partnership, which has many times put me in the position of a figurehead in various of our publications.

MUZAFER SHERIF

Institute of Group Relations
Norman, Oklahoma
May 10, 1962

CONTENTS

I

PROBLEMS OF APPROACH AND THEORY

1 INTERGROUP RELATIONS AND LEADERSHIP: INTRODUCTORY STATEMENT

by Muzafer Sherif

This introductory statement to problems of intergroup relations and leadership will start by pointing them out—the safest step we can take, at the start, in approaching the study of complex human problems. Then, a little brush clearing will be done to prepare the ground for an adequate conception of intergroup relations. The implications of this conception for interdisciplinary research strategies conducive to generalizations pertinent to the actualities of various areas of the social scene will be mentioned. Leadership, delegation, representation, bargaining, decision making, and policy making will be viewed as part processes within the framework of group functioning. The statement will close with application of the foregoing formulations to assessment of effective steps in the reduction of prevailing intergroup conflicts.

Importance of Intergroup Relations in Human Affairs Today

Obviously, intergroup relations refer to states of friendship or hostility, cooperation or competition, alliance or enmity, peace or war between two or more groups and their respective members. Such states between groups have always been important and fateful in human affairs. History books have been written chiefly as records of them.

But today, we hear repeatedly from policy makers and analysts of current affairs that the very fate of human beings de-

3

pends on the state of relations between groups and blocks of
nations. The impact of these relations is reflected even in the
way our family expenditures are budgeted and our personal
goals are regulated relative to the uncertainties of the future.

Groups and nations are no longer closed systems. The internal affairs of groups and nations, the rise or fall of leaders are
demonstrably affected by the impact of their intergroup relations. This is being strikingly demonstrated in a study of the
recent presidential election we have completed on the West
Coast and in the Southwest. Guided by the hypothesis that
various campaign issues (such as foreign relations issues, peace
issue, farm, labor, and civil rights issues) would have different
weights for voters, we arranged for our samples to rank these
issues in order of their importance. The data indicate that
peace and foreign relations rank higher than other issues.

Demarcation of the Problem Area of Intergroup Relations

Since we have noted the importance of intergroup relations,
we can turn to the demarcation of the problem. What states
of friendship or hostility, what kind of positive or negative functional relations between human beings, are characteristic of
intergroup relations? This is not an idle question. Many technically excellent studies have fallen short in dealing with the
problem because they were not initially designed on the basis
of an adequate characterization of intergroup relations.

Not every friendly or unfriendly act toward others is a case
of intergroup relations. We have to differentiate those actions
which can properly be called intergroup behavior.

Let us start by specifying the main concepts involved. This
specification must begin with an adequate conception of the
key term "group" itself. We define a group as a social unit
(1) which consists of a number of individuals who, at a given
time, stand in more or less definite interdependent status or role
relationships with one another, and (2) which explicitly or implicitly possesses a set of values or norms of its own regulating
behavior of individual members, at least in matters of consequence to the group. Shared attitudes, shared sentiments, shared

aspirations and goals are related to and implicit in the common values or norms of the group. For, group norms are expected, and even ideal modes of behavior, defining for members the limits or latitude of acceptable behavior. Thus defined, a norm is not *necessarily* a statistical average of behaviors in a group. The expected or ideal modes of behavior defined by norms relate to motives and goals that members share in common, or concern the existence and perpetuation of the group itself, along with the reciprocal expectations that regulate the functioning of the organizational pattern.

The term "intergroup relations" refers to relations between two or more groups and their respective members. Whenever individuals belonging to one group interact, collectively or individually, with another group or its members in terms of their group identification, we have an instance of intergroup behavior.

The appropriate frame of reference for studying intergroup behavior is the functional relations between two or more groups, which may be positive or negative. The functional relationship between groups whose members perceive them as *in-groups* has properties of its own. These properties are generated during interaction between particular groups. Intergroup situations are not voids.

Though not independent of the relationships within the groups in question, *the characteristics of functional relations between groups cannot be deduced or extrapolated solely from the properties of relations prevailing among members within the group itself.* Prevailing modes of behavior within groups, in the way of cooperativeness and solidarity, or competitiveness and rivalry among members need not be the prevalent modes of behavior in their relations with other groups. Hostility towards out-groups may, at times, be proportional to the degree of solidarity within the group. Democracy at home need not imply democratic attitudes toward out-groups.

Some Blind Alleys in Intergroup Conceptions

In recent years, intergroup relations have sometimes been explained through analysis of individuals who have suffered unusual degrees of frustration, or who have received extensive authoritarian treatment in their early life histories. Such views are discussed and evaluated by Robert Faris in his chapter, "Interaction Levels and Intergroup Relations."

There is good reason to believe that some persons growing up under unfortunate life circumstances may become more intense in their prejudices and hostilities. But such cases are not the crux of the problem of intergroup relations. At best, they can explain the intensity of behavior in a given dimension. On the whole, established stereotypes of out-groups are not the doings of a few frantic or frustrated individuals.

When there is conflict between two groups, such as a strike or a war, it is usually the more responsible, the more talented, the more exemplary members of the group who are in control. Activities in conflict are conducted by individuals who can withstand the strains imposed by the conflict. When members of a group correctly or incorrectly perceive threat, unjust treatment, or invasion of their rights by another group, opinion in their group is consolidated, slogans are formulated, and decisions are made for effective measures—but not usually by a few neurotic or deviate individuals. Those recognized as the most responsible take the lead. Deviate personalities or frustrated members ordinarily exhibit their intense reactions within the latitudes for acceptable behavior established in their respective settings, which may include hostility toward other groups as well as sacrifice for one's own.

If intergroup behavior were first and foremost a matter of deviate behavior, it would not be the issue of vital consequence that it is today. I repeat: *Intergroup behavior is not primarily a problem of deviate behavior.* It is primarily a problem of participation by individual members within the social distance scale of their group in more stable times, and in the developing trends in relations between their group and others in periods of flux and change, such as that characteristic of our own times.

On the basis of UNESCO studies in India, Gardner Murphy (1953) concluded in his book, *In the Minds of Men,* that to be a "good" Hindu or a "good" Muslim implied believing all the nasty qualities and practices attributed by one's own group to the adversary. The "good" members, who usually constitute the overwhelming majority, remain deaf and dumb to favorable or correct information disseminated concerning their adversary.

On the whole, occasions for further conflicts arise by making social contacts and opening the avenues for communication.

It has been argued that aggressive behavior directed against other groups is a result of pent-up aggressive impulses accumulated by group members owing to their individual frustrations. If this be so, how can we explain the fact that acts of violence against other groups do not necessarily occur where the probability of individual frustrations is greatest?

Otto Klineberg, whose chapter in this volume deals with "Intergroup Relations and International Relations," asked penetrating questions in this regard in his survey of *Tensions Affecting International Understanding* (1950). He noted that white Brazilians are, on the whole, much more frustrated economically than white Americans, that economic standards in Brazil are much lower, that Brazilians, too, endure the fluctuations of the business cycle. He asked why, then, were there no lynchings of Brazilian Negroes? "This fact," Klineberg stated, "makes it clearly inadequate to explain aggression against the Negro, or in more general terms, hostility against other groups (which may take the form of war in extreme cases) entirely in terms of the aggressive impulses developed within the individual as a result of his frustrations" (p. 198).

Klineberg continued this line of questioning: "Why, if war is due to these factors within the individual, are the majority of individuals opposed to war? Why must they be made to fight? Why must every country, in seeking to build its army, have recourse to conscription?" (p. 199).

Modern warfare is conflict between modern states with definite organizations and value systems. As the English psychologist, Pear, noted in *Psychological Factors of Peace and War* (1950), a solely psychological theory of war "fails to distinguish between the aggressiveness of the warmakers, which can be very real indeed . . . and the attitudes of the general population" (p. 40).

L. F. Richardson (1950) compiled statistics on the number of wars engaged in by major world powers from 1850–1941. Britain heads the list with twenty wars—more than the Japanese (with nine), the Germans (with eight), or the United States (with seven). We often hear explanations of Germany's war-like tendencies on the basis of the authoritarian character of the

German family and educational training and the resulting frustration to the individual German. Do these statistics indicate that the British people are more frustrated than the Germans? In this connection, it seems reasonable to ask a question which historians and other social scientists can help us answer: "Doesn't having an empire with far-flung interests to be protected and expanded have anything to do with this frequency of war?"

Today we are told that it would be extremely difficult for the United States to remain aloof from a major conflict in any part of the world, since it is one of the two major powers. Does the democratic or authoritarian upbringing of individual Americans in Iowa or Maine or Arizona have anything to do with the likelihood of the United States being involved or not being involved in a war?

Level of Interaction in Intergroup Behavior

Such considerations lead to conclusions concerning the effects of motivational components, that is, of aspirations, frustrations, aggressive impulses, at different levels of interaction—individual, group, and intergroup interaction:

We cannot legitimately extrapolate from the effects of the individual's motivational urges and frustrations to group situations, as if a group situation were a void and the interaction processes and reciprocities within it were a play of shadows. Similarly, compelling material conditions (technology, socioeconomic forces) influence human relations as affected by the existing organizational structure and the system of beliefs or norms. Oscar Lewis has demonstrated this in a striking way in his book, *Five Families* (1959), which has in its subtitle the phrase "the culture of poverty." In his chapter in this volume, Raymond Crist deals with organizational problems tied directly to land, its distribution and use.

We cannot extrapolate from the properties of individuals to the characteristics of group situations. It is equally erroneous to extrapolate from the properties of relations within a group to explain relations between groups, as though the area of interaction between groups consisted of a vacuum, or even of the cozy atmosphere of a conference room. The character of relations and norms that prevail within groups does influence their relations with other groups, but intergroup relations are potently determined by the process of interaction between the groups. The give-and-take between groups may be full of conflict or in a state of flow. And it is this area of conflict, in the case of negative relations, or of flow, in the cases of cooperation or alliance, which may produce consequential reverberations within the groups themselves (Sherif and Sherif, 1953).

What determines the positive or negative nature of interaction between groups? In large part, it is determined by the reciprocal interests of the groups involved and the degree of their significance to the groups in question. The issues at stake must be interests of considerable concern to the groups, if they are to play a part in intergroup relations. A matter of concern may relate to values or goals shared by group members. It may be a real or imagined threat to the safety of the group as a whole, an economic interest, a political advantage, a military consideration, prestige, or a number of others. Once a particular issue comes to the foreground as the dominant influence in intergroup relations, it may become the *limiting factor,* the main anchorage in the interaction process between them.

Empirical Generalizations

The foregoing approach to in-group and intergroup relations was formulated on the basis of extensive surveys of pertinent theoretical works and empirical research. Empirical field studies are full of pregnant leads for experimentalists in formulating valid and testable hypotheses. A series of hypotheses was derived concerning formation and functioning of in-group structure or organization (that is, status or leader-follower behavior and ensuing member attitudes), concerning conditions conducive to positive and negative intergroup attitudes, and concerning measures for the reduction of intergroup conflict (Sherif and Sherif, 1956; Sherif et al., 1961).

In order to study the effects of aspirations, deprivations, frustrations, and other goal-directed components within an appropriate level of interaction, as the first step in our research, autonomous in-groups were formed experimentally. Then these groups, whose natural history was ascertained step by step, were brought into functional contact under reciprocally competitive and frustrating conditions. Finally, study of reduction of intergroup conflict was undertaken. Our large-scale experiments were carried out in 1949, 1953, and 1954. In 1954 the research was sufficiently advanced to tackle the difficult task of reducing intergroup conflict.

As a background to points raised later in this introductory statement, only the generalizations pertinent to the major hypotheses will be stated here in brief.

Generalizations concerning group formation:

1. A definite group organization (structure) manifested in differentiated status positions is produced when a number of individuals (even without previously established interpersonal relations) interact with one another under conditions (a) which embody goals with appeal value to the individuals, and (b) which require interdependent activities for their attainment.

2. The structure or organization is reflected in a consistent pattern of communication among group members. The higher the status of a group member, the greater the frequency of suggestions concerning group activities addressed or relayed to him.

3. Concomitant with the formation of a group organization, group norms emerge and are stabilized, regulating the members' behaviors within specifiable *latitudes of acceptable behavior*, in practices and activities commonly engaged in.

Generalizations concerning negative intergroup relations and the rise of prejudice and stereotypes of the out-group:

1. When groups engage in reciprocally competitive and frustrating activities, such that the victory or gain of a desired goal by one group results in the defeat or loss for the other group, unfavorable stereotypes come into use in relation to the out-group and its members. In time, these unfavorable stereotypes are standardized in a group, placing the out-group at a prejudicial distance (proportional to the degree of negative relations between them).

2. Concomitant with the rise of mutually prejudicial attitudes between groups, self-glorifying or self-justifying attitudes toward the in-group are strengthened. The performance of the out-

group is deprecated and the moves of the out-group and its members are perceived in a suspicious light.

Note that in the research on which these generalizations are based the members of the groups were meticulously selected to be socially well-adjusted and academically successful individuals from established families. They were not from broken homes or families with undue behavior problems. Therefore, it would be decidedly off the mark to explain their behavior in intergroup relations on the basis of severe frustrations or instabilities during their prior life histories.

Now, generalizations concerning reduction of intergroup conflict:

1. *Contact* between groups in close proximity in activities which are individually enjoyed by the members of each group does not produce a decrease in the existing state of intergroup hostility. In fact, such occasions of intergroup proximity may be utilized for further exchanges of invectives across group lines and for attribution of the blame for the existing state of affairs to the out-group.

2. The next generalization concerns the measure that proved effective in this research: introduction of superordinate goals. *Superordinate goals* are defined as goals which are compelling for all and cannot be ignored, but which cannot be achieved by the efforts and resources of one group alone. They require the coordinated efforts and resources of the groups involved. The generalization in this regard is: When groups in a state of friction come into contact under conditions embodying superordinate goals, they tend to cooperate toward the common goal.

But reduction of intergroup conflict is not a one-shot affair. The next generalization brings in the *time* dimension.

3. It was necessary to introduce various superordinate goals over a time span to sustain cooperation and, along with it, to decrease friction and weaken unfavorable stereotypes. Examples of superordinate goals used in our 1954 experiment were a crisis due to shortage of one of the basic necessities of daily living, breakdown of the available transportation that affected everyone, and opportunities for greatly desired activities.

4. The last generalization to be mentioned from these experiments concerns the impact of the state of intergroup relations

on in-group relations and organization. It was found that functional relations between groups which are of consequence to the groups in question bring about changes in the pattern of relations within the groups involved. Illustrative of this generalization are the following: When defeat followed defeat for one group in the 1949 experiment, the leader of that group, even though daring, became demoralized. Operational leadership was undertaken by another group member, who, out of friendship for the leader, had not taken the reins earlier, even though he could easily have done so. In the 1954 experiment the leadership changed hands when the peace-time leader could not live up to the requirements of conflict to be in the front lines leading his group in engagements with the adversary.

This finding illustrates the inadequacy of extrapolations from practices and trends within groups to the explanation of intergroup relations and practices. Practices and trends within groups are themselves affected by relations with other groups. The practical implication is that in-group democracy, friendship, and solidarity need not be extended to cooperativeness, friendship, and solidarity with out-groups.

The generalizations just presented may warrant the following summary of the rise of favorable and unfavorable attitudes toward the in-group and toward out-groups:

In the process of interaction among members, the group is endowed with qualities which tend to be favorable, and may be self-justifying and even self-glorifying. Individual members, in their strivings to get along well in their interpersonal relations, to be accepted or rewarded, tend to develop qualities or traits put at a premium in their reference groups through the example of other members they look up to, through verbal dictums and through a set of sanctions applied to cases of deviation from the prevailing acceptable modes of behavior.

Out-groups and their respective members are attributed favorable or unfavorable traits depending on the positive or negative nature of functional relations between the groups in question. Are the groups or a combination of groups competing with each other to excel in prestige, towards economic ends, political ends, territorial ends, so that the gain of one party is necessarily the loss of the other? Does the victory of one party mean the sure

defeat of the other? Does possession by one party mean deprivation or humiliation for the other? Or are the attainments of
such ends by one party compatible with the ends of the other?
These possibilities are illustrative of the situations conducive
to positive or negative functional relations between groups. Experiments indicate that negative functional relations between
groups give rise to hostile attitudes and unfavorable stereotypes
toward the out-group irrespective of the objective qualities of
the individuals involved. For example, if the enemy kills fifty
of us he is labeled "fanatic" and "cruel," but the in-group member is cited as "brave" or "heroic" for killing the enemy.

Hence, upholding the conception that one's reference group
maintains about an out-group is not essentially a problem of a
deviate or highly frustrated individual. It is a problem of participation by in-group members in evaluative processes and activities directed toward the out-group on the part of "good"
members, who ordinarily constitute the majority of membership
so long as group solidarity and morale are sustained.

It is in states of transition, rapid change, or acculturation that
cases of nonconformity and lack of consensus increase in frequency. At such times, development of schisms and factions
within social units becomes accelerated. For adequate formulations about such periods of transition and the rise of factions,
we need a great deal of information from anthropological field
observations, of the kind presented in the chapters by David
French and Alan Beals.

Once hostile attitudes and unfavorable stereotypes are stabilized toward another group and its members, they become a
part of the cultural repertory of the group, coloring the light in
which the out-group is seen and outlasting the actual intergroup
relations in which they originally developed. Lewis Killian's
chapter on Leadership in the Integration Controversy provides
evidence of the importance of this heavy hand of the past in a
period of changing intergroup relations.

Problems of Research and Validity

The formulations presented so far have been based primarily
on surveys of theory and factual evidence concerning relatively

small social units and experiments on small groups of young people. Therefore, Robert Blake and Jane Mouton's chapter dealing with problems of intergroup conflict among adult groups in industrial settings through experimentally created discussion and representation techniques is indeed instructive.

To insure that generalizations from small group research have relevance for actual groups, small and large, it is necessary to raise the much neglected problem of *validity* of experimental findings. The validity of research findings should be a major concern of interdisciplinary efforts, provided that members of each discipline have learned enough about intergroup relations that we can talk with one another, rather than at each other across the particular brand and jargon of our respective disciplines.

The problem of validity includes the question of the relative adequacy of experimental and empirical findings for understanding and predicting problems of leader-follower relations, friendship, and hostility among groups, reduction of conflict and unfavorable stereotypes in actual settings of political, economic, and social life.

Doubts and negation of the validity of small group research have been stated by authors dealing with hard "facts of life"— for example, by David Truman in his chapter in *Research Frontiers in Politics and Government* (1955), following in the footsteps of V. O. Key. They are raised by the Columbia anthropologist, Conrad Arensberg (1951), in his discussion of small group research and large organizations, and by the sociologist, Arnold Rose (1954), in his comments on intergroup experiments.

On the other hand, it is contended by confirmed experimentalists that experimentation lends itself to greater generality of results—to generalizations applicable in a wider variety of situations. I propose that neither party to this discussion presents an adequate picture. In their revised *Group Dynamics* Cartwright and Zander (1960) illustrate the wide generality of experimental findings with studies on norm formation utilizing the autokinetic effect. If these experiments have generality, I think it comes from the fact that they were preceded by extensive surveys of the phenomena in question and the conditions in which they occurred. They were not undertaken for the mere sake of testing hypotheses derived by analogy from physical models, which may or may not be valid models for actualities of social happenings in the problem area.

The validity of both experimental and empirical findings is bounded by the special conditions under which the study is conducted. This limitation applies to field research just as much as to experimental research. In reporting experiments, the usual practice has been to specify only those variables actually manipulated by the experimenter. On the whole, such meticulous concern has not been shown in specifying variables or conditions which are not intentionally manipulated but which, nevertheless, enter into determining the results. The practice of plunging into hypothesis testing because certain techniques have become fashionable at the time and without sufficient grounding in the background and actualities of the problem area invites justified criticism of experimentation. The price of such practices is reports of contradictory generalizations, each of which might be true, but only for the particular conditions of the study, which are unspecified and may be unrepresentative. No wonder, then, that even the relatively brief history of experimental social psychology is in part the graveyard of artifacts lacking in validity from the point of view of problems purportedly claimed to be studied.

For example, if we are intent on proving that leadership quality is specific to situations, we can do so by choosing subjects who are not, at the start, acquainted with one another and setting them to a variety of motivationally neutral tasks called "problem solving" situations. On the other hand, if we are set to prove the generality of leadership quality, we can define experimental conditions conducive to showing it, namely, by having members of a group with established reciprocities face genuine problem situations such as tasks which have been of real concern to them day in and day out.

This does not mean that experimentation is necessarily invalid and fruitless. On the contrary, experimentation is the "crowning touch in analysis" when we can attain that level of analysis without mutilating the very problem we intend to study. The contradictory results of leadership studies fall into a meaningful pattern if evaluated in the light of the conditions of the studies—namely, the presence or absence of established relationships and expectations among individuals and the motivational relevance of the problem situations faced. The point could be illustrated further with the topics of the relative achievement in individual versus group performance, the relative efficiency of decision making in small and relatively larger groups, and other measures of decision making in role playing and conference situations.

The remedy, in my opinion, is not concentration on experimental work or on field work to the exclusion of the other, but constant evaluation of the *formulation* of the problems of intergroup relations and constant evaluation of the *conditions* in which they are studied in the light of persistent problems and persistent findings encountered in labor-management relations, in existing and emerging factions in societies in the throes of transition, in events ensuing under the magic spell of nationalism, and between nations encountering the sometimes grim problems of internationalism.

Needed Perspective for Study of Intergroup Relations

In order to evaluate properly the conditions bounding particular intergroup relations in various areas (political, cultural, ethnic, etc.), one of the greatest needs is placing them in proper perspective. Operationally, this amounts to explicit recognition and assessment of part processes relative to the total system of relationships. This oft-repeated dictum not infrequently remains only lip service. Its urgency is compelling as soon as one tries to coordinate generalizations concerning large social units with those concerning small units which operate within them. Robert Dubin has dealt with such problems in terms of "linkages" within a large system, for example, in his chapter in the book edited by Haire on *Modern Organization Theory* (1959). His present chapter on "Leadership in Union-Management Relations as an Intergroup System" can be effective in broadening our research strategies, both for those using primarily field methods and for those using experimental techniques.

In seeking perspective on special areas of intergroup relations through consideration of the systems of which they are parts, we immediately encounter the *power* dimension, which has been one of the most neglected aspects of small group research. We share the conception of those writers who characterize *social power* in terms of the *initiation or suppression of activity in others in requested or expected directions, with means and instrumentalities to apply sanctions when there is noncompliance.* Thus defined, the problem of power becomes integral to the study of any organizational framework, small or large, formally or informally organized. The initiation of activities in others without the possibility of sanction may be usefully designated by another term, such as *influence.*

The differentiated statuses which define any organization from an operational point of view are positions in a power dimension, whatever else they may be. As such, every group is a power group, even though means and instrumentalities of sanctions do differ in formal and informal organizations. For this reason, exploration of leader-follower relations within groups and in intergroup relations is fanciful without bringing the power aspect prominently into the picture.

Since problems of power have long been the main domain of political scientists, Robert North's chapter on "International Conflict and Integration: Problems of Research" in this volume will provide us with considerations to ponder seriously in our future work.

Leadership, Policy Making, and Representation as Group Functions

Within groups, small or large, formal or informal, the focus of power resides in the leadership and other high status members. But the leadership status itself is within a group, and not outside of it, as Cecil Gibb (1954) maintained in the most comprehensive survey of leadership studies to date. The leader himself is not immune from sanctions if he deviates too far from the bounds of acceptable behavior prevailing in the group. Leaders, delegates, and representatives of the groups must remain a part of the power structure of the group if their actions are to be effective. The significance of the power structure for assessing the behavior of individuals in such positions is immediately seen when their actions deviate widely from the expectations of the membership. The newspaper accounts of the business leader who has arrangements with a supplier, of the union leader who makes a deal with company representatives to his own advantage, of the prime minister who appears to succumb to the inducements of the enemy, tell us what happens in such cases.

Delegation and representation of authority are integral aspects of group functioning, especially in relations with other groups. Studies by Ralph Stogdill and his associates show that within a large organization, subordinate members expect superiors to delegate authority and regard those who delegate more freely as better leaders. Yet Stogdill, in his recent book, *Individual Behavior and Group Achievement* (1959), observes that there are limiting situations "where a high degree of co-ordination is required," and delegation may result in "confusion and mis-directed effort" (p. 189).

Thus, in critical situations, leaders tend to take over the reins. If representatives in a collective bargaining situation are not making effective headway, the top leaders may, for the first time, get *directly* into these procedures. Similarly, a critical international situation temporarily reduces the authority of representatives on international councils, and at such times top leadership may step to the front line of negotiations.

In dealings between groups, the problem of power is manifested in different ways. Within a large organization or within a society, relations between groups are ordinarily subject to sanctions by the still larger organization. However, in a "casually patterned" society, to use the sociologist Lynd's characterization, the relations between some of the constituent organizations may not be regulated by sanctions applicable to all parties within the all-embracing organization. These areas of intergroup relations—in what Bierstedt (1957) has called the "unorganized interstices" of society—are in the foreground of major social problems in this country today.

In the relations between nations, the extent of regulation by commonly accepted sanctions is still smaller. Thus, power is not infrequently manifested in the form of force and threat of force. It is in such contexts that relationships between groups become vital to the survival of the groups in question. It is in such contexts that the problems of reduction of intergroup conflict, hostility and its by-products become the urgent problems of our time.

Superordinate Goals in Reduction of Conflicts

In concluding, I venture to state some of the things that we have learned about the reduction of intergroup conflict. It is true that lines of *communication*, that is, *contact*, between groups must be opened before prevailing conflicts can be reduced. But if contact between groups takes place without superordinate goals—that is, goals which are *urgent* and *compelling* for *all* groups involved, under the circumstances—the communication channels and the contacts serve as mediums for further accusations and recriminations. The discussion becomes bogged down in direct and indirect reference to the vicious circle of "Who's to blame?"

When contact situations involve superordinate goals, communication is utilized in the direction of reducing conflict in order to attain the common goals.

In regard to dissemination of *information*, favorable information about a disliked out-group tends to be ignored, rejected or reinterpreted to fit prevailing stereotypes. But when groups are pulling together toward superordinate goals, true and favorable information about the out-group is seen in a new light, and the probability of information being effective is enormously enhanced.

When groups cooperate toward superordinate goals, *leaders* are in a position to take bolder steps toward bringing about understanding and harmonious relations. When groups are directed toward goals which are mutually incompatible, genuine moves by a leader to reduce intergroup conflict may be seen by the membership of his own group as out-of-step and ill-advised. He may be subjected to severe criticism and even loss of faith. When compelling superordinate goals become articulated, the leader can make moves to further cooperative efforts, he can more freely delegate authority, and representation processes can proceed more effectively. The decisions reached are more likely to receive support from other group members.

In short, various measures suggested for the reduction of intergroup conflict, such as dissemination of information, increasing social contacts, and conferences of leaders and representatives, acquire new significance and new effectiveness when they become part and parcel of interaction processes between groups oriented toward superordinate goals which have real and compelling value for all groups concerned.

Over a period of time, the interaction of groups toward superordinate goals which have genuine and compelling value for all groups concerned should assume organizational forms. If the tasks of building such organizations seem formidable, they are no more formidable, I think, than those which a modern war might impose. And surely there can be no doubt that man's potentialities can be realized better in the course of such efforts than in preoccupation with assigning blame for the state of affairs, in pursuits of old fears, old hostilities, and old conflicts with their awesome possibilities in this present world.

Concentrated efforts of all parties toward superordinate goals, rather than preoccupation with assessment of blame and clearing away all existing grudges, have a psychological implication as well. In the process of such efforts, man will be creating new organizations, new values, and thereby transforming himself. Just as the properties of part of a pattern are colored by the overall system of which it is part, the old grudges and stereotypes will acquire a different significance in the context of joint efforts toward common goals and their by-products. This is the plea made so eloquently by Gardner Murphy in his book, *Human Potentialities* (1958), of which the Yale physicist, Henry Margenau, wrote: "Here a psychologist of vision casts knowledge of man's present abilities into temporal perspective and portrays the forms which human development may take."

References

Arensberg, C. H., 1951. Behavior and organization: industrial studies. In J. H. Rohrer and M. Sherif (eds.), *Social psychology at the crossroads.* New York, Harper.

Bierstedt, R., 1957. An analysis of social power. In L. A. Coser and B. Rosenberg (eds.), *Sociological theory: a book of readings.* New York, Macmillan.

Cartwright, D., and A. Zander, 1960. *Group dynamics: research and theory.* Second edition. Evanston, Ill., Row, Peterson.

Dubin, R., 1959. Stability of human organization. In M. Haire (ed.), *Modern organization theory.* New York, Wiley.

Gibb, C. A., 1954. Leadership. In G. Lindzey (ed.), *Handbook of social psychology.* Volume II, Reading, Mass., Addison-Wesley.

Klineberg, O., 1950. *Tensions affecting international understanding.* New York, Social Science Research Council Bull., 62.

Lewis, O., 1959. *Five families: Mexican case studies in the culture of poverty.* New York, Basic Books.

Murphy, G., 1953. *In the minds of men.* New York, Basic Books.

——, 1958. *Human potentialities.* New York, Basic Books.

Pear, T. H. (ed.), 1950. *Psychological factors of peace and war.* New York, Philosophical Library.

Richardson, L. F., 1950. Statistics of deadly quarrels. In T. H. Pear (ed.), *Psychological factors of peace and war.* New York, Philosophical Library.

Rose, A. M., 1954. *Theory and method in the social sciences.* Minneapolis, University of Minnesota Press.

Sherif, M., O. J. Harvey, B. J. White, W. R. Hood, and Carolyn W. Sherif, 1961. *Intergroup conflict and cooperation. The Robbers Cave experiment.* Norman, Okla., University of Oklahoma Book Exchange.

Sherif, M., and Carolyn W. Sherif, 1953. *Groups in harmony and tension.* New York, Harper.

——, 1956. *Outline of social psychology.* Revised edition. New York, Harper.

Stogdill, R. M., 1959. *Individual behavior and group achievement.* New York, Oxford University Press.

Truman, D. B., 1955. The impact on political science of the revolution in the behavioral sciences. In *Research frontiers in politics and government,* Washington, D.C., Brookings Institution.

2

INTERGROUP hostilities, prejudices, and strife are frequently attributed to individual characteristics or impulses without due consideration for the sociocultural context in which individuals develop and function. In the following chapter, Robert E. L. Faris examines evidence offered in support of the more influential approaches of this kind. In doing so, he exposes the fundamental errors of all attempts to build theories of man's social behavior without regard for the patterned constellation of his relations with other individuals and other groups.

Beyond a critique of one-sided "individualistic" approaches, Faris points to the organizational patterns of the social groups in which an individual develops, their values, the individual's roles in them, and to the position of his group vis à vis others as the context in which social attitudes form and social behavior occurs. The implication for theory and research is that the established patterns and developing trends in relations among human groups, studied at their appropriate level of interaction, are the necessary framework for understanding the hostile or friendly character of intergroup attitudes and behavior of individual members.

Indeed, Faris concludes that analysis of organizations and their interrelationships, as well as prediction of the direction of member attitudes, are entirely feasible without reference to the psychological make-up or dynamics of the particular individuals composing the groups. If this were not the case, sociology, economics, anthropology, political science, history, and other social science disciplines would be simply "applied psychology," as, for example, Freud would have had it.

The choice of *units of analysis* (whether individual behavior, or a group, or an intergroup system) shapes the questions that are asked and, thus, the formulation of problems in research. The issues raised by Faris concerning approach and theory recur in this book in discussions of specific research areas, particularly in the chapters by Stogdill, Dubin, Blake and Mouton, and Killian.

EDITOR

2 INTERACTION LEVELS AND INTERGROUP RELATIONS

by Robert E. L. Faris

Scholarly interest in intergroup relations historically arose in a context of concern about objectionable behavior—interracial hostility—which we desired to control. In such situations humanitarian zeal has tended to set the direction of early efforts of investigation, and so it has been with race relations. Perhaps it was inevitable that the efforts of social scientists had to pass through a stage of emotional oversimplification of the nature of the problem. There is an ancient human tendency, which even a Ph.D. does not always suppress, to look for the basic cause of objectionable behavior in sheer wickedness of people, and academic investigators have not been entirely immune to this. Nor have we avoided the slightly more sophisticated Marx-inspired conception that a brutally selfish exploiting class deliberately foments race hatred in order to exploit a subject class.

Such attribution of undesired behavior to evil human nature is more compatible to the theological mind than to the scientific intellect. Science has undertaken the difficult but more rewarding responsibility of an objective search for causes apart from any original sinfulness in the human species. This approach has less of the appeal of simplicity, but more promise of eventual acquisition of sound knowledge.

The human race does not gain sophistication in a series of grand leaps, but makes progress by erratic and mincing steps, committing most of the possible mistakes along the way, always collecting the full penalties of its errors. Thus, to explain unfairness in the treatment of population categories, we were apparently destined to spend a generous part of research time and effort in seeking the relevant causation within the individual

24

person. At this early stage, nothing appeared more obvious than the proposition that a complete inspection of the internal nature of a person would furnish an explanation of whatever actions he performed.

Thus we have experienced, in the past half-century, the grand surge of effort into accounting for intergroup relations through research with an entirely individualistic focus, ranging from the naive instinctivism implied in a once-popular notion that races smell offensively to one another, to the implicit instinctivism embedded in psychoanalysis and in some of the individualistic schools of psychology. Doctrinaire investigators ranged far in search of supporting evidence and, as always, turned up enough to persuade themselves that they were on the right track. It is instructive to review a few of these experiences.

Some Individualistic Approaches

The appealing frustration-aggression formula, inspired by Freud and skillfully marketed by Dollard and his associates (1939), provides one such instructive example of wasted energy. This group appeared to conceive of aggression as a sort of indestructible fluid which accumulates within a person and which has to be discharged in some kind of aggression. Goal responses suffer interference, and cause actions which have the goal response of inflicting injury to an organism, or organism surrogate—to employ the vocabulary of the Yale scholars of the late 1930's. The mechanism is specifically connected with such forms of intergroup conflict as "lynchings, strikes, and certain reformist campaigns. . . ."

The concept of *displacement* has been offered to provide a mechanism which turns the accumulated aggression against objects which were not responsible for the originating frustration. The innocent target has come to be known as a *scapegoat,* and the practice of discharging the aggression on such a victim became known as *scapegoating.* Enthusiastic promotion from both academic and humanitarian sources gave this concept high popularity in action organizations during the 1940's. According to the authors of a popular research methods textbook it was used in Roman times to account for the persecution of Christians. Another pair of academics observed in 1940 that if the per-acre value of cotton in the southeastern section of the United States is low, the number of lynchings of Negroes in that area is high (Hovland and Sears, 1940). The helpless anger caused by economic troubles is displaced, in these views, on such scapegoats as Christians or helpless Negroes. The textbook authors display their confidence in the scapegoat theory by stating: "That this theory explains a number of observations gives us confidence in using the general principle it embodies for the purpose of prediction." This notion became widely applied, partly through a manual of *ABC's of Scapegoating* which provided practical directions for workers.

The fragility of the method used to support the scapegoating and displacement theory of intergroup hostility is conspicuous. No satisfactory direct method of supporting the theory has been found. There is a report, however, of a flatly contradictory finding. Lindzey (1950) has reported an elaborately controlled experiment on the scapegoat theory of prejudice which found that persons who are highly prejudiced do not differ significantly from those with little prejudice in their tendency to employ the mechanism of displacement.

This finding brings out one of the central arguments of the present article: that the attempt at explanation of intergroup hostility on the basis of psychological mechanisms in the individual, by pointing to the presence of such mechanisms among persons who show hostility, is wholly inadequate because of the lack of controls. When, in time, investigations include a wider range of subjects, it turns out that such mechanisms tend to be found in most normal persons and do not differentiate between prejudiced and unprejudiced persons, or any other such broad categories.

It is relevant here to comment on the closely related concept of *catharsis*. The emphasis here is on the indestructible character of the pent-up aggression within the person. If it accumulates it inflicts damage on its possessor, and it can supposedly come out only in some form of conflict—a fight, a quarrel, or a reasonably similar substitute for these, such as the vicarious battles fought mentally by the spectators at a lively prize fight. The theorists who display an interest in catharsis seem to differ from those who emphasize displacement and scapegoating, mainly in discussing the matter from their interest in the psychological welfare of the individual rather than in the subject of peace and harmony between groups. In fact, it is not uncommon for catharsis theorists to recommend overt display of hostility in the interest of mental health. The authors of a considerable amount of material on family behavior have, for example, advised married couples to have a good quarrel from time to time (Duvall and Hill, 1945), and the physician-author of a best-selling baby and child care manual advises that children should play at hurting and killing to avoid bottling up hostile feelings (see Goldsborough, 1949). Moreno (1940) has claimed to get the benefits of catharsis by having persons act out their hostility on the psychodramatic stage.

Like the frustration-aggression and the displacement-scapegoating concepts, the catharsis theory is based on doctrine without satisfactory support of methodical research. In fact, in most of the literature on catharsis the authors appear not to know that there is also a contradictory doctrine—that overt expression of hostility increases aggression rather than reducing it. A leading medical authority advises irritated persons to "burn their own smoke" and cultivate an attitude of serenity, and another clinician advises keeping cheerful, learning to accept adversity in the manner of Pollyanna. These experts also fail to provide research support for their doctrine, but show that reasonable views of experienced experts cannot be relied on to provide certain knowledge.

Experimental research on catharsis, in the sense used in the above paragraphs, is almost totally lacking. Stouffer and his colleagues (1949) did make an attempt in the American Soldier research, by administering before-and-after questions on personal adjustment and attitudes toward the army to an experimental and a control group. The control group was given a special opportunity to discharge aggression, but no significant differences resulted, and so, as far as their experiment indicates, no research support is given to the catharsis theory.

It is the opinion of the present writer that the most applicable evidence on the catharsis theory has been provided, perhaps to some extent inadvertently, by two of the admirable summer camp studies of Sherif (Sherif et al., 1954). In each case, matched groups of boys were placed in a situation of rivalry between the groups so that hostility quickly broke out. Full expression of the boys' aggression in overt activity clearly had no effect in decreasing it, but always seemed to generate more hostility.

It is thus argued here that the weight of what evidence we now possess is opposed to the theory of catharsis, and that there is no reason to employ any notions about an indestructible, fluid hostility in the attempt to account for relations between collectivities of persons.

Also a part of this individualistic approach to the explanation of intergroup relations is the attempt to isolate a fundamental personality type inclined toward improper prejudice and hostility—the *authoritarian personality* (Adorno et al., 1950).

The literature on the authoritarian personality is large and need not be treated here, but a brief evaluative comment is offered. In spite of some disclaimers—Hartley and Hartley (1952), for example, say: "these studies emphasize that 'prejudice' is not to be identified as psychologically abnormal"—it seems obvious that the summarized findings constitute an attempt at identifying an unhealthy type of personality at the bottom of most of our troubles in intergroup relations. From a summary by Flowerman (1950), a number of key descriptive terms may be quoted to illustrate the emotionally pejorative characterization. The Authoritarian Man is said to be "a supreme conformist" merging with the herd, compulsive and irrational, unable to risk being different and unable to tolerate differences in anyone else. He shows compulsive submission to authority, acting like a sheep, doing the bidding of a Hitler even if it means oppressing and killing. He sees the world and its inhabitants as menacing and unfriendly. He is rigid and shows limited imagination, and is a mechanical man, a kind of robot. He is a "phony conservative" who may be more destructively radical than the radicals he is attacking, a "counterfeit flag-waver." He is a moral purist, who has buried his smoldering resentment and hostility within himself. This can hardly be interpreted as a description of a normal person.

It must be immediately pointed out that the literature of criticism of the above studies is also large, and that there are devastating challenges of the research method and of the key findings, so that it is not at all granted by contemporary scholars that there is any such entity as described above. To many, including the writer, the authoritarian studies appear to be mainly the result of emotional enthusiasm, nobly motivated, producing an almost completely artificial and thoroughly useless result.

Social Sources of Conflict Attitudes

The foregoing section has described what may be regarded as a great false trail. The *explanation* of social attitudes was vainly sought where it is not—in the character of the individual. It seems impossible to understand how this error could be made other than through ignorance of the accumulated evidence of decades of published research and discussion indicating the *social* nature of the bulk of our personal stock of attitudes. From the time of Newcomb's noted Bennington political attitude studies (1943), if not earlier, it should have been clear that political attitudes are determined not primarily by a fundamental personality type, but by membership in a reference group —first the family in most cases, and then, among college students, the social groups within the college in which membership is valued. The same principle has been realized, and to some extent demonstrated in research, with reference to religious and moral attitudes, esthetic standards, food prejudices, and other sentiments.

To some scholars there has appeared to be a mystical implication in the foregoing generalization. Floyd Allport (1924), for example, at one time vigorously insisted that groups are not real, only individuals exist and can function as causes. Attitudes are only inside individuals, and cannot be caused by a nonexistent group.

This brings up the concept "misplaced concreteness," but epithet can generally be matched with epithet, and against the charge of "group fallacy" can be thrown the reproach of "reductionism." If it is insisted that all social phenomena are in reality only multiple manifestations of individual behavior, the same form of argument can be, and has been, used to assert that the organism is composed of cells, and these are made of molecules, and these are nothing but assemblies of atoms, and these are made up of even smaller things—subatomic particles. This

is as far down the reduction line as we can go at present, and
we find that instead of touching rock bottom reality we encounter inconsistent, confusing, frustrating fantasy, with absolute knowledge forever blocked by a principle of uncertainty.
After we have recognized the futility of reductionism, we can be
free to perceive the practical value of searching for causes on
the appropriate level of organization for each field.

An organization is a functioning pattern, not a sum, of elements which possesses characteristics that are not present in
the elements when isolated. This is true of a machine (a clock
and its parts), of an organism (a sponge and its cells), and a
colony (a hive and its bees), as well as a human group or
society. In a human organization the elements would be supposed to be persons, but the statements require one important
qualification. Most of us have membership in a number of organizations—a man may be a bank official, a father of a family,
member of Rotary, P.T.A., two recreational clubs, deacon of a
church, and district leader in a political party. It seems most
realistic to hold that he does not participate in each of these
as a whole person but with a distinguishable *aspect* of himself,
and in some cases these aspects have little overlapping and may
even be in some conflict. The bank, thus, is an organization not
truly composed of complete persons, since, for example, the
father aspect, the deacon aspect, or the poker club aspect of its
vice president are normally kept utterly separate and play no
part in the pattern that makes up the bank organization. The
elements of the social organization that makes up the bank are
the banker aspects, and these differ from person to person, among
the bank's members, according to each person's position in the
organization.

A parenthetical question may be raised concerning whether
there is any use at all in thinking of a person as a unity; do these
various aspects of a person constitute some kind of a whole?
The answer would seem to be that they may in some cases, but
that there is nothing necessary about this. Aspects in this sense,
and there is no harm in using the term "roles," can be and frequently are entirely independent of one another in the same
human being. This is no freak phenomenon of "dissociated
personality" but the way human life operates.

The concept that a whole, or organism, can be nothing more

than a sum of its parts is deficient in another important respect. A functioning whole may have the ability to select new parts, and to transform the elements by assimilation. This has been dramatically shown in zoology at the subhuman level. A fascinating example is furnished by a species of social amoeba, *Dictyostelium discoideum*, which spends part of its life cycle as separate cells, each going its own way, moving and feeding in the manner of amoebae (Bonner, 1949). At certain periods, however, a number of these cells will gather and form a sausage-shaped coordinated mass, which is capable of a new kind of locomotion, something like the crawling of a caterpillar. After migrating a moderate distance, the mass assumes an upright and stationary position and a pointed tip is thrust upward. The cells in the mass change their shapes and their nature according to where they are located in the pattern, and those in the upper stalk change into pill-shaped spore cells, encased in a hard, resistant capsule. Here then is an organic whole in which the pattern of the organization reacts back upon, and transforms, the character of the elements of which it is formed.

The biological or physiological process in which an organism alters the nature of its elements is known as assimilation, and it is efficient to use, as sociologists do, the same term to denote the transformation of persons by the groups in which he participates.

Social organizations create the human and social characters of their members to begin with, first through the agency of the family. Later assimilation then produces in the child aspects which belong to schoolroom life, to peer groups, and to such organized social systems as Boy Scouts, Sunday Schools, and others. In the normal course of life, each of us picks up from definite groups organized roles or offices which partially control our thoughts and behavior and constitute the fundamental materials of personality and character. We need not share Floyd Allport's concern about attributing reality to a social organization if we can show, as we have done abundantly, that it produces real consequences.

Of course this argument, in its general form, is ages old and has been fully stated and restated in the literature of sociology for a century and a half. It is no longer controversial in this discipline, mainly because systematic research has confirmed it.

The point has not been fully appreciated by some of our colleagues in sister disciplines, however, and is really not grasped at all by the concerned public, which still holds fondly to the primitive tendency to account for human troubles by the goodness or badness of individuals.

The Mechanism of Social Attitudes

It has long been known that people respond to objects not in terms of objective reality but in terms of the particular way in which the object is perceived. The attitude, in guiding our perception, defines the object for each of us, and this definition, however arbitrary it may be, is the reality that influences our behavior. This statement is supported by a massive amount of research familiar to all social psychologists, but it appears to be easy to forget, especially in its application to ourselves. Each person, unless disciplined by an unusual sophistication in social psychology, holds an intuitive conviction that his own senses and clear logical facility puts him in direct touch with things as they are. Even a laboratory demonstration, such as the Sorokin music experiment (1932), in which students were influenced to judge the same record played twice as two different compositions of contrasting merit, does not generally alter this conviction. A common escape from the correct conclusion is afforded by a process of explaining away this particular result as exceptional.

Granting that there are attitudes which are constructed in consequence of unique individual experiences, most attitudes of most persons are created in a social process and transmitted to each individual through instruments of group influence. This fact is also much more visible in others than in ourselves. The Vermont merchant has little trouble in understanding how social influences compel a Georgia textile worker to be a Democrat, but tends to feel confident that clear unaided observation and reasoning has brought him into essential political agreement with his Republican friends and neighbors.

This very fact—that we perceive the influence of social attitudes mainly among those persons with whom we disagree—may be partly responsible for a widespread habit of conceiving of it as essentially abnormal. It distorts reality, creates error, and seems obviously a bad thing. And so we may fail to recognize the essential normality and inevitability of the principle.

There is in fact no hope of a situation in which each person faces the world of reality entirely on his own efficient mental equipment. The infinite complexity of things-as-they-are would utterly defeat the best of us. Just as the collective history of mankind has evolved material culture objects in a slow accumulation, so it has culturally selected and defined and standardized the definitions of things and nonmaterial concepts which make social teamwork, and therefore survival, possible. For each new member of the society, throughout infancy, childhood and youth, there is no escaping the principle of *authority of organized social influence* in the creation of the world which he is to perceive and respond to. At the frontier of knowledge, where new conceptions have to be sought, we rightly seek to break out of this domination by group authority, but elsewhere this is neither desirable nor possible. The invidious connotations of such words as "prejudice" and "stereotype" are intelligible in terms of the special situations to which these words are applied, but it is important not to lose sight of the fact that as processes of social psychology, these are the normal ways in which a human mentality simplifies the overpowering complexity of his universe.

Man's physiological inferiority and dependence in fact makes this principle an indispensable basis of all social life and thus of survival. We cannot act in concert unless we share a large body of concepts and definitions. The general harmony or conformity of these with metaphysical reality is of course not irrelevant, but standardization among the coacting society is absolutely essential. We may think of race prejudice as a perversion of a normal process, if we like, but we go fatally astray if we regard the operation of social authority over attitudes as psychologically abnormal.

A child, not having been exposed to the pressure to appear individually self-sufficient in opinion formation, can naively acknowledge this dependence on group authority. He may ask a parent, "What do these words 'Republican' and 'Democrat' mean?" And, after an explanation of the beliefs associated with each party, will ask, "What do *we* believe?" In adulthood he may feel the necessity to make such an inquiry a little less directly by putting it, "What is the liberal (or conservative) position on this issue?" If he changes his group affiliation, a person normally tends to develop a general evaluative attitude toward that group and then may alter subsidiary attitudes to conform to this ruling loyalty (cf. R. Hartley, 1956). For example, judgments concerning the propriety of a President seeking his regular exercise on a golf course may be dominated by political party affiliation. Or again, the reference to a family dog in a major political speech would be in bad taste according to whether judgment is made by Democrats who heard Richard M. Nixon's television mention of Checkers, or by Republicans some years earlier who heard Franklin D. Roosevelt refer to his dog Fala in a campaign speech.

The Creation of Group Attitudes

A pluralistic conception of social attitudes would hold that these could be nothing more than a sum of individual attitudes. Attitudes, it has been argued, can arise and exist only in individual minds. To speak of any kind of collectivity creating an attitude would seem on the face of it to be hopelessly mystical.

Such an assumption apparently underlies some of the well-known studies of international and intergroup tensions. In order to forecast the outbreak of overt conflict, a survey or poll could establish the trend in number and strength of individual expressions of hostility, and by extrapolation estimate a date for the beginning of war. Similarly it has been suggested that interracial violence might be predictable from the frequency of individual expressions of attitudes. S. C. Dodd (1951), for example, attempted to measure the degree of approach to hostile action between Negro and white inhabitants of a housing project, using as a unit of tension measurement among whites "one anti-Negro opinion offered by one white respondent in reply to a non-directive question." The *sum* of such units constituted the measure of the group tendency toward violence.

But as previously asserted, organization is not an addition of like units, and there are other mechanisms than summation that produce a group attitude. Opposing armies of soldiers do not undertake to fight each other merely as a consequence of a high proportion of the men on each side reaching an emotional boiling point. In fact, most modern soldiers have to be drafted, and many show no initial enthusiasm for combat—one of the great military problems is how to make soldiers want to fight. Hostile attitudes may be generated during the conflict, however, without having been the initial cause of it. The causal sequence most commonly appears to begin with a clash of nations as entities, with individual attitudes of hostility generated in a collective process within each nation. The U.S.–Cuba irritation of 1961, for example, followed such a sequence. Cubans *en masse* shout epithets against the *Yanqui* not as a consequence of person-to-person experiences but in consequence of a prior interaction of nation to nation.

This is in fact a general principle of the sociology of organization. The policy, the characteristic actions, of an organized group are determined in a collective process that is not only *not* produced by summation of individual attitudes and actions but often may depart to a considerable extent from the average individual preferences. In recent years, for example, a referendum was held in a large western city to decide whether daylight time should be observed in the summers. Among the organizations publicly and actively opposing the adoption of daylight time was the city Parent-Teacher Association. No poll or vote, however, was taken among its members, and it could not be known whether the majority of them would favor or oppose the measure. How, then, could it happen that the officials of the organization came to speak against the measure? The answer would seem to be, at least in part, that the officials are not representative of the membership, but are in fact a highly unrepresentative selection, not as a consequence of sinister plottings but in accord with the normal behavior of organizations.

The P.T.A. membership may be differentiated according to degree of interest in the organization's activities and purposes. The largest number consists of essentially nominal members, who have been urged to pay dues and support a worthy association, and lured into attendance at an occasional meeting by pressure on their children in school, such as a prize for the room with the highest rate of parent attendance. A smaller fraction of the membership attends meetings regularly because of actual interest in the proper business of the organization. Within this

number are circles and inner circles of members who maintain
active participation for years, work on committees, and hold the
top offices. It is among these of the inner circles that the policies evolve, and they not uncommonly find that the inner logic
of the organization's situation, as they see it, require them to act
in a way which they realize would not be in accord with the
sum of members' attitudes. For instance, if this were not so,
many an organization would find it extremely difficult to raise
the rate of dues.

A fringe member of the P.T.A. might vote for the daylight
time measure because of his fondness for outdoor sports, or, if
he is a filling station operator, because another hour of evening
driving by the public would increase profits. This man is a
whole person on the membership books of the P.T.A., but socio-
logically is only a small fraction of a person in that organization. A member of the P.T.A. inner circle, however, comes to
act in an *office*, which means that he does not feel free to follow
his personal inclinations, but must sense the responsibilities that
bear on him and act accordingly.

Thus, as stated earlier, an organized group is not composed
of persons, but of aspects of persons, and the aspects are quite
different according to the place each person has in the organization. Attempts to predict behavior of an organization from
the characteristics of the members as whole persons fail because
a considerable part of the whole person is irrelevant, and also
because the behavior of the man who acts in an office may be
detached from other aspects of his personality.

The behavior of organized groups, then, cannot be predicted
from complete knowledge of the characteristics of their members.
The relations *among* groups must be known if causation is to
be understood, and to a considerable extent individual behavior
follows as effect. The office makes the man, not the man the
office, in the normal experience of persons in organizations.

The Character of Hostile Attitudes

In the early years of the century William Graham Sumner
(1906) made a case for the universality and normality of ethnocentrism. The basic naive attitude of people everywhere has

been to regard themselves as men, and persons of other groups as *somewhat less than men.* In fact, the names for their own people often consisted of their own native word for man, or human being. The name for any particular outsider is frequently some epithet calling attention to his peculiar and offensive ways. This basic classification into the division "ourselves" and "others" dominates perception and guides the nature of appropriate activity. Among some peoples the appropriate activity toward the "others" was to kill them, but even among those with less drastic concepts of the outsider the treatment has always been distinctly different from that appropriate to their own people.

To most of us, it is hard to watch a person die. The newspaper reporter sent to cover an execution does not relish his assignment. But swatting a mosquito involves emotional strain for few persons. The more we can see human characteristics in animals, the more unpleasant it is to inflict injury and death on them—it is easier on our feelings to lop off a turkey's head than to guillotine a monkey. Similarly, if we have to kill, the task is made less painful to the extent that we can define the victim as nonhuman. A soldier has to be taught to think of the enemy as somewhat subhuman if he is to bring himself to willingness to use a bayonet on him. The designation of the enemy as "beast," "Hun," or "ape" serves a function, then, of permitting a normally sociable and sympathetic man to kill a similar human who has not necessarily ever offended him personally.

To the extent that this works, the soldier who learns to kill is no more brutalized than the gentle wife who finds calm diversion in watching television westerns which involve routine shootings of anonymous black-moustached bad men. The distinction between "our side" and "their side" is sufficient with normal persons to make the difference between agonized weeping at a death of one of ours, and good-humored cheering when an enemy falls. Sympathy has a range which in most persons is far from all embracing—the definitions presented to us by our group affiliations draw the effective boundaries beyond which soft feelings do not apply (cf. Ansari, 1956).

We understand hostility better, then, if we see it not merely as a characteristic of a person's inner nature, but in terms of the relationships between him and the objects arbitrarily defined for him by his group. The same person, seen from a completely objective point of view, is sympathetic and brutally cruel in every possible degree, but with the help of social attitudes is ordinarily able to think of himself in the more favorable image.

In the light of an abundance of relevant experimentation by Sherif, Asch, and others, we are not surprised that the group definition of an object may have great power in individual perception. But this has limits, as the experiments also show—beyond a point the group authority cannot make a man find an obviously shorter line the longer. And, in the experience of war and other forms of intense conflict, it can and does happen that a person will perceive that a particular enemy soldier does in fact have all the indications of humanity that are characteristic of an in-group. Such a discovery, however, does not always automatically destroy the cliche of enemy characteristics— a common resolution of the inconsistency is achieved by seeing this particular person as an exception. Similarly in the investigation of racial stereotypes we find a tendency to separate the inconsistent perceptions so that the group attitude remains intact (Cooper and Jahoda, 1947).

Ethnocentrism thus generally involves, in its most primitive form, a double or even multiple standard. Moral rules apply to the in-group, and a separate and less sympathetic set of rules, sometimes no rules at all, apply to the out-group. To some isolated preliterates, in fact, strangers, not being considered human, are to be put to death if possible. Civilized man does not go so far, but historians point out that, in the high-minded times of chivalry, the idealistic morals of the knights governed only their behavior among their own class; toward others of lesser breeding, roughness, exploitation, cheating, and other behavior dishonorable in the chivalric tradition was not considered inconsistent with the idealism of knighthood.

All this is to support further the general point that hostility is not something that exists in, or proceeds from, the inner character of the person. Hostility is not principally a personality component, but at least in part is a relation to a specific group or groups. This distinction between social distance as a product of ethnocentrism and as a characteristic of an "authoritarian" character is exemplified by a study in Lebanon where hostility among national and religious groups is abundant (Prothro and Melikian, 1953). Two groups of university students, totaling

232 in all, and representing a range of nationalities and religions, were scored anonymously on both "authoritarian personality" scale and a social distance scale toward twenty categories of national and religious affiliation plus two fictional nationalities. No correlation was found between mean social distance of national groups and score on the "authoritarian personality" scale (coefficient of .01). Similarly the correlation between mean social distance of religious groups and the scale was too low to be significant (.14). Of the 102 students who were presented with the fictitious nations along with the real ones, only seven rated them at all and four of the seven ratings were neutral. All others checked the response "I know nothing about this group; I cannot express an attitude." The authors of the study conclude that "None of the American evidences of a generalized ethnocentric factor of personality are found in our Near Eastern subjects." In short, in this part of the world where intense intergroup hostilities are abundant, objective research finds these to be entirely specific to relations among groups rather than properties of individual characters.

Origins of Hostility in the Group

If we agree with the foregoing elaborate argument that group hostility does not originate within the minds of its individual members, we incur the obligation to explain the existence of hostility in the group. If hostility flows from group to member, how could it have come to be a property of the group in the first place?

The answer would seem to be that the relations of *group-to-group* generate in each of the groups certain unique and emergent qualities which come to find verbal expression in policies, ideologies, stereotypes, and social attitudes. These products of a collective process thus achieve a form which can allow them to be a part of the content of the individual minds of the members of the groups.

Before proceeding with this point, let us be reminded that there is abundant reason to recognize that where no such group mechanisms have operated and no previously defined attitude is present, differences among persons are not only inadequate to produce hostility, but may not even be noticed. Individually, and naïvely, we do not automatically categorize persons on the basis of visible differences.

In support of this assertion we may recall that history records that interindividual relations of Indians and early white migrants to America were originally friendly, and that Indian-white hostility had at least part of its origin in the group competition for land (McNickle, 1937).

For a more familiar example, we may observe that small children who have no previous knowledge of other ethnic groups, have frequently been reported to be unaware of differences and therefore unable to create categories. Observations at an international children's gathering in 1951, for example, indicated that among 5,040 recorded contacts between individual children of varying nationalities, there were twice as many contacts outside of a child's national group as within, and that there were twice as many friendly contacts as there were neutral and hostile contacts combined (Allen, 1956).

Perhaps even more convincing is the common observation that preschool children who are permitted to engage in mixed nude swimming parties are sometimes reported not able to draw sex distinctions for lack of the conventional differentiation by clothing.

Thus it is not an individual tendency of the human species nor a product of person-to-person interaction that we find at the bottom of intergroup hostility, but causation on the higher interaction level of group-to-group interaction. Sociologists have for some time insisted that the broad pattern of Negro-white relations, for example, must be accounted for on the basis of the history of contacts between the races. This explanation involves the experience of slavery and of colonization, with the evolved adaptations and rationalizations on both sides, and involves also the various processes following emancipation of slaves and the social and political movements about the world which are directed toward independence and equality (Frazier, 1957; Yinger, 1959).

The causal significance of the group-to-group interaction level is also shown in a variety of contexts, including race discrimination among college students. Noel P. Gist (1955), who has studied the phenomenon in college fraternities, states that "The fraternal system is a series of interrelated power structures with centralization of authority in the governing body of each national organization." Attempts on the part of college authorities to eliminate discrimination in fraternities have had success mainly through exerting force on the national systems of alumni control. Studies have shown that even where students in local chapters have wished to abandon a policy of racial exclusiveness, they have often been prevented by the control of the national organization.

Herbert Blumer (1947), among others, has pointed to the dominance of the collective process over the individuals involved in labor conflicts. Indicating the error of focusing attention on the relations of individual employers and employees, he explains

That bare fundamental relation has been elaborated in our society into an extensive, diversified, complex and indirect network of relations in which the individual worker becomes an insignificant and inconspicuous figure. With unionization, especially with industrial unionization, workers have become incorporated in organizations, usually of vast dimensions. The relations of workers to management become increasingly led by, directed by, mediated by and expressed through such organizations. The organization as such functions through a hierarchy of officers and central committees who formulate policies, establish objectives, decide on strategy and tactics, and execute decisions. On the side of management one finds similar organization which takes out of the hand of the individual manager the determination of the major outlines of his relation to the worker. Relations between workers and management become primarily a matter of relations between organized groups (p. 272).

At this point it is appropriate to reiterate that it is of minor consequence in the course of affairs in industrial relations whether certain workers or employers as individuals have authoritarian tendencies in their personalities, or suffer from bottled-up aggression demanding discharge or catharsis. Whether he is belligerent or peaceful by nature, the union leader in a period of industrial turmoil will be forced by his office to turn a conflict face toward his opponents and stimulate the members of his organization to do the same.

All the above principles seem to apply as well to much smaller groups in conflict, and the point concerning the origin of personal attitudes of hostility in group-to-group relations is even experimentally shown in the Sherif Robbers Cave study. Here we can perceive the process in all of its stages, from the initial formation of an organized unity in each of the separate groups of boy campers, mutual discovery of the existence of the groups, the experimentally arranged collision of interests, and the consequent generation of intense individual hostility toward all members of the opposite group.

A further, and unparalleled, contribution of the Robbers Cave study is the experimental demonstration that the reduction of hostility is also a collective process. Artificially arranged interpersonal contacts between hostile boys had no observable effects on reducing hostility, but the replacement of the antagonistic collision of the groups by a succession of external crises requiring organized cooperation across group lines succeeded in rapidly transforming the entire process, so that the hostility dissolved almost entirely within two or three days and was replaced by friendliness and admiration.

It appears consistent with the best of current knowledge that the above analyses of industrial relations and boy campers' hostilities fit equally well the analysis of race relations. To quote Blumer (1958) again:

> . . . race prejudice exists basically in a sense of group position rather than in a set of feelings which members of one racial group have toward the members of another racial group. This different way of viewing race prejudice shifts study and analysis from a preoccupation with feelings as lodged in individuals to a concern with the relationship of racial groups. It also shifts scholarly treatment away from individual lines of experience and focuses interest on the collective process by which a racial group comes to define and redefine another racial group . . . race prejudice is fundamentally a matter of relationships between racial groups (p. 3).

This statement is representative of the position of modern sociology, and directs attention to the level of interaction that is of highest significance in accounting for the conflict behavior with which the present paper is concerned.

Summary

It is the contention of this paper that many prominent and influential investigators of the character of intergroup interaction made an early choice of the wrong path in seeking the explanations in the processes of individual psychology and psychoanalysis. It is not claimed here that all this material is entirely irrelevant to science, but that it is inadequate to account for the major part of hostile behavior across group lines. Part of the difficulty appears to lie in defects of knowledge and theory in the above fields, but the more important part stems from failure to recognize the nature of collective processes. The content of human minds is of course influenced by unique patterns in individual experiences, but far more by elaborately organized social experience. Persons can make distinctions, and invent categories which influence actions, but most of these are in fact made for them by the groups in which they have membership.

We are told by our groups who and what to like and dislike, but in a process generally subtle enough to allow us to feel that we have arrived at these judgments individually and logically. Our organized groups, in turn, achieve the content of collective judgments, not from summing the contributions of the separate members, but within an emergent process of group-to-group interaction which can only be fully investigated on the sociological level. We thus require a concept of causation in which groups, which are entities real enough for our purposes, interact in collisions, generate materials of psychological content, and diffuse these among their members. Any hope of control of psychological aspects of hostility necessarily lies in the comprehension and control of the processes involved in the group-to-group interaction.

References

Adorno, T. W., et al., 1950. *The authoritarian personality.* New York, Harper.

Allen, Doris T., 1956. Action research with children of different nationalities. *Psychological approaches to intergroup and international understanding.* Austin, Texas, The Hogg Foundation for Mental Health.

Allport, F. H., 1924. The group fallacy in relation to social science. *Amer. J. Sociol.,* 29, 688–706.

Ansari, A., 1956. A study of the relation between group stereotypes and social distances. *J. Educ. and Psych.,* 14, No. 1, 28–35.

Blumer, H., 1958. Race prejudice as a sense of group position. *Pacif. Sociol. Rev.,* 1, No. 1.

Blumer, H., 1947.   Sociological theory in industrial relations. *Amer. Sociol. Rev.*, 12:3, 271–278.

Bonner, J. T., 1949.   The social amoebae. *Sci. American*, 180, No. 6, 44–47.

Cooper, E., and Marie Jahoda, 1947.   The evasion of propaganda: How prejudiced people respond to anti-prejudice propaganda. *J. Psychol.*, 23, 15–25.

Dodd, S. C., 1951.   A measured wave of interracial tension. *Soc. Forces*, 29, 281–289.

Dollard, J., L. W. Doob, N. E. Miller, O. H. Mowrer, and R. R. Sears, 1939.   *Frustration and aggression.* New Haven, Yale University Press.

Duvall, E. M., and R. Hill, 1945.   *When you marry.* New York, Heath.

Empey, L. T., and W. L. Slocum, 1955.   Stability of farmers' attitudes in a conflict situation involving farmer-hunter relations. *Rural Sociol.*, 20, 242–248.

Flowerman, S. H., 1950.   Portrait of the authoritarian man. *New York Times Magazine*, 2, 179–204.   (Quoted in E. L. Hartley and R. E. Hartley, 1952. *Fundamentals of social psychology*, 711–713.)

Frazier, E. F., 1957.   Race relations in world perspective. *Sociol. soc. Res.*, 41, 331–335.

Gist, N. P., 1955.   Fraternal membership policies and minority groups: the case of Missouri University. *Soc. Prob.*, 2, 165–172.

Goldsborough, L., 1949.   Better toys for your child. *Reader's Digest*, December issue.

Goldsen, Rose K., E. Suchman, and R. Williams, 1956.   Factors associated with the development of cross-cultural social interaction. *J. soc. Issues*, 12, 26–32.

Hartley, E. L., and Ruth E. Hartley, 1952.   *Fundamentals of social psychology.* New York, Knopf.

Hartley, Ruth E., 1956.   The acceptance of new reference groups. (Mimeographed.)   Summarized in *Psych. Abstracts*, 1958, 6, 234.

Hovland, C. I., and R. R. Sears, 1940.   Minor studies in aggression: VI. Correlations of lynchings with economic indices. *J. Psychol.*, 9, 301–310.

Jahoda, Marie, M. Deutsch, and S. Cook, 1951.   *Research methods in social relations.* New York, Dryden.

Lindzey, G., 1950.   An experimental examination of the scapegoat theory of prejudice. *J. abnorm. soc. Psychol.*, 45, 296–309.

McNickle, D'Arcy, 1937.   Indian and European: Indian-white relations from discovery to 1887. *Ann. Amer. Acad. pol. soc. Sci.*, 311, 1–11.

Moreno, J. L., 1940.   Mental catharsis and the psychodrama. *Sociometry*, 3, 209–244.

Newcomb, T. M., 1943.   *Personality and social change.* New York, Dryden.

Prothro, E. T., and L. H. Melikian, 1953.   Generalized ethnic attitudes in the Arab Near East. *Sociol. soc. Res.*, 37, 375–379.

Sherif, M., O. J. Harvey, B. J. White, W. R. Hood, and Carolyn W. Sherif, 1954.   *Experimental study of positive and negative intergroup atti-*

tudes between experimentally produced groups: Robbers Cave study. (Multilithed.) Norman, Oklahoma.

Sherif, M., and Carolyn W. Sherif, 1953. *Groups in harmony and tension.* New York, Harper.

Sorokin, P. A., 1932. An experimental study of the influence of suggestion on the discrimination and the valuation of people. *Amer. J. Sociol.,* 37, 720–737.

Stouffer, S. A., et al., 1949. *The American soldier: Adjustment during army life,* Vol. I. Princeton, Princeton University Press.

Sumner, W. G., 1906. *Folkways.* Boston, Ginn.

Yinger, J. M., 1959. The sociology of race and ethnic relations. Ch. 17 in R. K. Merton, L. Broom, and L. S. Cottrell, Jr. (eds.). *Sociology today.* New York, Basic Books, 376–399.

3

"NO MAN is an island."

"A system (or a group or a 'whole') is not the same as the sum of its parts."

"Groups are open, not closed systems."

These aphorisms receive lip service from many social scientists and psychologists today. It is far more difficult to make such notions operational through concepts, methodology, and procedures suitable for research on individual, group, and intergroup levels of interaction. The authors of this book reveal some of the difficulties in discussing problems they have faced in their own research programs.

In this chapter Ralph M. Stogdill takes us through programmatic theory and research developed for the study of leadership, especially in industrial organizations. Problems of leadership, possibly more than any others, virtually demand the integration of concepts and findings from different levels of analysis. Leaders, their representatives, or their delegates are frequently involved in *intergroup* transactions. Leadership is a position *within* an organization and is subject to its sanctions. A leader is also involved in repeated *interpersonal* interactions with other members; and, in the ordinary run of affairs, the leader position is undeniably occupied for considerable periods of time by the same *individual*.

With a critical eye on related approaches and research, Stogdill summarizes a conceptual scheme found useful in dealing with interpersonal and group interaction. Then he proposes extensions of the scheme to the level of intergroup interaction, pointing to existing gaps in research. The latter include, notably, persistent issues concerning the power structures within groups which affect leaders and their representatives in transactions with other groups, especially in committing their groups to some course. Such issues become focal in later chapters by Dubin and Killian and are inevitably crucial in the enormous problems faced by the political scientist who, like Robert C. North, undertakes research on policy and decision making in international affairs.

EDITOR

3 INTRAGROUP-INTERGROUP THEORY AND RESEARCH

by Ralph M. Stogdill

The scientist attempts to make verifiable statements about the nature of things. Such statements, when advanced as theories, are expressed in terms of the relationships between events. Increase in understanding is dependent upon the development of methods for demonstrating that theories are not only verifiable, but are also logically consistent. Understanding is further increased when two or more separate systems can be put together in such a manner as to form an integral system of verifiable and logically consistent statements.

Strong efforts are being made in the social sciences to bring about the integration of subsets of statements heretofore regarded as separate and independent theories. The convergence of theories relating to individual with those relating to group events is apparent in research on interpersonal perception and interpersonal reinforcement. Much other integrative work is being done at different levels of generality.

All of this is encouraging, particularly in view of the fact that no more than a decade ago a considerable number of social scientists indicated doubt that any attempt should be made to develop structured theories. The fear was expressed that premature structuring might close important avenues to discovery. Of course, this danger exists with theories that are formulated independently of designs for empirical research. Fortunately, this kind of theorizing is not as popular as it once was. We now tend to keep the factor of testability firmly in mind in the development of theories.

In the Ohio State Leadership Studies, we have tended to move slowly in the development of theory. This does not mean that we worked without any theoretical orientation. At the very beginning of our research, we developed a set of guiding principles relative to content and method; in regard to method, we set down the following working principles:

1. Description should precede evaluation. Let us discover what exists before attempting to evaluate it.
2. Understanding is based on the demonstration of relationship. Theory should be based on an empirically established system of interrelationships.
3. Methods should be developed for the measurement of all variables thought to be necessary for a logically complete and coherent system. Whenever possible, scaled measures should be developed for every variable thought to be essential to the system. That which cannot be categorized or quantified cannot be related to other variables.
4. Empirical research should be conducted on a systematic basis.
5. Structured designs are necessary for systematic research.

In regard to content, we worked on the assumption that our predecessors might not have been totally in error in what they thought important to an understanding of leadership and group endeavor. Analysis of a variety of sources suggested the need for measures or categorizations of the following sets of variables:

(1) Group structure and functional differentiation
(2) Responsibility, authority, and delegation
(3) Individual work performance
(4) Member role behavior, including leader role behavior
(5) The structure of working interactions
(6) The structure of informal interactions
(7) Member expectations and satisfactions
(8) Group outputs, including productive effectiveness

We omitted two sets of variables which I now think must be given consideration. One is the factor of personality. The other is the individual's system of values in terms of which he evaluates issues and events. Upon completion of research now in progress, we plan to expand our design to include these two sets of variables.

Two matters of prime importance will not be included in our

new research design. One is concerned with ecological and environmental factors bearing upon a group. The other is concerned with intergroup relations. Sound progress in what we are doing requires that we limit our design to manageable propositions. Our work suggests a number of research problems that may be of interest to the intergroup theorist. But my comments will not be based on any research that we have done in the area. They will be based on the assumption that any variables that are important in intragroup theory may also be relevant to intergroup theory.

The Convergence of Individual and Group Theories

The social sciences have developed separate theories relative to personality, value, role, and social group. None of these theories in isolation has proved to be as powerful as we once hoped it might. Perhaps one reason for this outcome is that none of the theories is a complete system in itself. For more than thirty years, personality has been defined in terms of interpersonal stimulus potentials, but we conduct our research as if personality resided solely in the isolated individual. Considerably better progress has been made in research designed to study social roles as interpersonal events. Much of the current research on values is of the static sort which attributes value solely to the individual. But thanks to Sherif's (1936) pioneering work, marked progress has been made toward the study of values as group and individual norms in interaction. Quite recently, the study of interpersonal expectation and its reinforcement has provided another approach to research on values and roles. It seems not improbable that further developments of norm theory and expectation theory may open up new avenues to research in personality.

The trend of the new research, in its most sophisticated form, is exemplified in Cattell's (1960) integration of theory relating to personality, role, and group; and in Sherif's (1960) integration of theory involving individual values, interpersonal norms, intragroup behavior, and intergroup action. There is unmistakable evidence on these developments that the concepts of personality, role, identification, value, norm, group structure, and group action are thought to belong in a single theoretical system. Once this integration has been accomplished, we should learn much more about each subset of the system than we can possibly know about it when it is considered in isolation.

Person-Interperson Theory

If several subsets belong in the same system, then it should be possible to demonstrate that they all can be generated by the same set of input variables. Two major problems are involved in such an attempt. The first involves speculations or decisions relative to what subsets actually belong in the system. The second concerns the selection and definition of basic variables capable of accounting for the system as a whole, as well as for all the subsets that it contains. The scientific method specifies no rules of procedure for this sort of work. It is a matter of judgment and invention. A correct solution, if attained, can as readily issue from a flash of insight as from a laborious period of trial and error, or from a combination of both. The scientific method becomes applicable after this work has been completed and advanced as an hypothesized solution in need of test and verification. But a theory is necessary for systematic inquiry and testing if the problem is at all complex.

As an aid to systematic research on some of the problems being considered by this symposium, an outline of personal-interpersonal variables might be of at least passing interest. One possible set of such variables is represented in Figure 1. It lists a minimum set of variables that appear to be needed for a coherent system, and outlines the structural, not the operational, requirements for a theory. It represents a broadly generalized statement of hypothesis relative to the structure of relationships between sets of personal, interpersonal, and group variables that appear to belong in the same system. It will be noted that performance, expectation, and interaction are regarded as basic inputs from which the remainder of the system is derived.

This outline expresses the general hypothesis that the three subsets of basic variables, acting in combination, are capable of

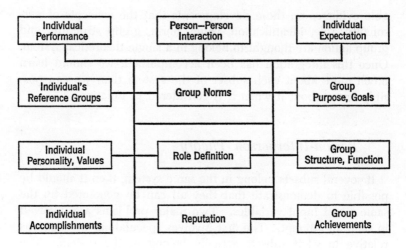

Figure 1. Conceptual structure for a person-interperson system.

explaining individual personality, values, and reference group identifications—as well as group norms and interpersonal role definition, and also group purpose, structure, and function. These six subsets may be regarded in turn as mediators. It is only through the mediation of these variables that the basic variables can be operated upon to generate a set of outcomes.

A system stands or falls on the definition of the concepts in each of the subsets. Any one of several variants of expectation theory could be entered in the upper right hand segment of the outline. The statistical theory of expectation can predict only the value of an outcome. Decision theory and utility theory are based on simplifying assumptions that seriously limit the validity of any outcomes generated by the theories. Only when expectation is defined as a learning or reinforcement theory does it appear capable of predicting response and accounting for the complexities of individual personality and group structure. This example is sufficient to suggest that the definition of a concept is an important determiner of the theory that can be produced with its use.

In this discussion, we are not interested in the definition of concepts, but in an examination of some of the considerations which lead us to believe that the variables outlined in Figure 1 belong in the same system. But this examination cannot be conducted in any greatly detailed or closely reasoned fashion.

It should be noted that group structure and operation cannot be accounted for by adding the characteristics of individuals. Intergroup theory amounts to more than a summation of the characteristics of groups. All the subsets in Figure 1 interact to produce individual and group effects of great complexity.

Money and materials may be regarded as inputs and outputs in many groups, but are not common to all groups. Energy is not properly regarded as an input from external sources, since it is released by stimulation. But performances, expectations, and interactions are basic conditions for the existence of any organized group. For this reason, they may be regarded as inputs. Any increase or decrease in performance, expectation or interaction accounts for a change in group inputs. The inputs of a system are merely concepts which when examined in all possible combinations account for the structural and operational characteristics of the system. Outputs, in turn, are concepts used to describe the consequences generated by the system. Such outcomes may refer to satisfactions, winnings, losses, services, or physical products. Whatever their referents, the inputs and outputs of a system are to be regarded only as abstract concepts.

The basic variables (performance, interaction, and expectation), as well as the mediating variables, have been subjects of extensive research and theory. Comparatively little is known about the structure of the output subsets. Recent research on creativity offers hope of increasing knowledge of the nature of individual accomplishment. Reputation has received little attention in the past two decades. However, prior to World War II, prestige was regarded as an important variable, especially in the theory of leadership. Both individuals and groups acquire reputations. These factors may have considerable weight in determining a member's acceptability to a group, as well as the group's acceptability to a prospective member. The proposed outline suggests the need for a renewed concern for the factor of individual and group reputation in our research. It is only within the past two years that a successful theory of group achievement has been produced. Stogdill's (1959) work suggests that the many apparently contradictory findings relative to the relationships between member satisfaction, group integration, and group productivity can be reconciled and explained if group integration, morale, and productivity are all regarded as group outputs. Research now in progress appears to offer strong support to this interpretation.

In Figure 1 the mediating and output subsets (reference groups, personality, and accomplishments) in the left hand column can be regarded as attributes of individuals; those in the middle column (norms, roles, and reputations) can be regarded as pertaining essentially to interpersonal relations, and those in the right hand column as pertaining to groups. But there is considerable overlap and blending between the three columns, as would be expected of subsets of variables generated by the same set of inputs. This blending effect probably accounts for the confusion and segmentation that has existed in the field of social psychology. Another factor that has acted to retard progress in the integration of theory is the tremendous complexity of each of the twelve subsets in the outline.

In comparison with those in the middle column, the variables in the outside columns appear to exhibit a high degree of structural stability. Individual personality describes characteristic patterns of valuing and coping that tend to persist from one situation to another. The formal structure of positions (status and function) in a group tends to endure, even with changes in the occupancy of the positions. This is particularly true in large, long established organizations. However, it has been shown that role performance and group norms tend to change in conformity with changes in interaction characteristics, task requirements, and situational structure. Supporting evidence is reported by Sherif and Sherif (1956). The primary direction of effect is considered to act from top to bottom. A secondary direction of operation acts from left to right. However, any subset, through feedback effects, can influence and modify any other subset, including the input variables.

If there is any merit in the hypothesis that all the twelve subsets belong in the same system, then it seems possible to account for the lack of progress in each one separately. No one of the twelve contains a firm anchoring point or criterion in itself. Its structure can be elucidated and verified only in terms of its relationships to the other subsets. Progress in the physical sciences has proceeded along these lines. Despite the arguments of those who claim that the social sciences constitute a separate breed requiring its own special rules and exemptions, there is reason to believe that progress here will be made only along the same lines as pertain in the physical sciences. There are no absolute criteria for any of the sets of events studied in the social sciences. For this reason, it seems hopeful that progress can be made through the demonstration of interrelationship between subsets of events considered to belong in the same system.

Leadership and Intragroup Theory

The person-interperson outline covers a wide area of theory and research. Definitions of many of the concepts, and the operation of parts of the model have been discussed in a prior publication (Stogdill, 1959). It should be capable of generating a theory of leadership. It seems only necessary to start with the assumption that leadership is based upon the performances and expectations of group members in interaction.

Every member of a group exhibits at least some minimal sort of performance, if no more than that of affiliating or paying dues. A member's interactions with other members is in itself an overt performance. The research of Bales (1950) exemplifies a large body of studies which indicate that an individual's performance is an important determiner of the part he will be permitted to play in a group. The same research indicates that a member's pattern of interaction with other members is a determiner of his role in the group. In recent years, it has been clearly recognized that roles are defined in terms of the expectations that members entertain relative to their own performances and interactions, and particularly relative to the contributions of other members of the group. The role concept is a central one in group theory.

The structuring of a member's role defines, at the same time, his position (status and function) in the group. A system of positions, thus defined, describes the formal structure of a group.

A member is expected to perform and interact in accordance with the specifications defined for his position.

But each member brings into a group a strongly preconditioned personality, value system, and set of identifications. These factors, in addition to a member's general ability, knowledge, and skill, may determine to a very high degree the adequacy of his performances and interactions, and the realism of his expectations in a group. Thus, an individual's prior experience and conditioning, as well as his immediate behavior in a group, plus his accomplishments and reputation, and his positions in other groups, combine to determine the role he will be able to play.

Once the members of a group become mutually task oriented or agree upon a common purpose, they tend to operate in such a manner as to achieve three distinctive outcomes—the creation of a product or service, the maintenance of structural and operational integration, and the maintenance of sufficient freedom of action for individual initiative in the performance of defined roles. These outcomes are not always positively correlated. In fact, there is extensive experimental evidence which indicates that integration tends to decrease as productivity increases, and conversely that efforts devoted by the group to the redefinition of structure tend to be accompanied by a decrease in productivity. Research now in progress confirms the same general relationship between integration and productivity in the different subunits of large manufacturing plants.

One means adopted by a group to cope with the complex and contradictory demands made upon it is that of role differentiation. Each member acquires a specified position and role. Leadership may be regarded as one aspect of such role differentiation. It is not an attribute of individuals as much as of positions and roles, all of which may differ in this respect from very little to very much. A single role may also differ considerably in this regard from time to time. About a decade ago, Homans (1950) and Hemphill (1954) presented the first operationally useful definition of leadership. They defined it as the origination or initiation of structure in interaction. More recent experimental and theoretical work suggests that the interactional concept alone is not adequate to generate a theory of roles or of group structure. Roles are defined in terms of mutual expectations. In view of this consideration, it would seem that *leadership* can be best defined in terms of *the initiation and maintenance of structure in expectation and interaction.*

The definition is of considerable theoretical significance, not only for what it includes, but also for what it omits. Leadership is defined in terms of its effects upon two of the input variables that generate group purpose, structure, operations, and achievement. If one may appeal directly to the experimental evidence, we see that the individual who emerges as a leader in an experimental group is one who succeeds in initiating structure and in reinforcing the expectation that he will be able to maintain such structure as operations continue. His role becomes differentiated from other roles in specific reference to group purpose, structure, and achievement. He is expected not only to keep the group moving toward task achievement but also to maintain the structural integrity of the group and to provide freedom for initiative in other member roles.

Now let us consider the input variable that was not included in the definition of leadership. This is the performance variable. Why do we not include the structuring of member performance in the definition of leadership? First, because the leader cannot do the work of all the members of the group. Second, because initiation of performance is not confined to leadership. It is a characteristic of every role in the group. In terms of our analysis, one of the prime functions of leadership is that of providing freedom for the initiation of performance in other roles. The only restriction of this freedom for initiative that concerns leadership is such restriction as may result from the maintenance of structure in role definition. Within this range of definition, initiative for performance remains with the occupant of each position in the group. Any serious violation of this freedom for initiative is likely to reduce group productivity, and possibly integration as well.

Research on the emergence of leadership in experimental groups suggests that the greater degree of freedom granted the high status member is directly concerned with the initiation, reinforcement, and maintenance of a structure of differentiated roles. Little progress toward task performance is able to take place until such structure has been achieved and stabilized. However, the group members, in granting greater freedom to fellow members in positions of greater leadership potential, do not thereby relinquish their rights to the initiation of task performance in their own positions. In fact, they tend to grant high status to the member who exhibits considerable tolerance for initiative in other members.

It appears, then, that the individual most likely to emerge as a leader in a group is one who is capable of reconciling the complex and contradictory demands involved in the maintenance of group productivity, structural integration, and freedom of action in goal striving. These three role requirements might be regarded as basic functions of leadership. They are to some extent mutually contradictory, and difficult to keep in balance. Perhaps the least well understood is that relating to individual initiative and group freedom from restraint in action toward a goal. One of the central issues in political philosophy is concerned with this problem. Intimately related to it is the problem of power. Struggles for power between individuals and subgroups have been largely treated as studies in the pathology of the vertical status structure of the group. But Dubin (1957) has shown that intragroup power struggles are directly concerned with the right to control the exercise of function—usually the leadership function.

In summarizing this brief discussion of leadership, it would appear that concepts and theory developed within the past five years should provide a basis for more systematic and effective research than has been possible in the past.

An Intragroup-Intergroup Model

We have followed the procedure, in discussing group theory, of exploring broadly rather than probing in depth. We shall follow along the same line in discussing intergroup theory. We shall be interested, not so much in developing new information, as in uncovering and clarifying some of the implications of intragroup theory for research in intergroup relations.

Figure 2 represents one possible set of structural specifications for an intragroup-intergroup model. It does not specify the formal operations necessary to generate a theory of intergroup relations. This outline is based on the hypothesis that

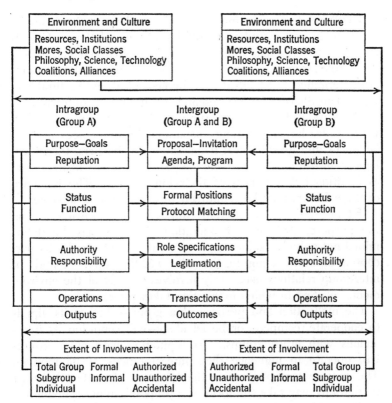

Figure 2. Conceptual structure for an intragroup-intergroup system.

groups interact on the dimensions that define intragroup purpose, structure, operations, and achievement. The comments presented here represent observation and speculation rather than any formalized attempt to develop theory. No argument is offered for their validity.

The outside columns represent condensed models of two separate groups. All the individual and interpersonal variables contained in Figure 1 are assumed to have been absorbed and stabilized by the two formally structured groups in Figure 2, but still capable of operating as in Figure 1. The middle column specifies some of the major variables of contact and interaction between the two groups.

The weaknesses inherent in the disregard of environmental

and cultural factors in intragroup theory become immediately apparent in any consideration of intergroup relations. Groups are open systems that interact with their environments. Their goals, role structures, norms, comparison groups, and operations are determined to a high degree by ecological and cultural factors. The Sherifs' (1960) research on groups in differentiated sociocultural settings strongly supports this point of view. When we consider larger groupings, separated by differences in race, language, and geographical demarcations or barriers, then ideological, institutional, and technological factors are likely to act as additional determiners of their interactions. The influence of these factors may be reinforced by coalition and alliance.

If two groups from different cultural settings are interacting, the purpose, structure, or operations of each may be determined not only by factors in its own culture but also by its perception of, and reaction to, the culture of the other. A study of intergroup relations necessarily involves a study of the environmental context in which interaction takes place.

The motivation and purpose of a group—whether its aim is to cooperate, compete, or be let alone—will condition its interactions with other groups. Its reputation with other groups will operate to influence their interpretations of its motives. The statement of purpose in the initiation of contact between two groups may take the form of a proposal, inquiry, invitation, challenge, demand, proclamation, and the like. It may or may not specify a detailed program of proposed action. Of course, there are circumstances in which the mere presence of two groups in the same territory is sufficient to stimulate action without any statement of intent, but each is likely to arrive at a purpose which it may or may not attempt to conceal.

The extent to which a group regards itself as committed to a given objective is related to the status in the group of the member who initiates policy or action in regard to intergroup relations. Sherif and Sherif (1956) report that the gangs of boys in the Robbers Cave study regarded themselves as committed by the decisions and actions of their respective leaders. They did not regard themselves as committed by the actions of low status members. However, one group might commit itself to avenge some aggression exhibited against one of its low status members by the rival group.

The higher the "within" group status of the members who are the locus of intergroup contact, the greater the degree of formality and protocol surrounding arrangement for the contact. Furthermore, as the discrepancy in status between the representatives of two groups increases, the resistance to communication and transaction also increases. Sherif and Sherif (1953) and Whyte (1943) have presented evidence which suggests that the high status members of a group may refuse to interact at all with low status members of a rival group. Whereas the highly skilled members of a group may exhibit great restraint in any competition with their own leader, they exhibit no such restraint when competing with status equals in their own or in rival groups.

Not only do the members of a group differ in function and status; the groups within a society, and the societal groups in the world environment, differ among themselves in status. The status differential between groups can serve as a mechanism by means of which an aspiring leader of a low status group can elevate his personal social status. Any success attained by such a leader in gaining recognition by leaders of high status groups serves effectively to elevate his personal status, whether or not it raises the status of the group that he represents. The legitimation of position can come about either as the result of mutual assent among the members of a group or as the result of recognition by the leadership of external groups.

The locus in the status structure at which two groups agree to interact determines not only the quantitative but also the qualitative aspects of the group power involved in the interaction. Ordinarily, less power is exerted by middle status than by high or low status representatives of interacting groups. Transactions by high status members tend to marshall comparatively high degrees of group power at the level of negotiation and commitment. Interactions by low status members may involve the application of high degrees of group power in physical transactions. This observation, or rather hypothesis, suggests the need for research on conditions that determine the power that can or will be applied by groups in their transactions with one another.

The positions in a group are differentiated according to status and function. Function defines the performances expected to pertain to a given position, regardless of its occupant. Successive occupants of the same position may not play identical roles in the group. They may not be assigned exactly the same responsibilities, and they may not be granted equal degrees of authority for the discharge of their responsibilities. Whereas positions define sets of high generalized and stabilized expectations relative to group purpose, roles define short range, changing expectations relative to the details of performance on behalf of the group. Positions are differentiated relative to status and function. Roles are differentiated in terms of responsibility and authority for specified classes of performances.

The member in a position of leadership is subject to group sanctions. He may be held to higher standards of accountability and respectability than other members of the group. He can deviate from expectation with impunity only when he holds dictatorial power over the members or when he becomes such a perfect exemplar of the member norms and aspirations that he is perceived to do no wrong. Even under these extreme conditions of legitimation, whether by force or common assent, the leader is expected to act in the interest of group survival and member welfare. Due to the peripheral positions of rank and file members in the communications system, it is often difficult for them to evaluate the consequences of a commitment to another group until long after a *fait accompli*. Considerable detailed information is available regarding the means by which a powerful leader may exploit or subvert a group. However, comparatively little is known about the measures that a group may take in order to abrogate a group commitment made by its leader in secret or in violation of the interests of the members. This problem has assumed increasing importance in the past two decades, especially on the international scene.

Knowledge of a member's position (status and function) may reveal very little about his responsibility and authority in a group. Knowledge concerning the role structure is also required. In addition, it is necessary to know whether a member has been granted special responsibility and authority for a specific task. Such knowledge is particularly important in intergroup relations. Progress in intergroup transactions may depend upon an exact knowledge of the authority of the participants to commit the groups that they represent. The firmness of commitment will be conditioned by the locus of authority in the group and the method of its legitimation by the group members. This is a matter of considerable complexity. Commitment and follow-through are likely to be most firmly established when the participants in an intergroup transaction are specifically authorized representatives of the group and its leadership in consensus. Commitments made by a leader or representative independently of group consensus are most easily evaded by that leader or representative. On the other hand, a leader with a strongly legitimated position in group consensus may bind a group to the most damaging commitments from which it has no recourse or escape. There is no problem within the realm of the social sciences so much in need of cleanly designed research as that pertaining to group commitment, particularly unauthorized commitment made under conditions of secret negotiation.

The transactions of the representatives of two groups represent operations of the groups. Such intergroup operations generate outcomes that feed back into both groups and affect their progress and survival capacity. It is in the group interest to specify clearly the roles of its representatives and the limits of their authority in committing the group to a decision or course of action. But this power of specification and legitimation is seriously abridged when the locus of authority resides in the leader who is himself acting as the representative of the group.

Observation suggests the hypothesis that the mutual agreements made by groups tend to involve high degrees of commitment. But exceptions are noted. Research is needed to determine the internal and external conditions under which a group regards itself as bound by, or free to violate, the agreements it makes. The ideology of the group relative to the importance, means, and ethics of goal attainment would appear to be an important determining factor. Any marked differential between two groups relative to the ethics of keeping agreements is likely to place one or the other at a disadvantage. If its cultural ethic requires the keeping of agreements, a group may not be able to renounce a disadvantageous commitment without such a marked change in its leadership structure as to alter the essential identity of the group. The identity of the German nation was not quite the same under Hitler as under the administration of his predecessor. Many other examples could be cited. Since the identity of a group may be profoundly affected by a change of leadership and administrative ideology, and the repudiation of a disliked agreement may require a change of leadership, intergroup commitments may be matters of critical importance to a group. The power of the group leader to make or break agreements may also be an important factor in group identity and survival.

Problems concerning the nature and extent of group involvement in intergroup relations have been discussed in different contexts. But they merit additional attention. Certainly the nature of any transaction will differ depending upon whether it involves two total groups, a subgroup from each, or an individual representative from each. It will differ depending upon whether the contact is a formal or informal one, and upon whether it is authorized, unauthorized, or accidental. A few examples will make this clear. When a subgroup from each of two larger groups meets on an informal but authorized basis, perhaps to play baseball or basketball, the contact can have positive prestige and integrative value for each of the parent groups. Of course, it can and occasionally does have the opposite effect. In a different situation, a subgroup making covert contacts with a rival group can place the parent group in serious jeopardy. Or again, the accidental collision of a single member with a rival group can mobilize the full force of both groups in active combat. Such examples could be cited for each of the 3 x 2 x 3 factors of involvement shown in Figure 2. Each of these separate conditions could be further elaborated in relation to several conditions of intragroup and intergroup purpose. When we consider the interactions between all the subsets of variables in the outline, which is far from complete, it becomes apparent that intergroup theory is indeed a complex matter. We have noted here only a few of the highlights.

Discussion

We have examined one approach to the integration of subsets usually regarded as constituting independent theories. We have concerned ourselves primarily with the structure of such an integrative system. A most casual examination of the operational possibilities of the outline suggests that a systematic theory developed along these lines should be capable of generating insights of great complexity.

Certain aspects of the system are well supported by empirical findings; others are greatly in need of intensive research. It would appear that a structured theory, far from closing the door to inquiry, can provide an effective framework for systematic research and can pinpoint areas in need of original investigation.

References

Bales, R. F., 1950. *Interaction process analysis.* Reading, Mass., Addison-Wesley.

Cattell, R. B., 1960. *Group theory, personality and role: a model for experimental researches.* (Mimeographed.) Urbana, University of Illinois, Laboratory of Personality Assessment and Group Behavior.

Dubin, R., 1957. Power and union management relations. *Admin. Sci. Quar.,* 2, 60–81.

Hemphill, J. K., Pauline N. Pepinsky, R. N. Shevitz, W. E. Jaynes, and Charlotte A. Christner, 1954. *Leadership acts: I. An investigation of the relation between possession of task relevant information and attempts to lead.* (Mimeographed.) Columbus, Ohio State University, Personal Research Board.

Homans, G. C., 1950. *The human group.* New York, Harcourt, Brace.

Shaw, C. R., and H. D. McKay, 1942. *Juvenile delinquency and urban areas.* Chicago, University of Chicago Press.

Sherif, M., 1936. *The psychology of social norms.* New York, Harper.

——, 1960. Conformity-deviation, norms, and group relations. In I. A. Berg and B. M. Bass (eds.), *Conformity and deviation.* New York, Harper.

Sherif, M., and Carolyn W. Sherif, 1953. *Groups in harmony and tension.* New York, Harper.

——, 1956. *An outline of social psychology.* Revised edition. New York, Harper.

——, 1960. *Theoretical and research reports on behavior in natural groups within differentiated sociocultural settings.* Reports II and III. (Mimeographed.) Norman, University of Oklahoma, Institute of Group Relations.

Sherif, M., and M. O. Wilson, 1953. *Group relations at the crossroads.* New York, Harper.

Stogdill, R. M., 1959. *Individual behavior and group achievement.* New York, Oxford University Press.

Whyte, W. F., 1943. *Street corner society.* Chicago, University of Chicago Press.

II

INTERSYSTEM AND
INTRASYSTEM RELATIONS:
THEIR RECIPROCAL IMPACT

4

THE IMPACT of intergroup confrontations upon the respective group organizations and, conversely, the significance of the particular patterns of authority and value within groups for the outcome of intergroup transactions are strikingly manifested in labor-management relationships. Indeed, it could be maintained with reasonableness that the origins of union and management groups in the United States, as organized subsystems with fairly explicit goals and memberships, lie, to a large extent, in successive collective conflicts between the parties involved.

Robert Dubin addresses union-management relations in the United States today as an intergroup system. He shows how the properties of this system as well as the organizing schemes and goals of its subunits affect leadership functions, especially the ranges of choice available to the respective leaders and the flexibility possible in intergroup negotiations. Certain characteristics of the system and of the subsystems as stabilized at present function, therefore, as "constraints" upon leaders in decision making processes.

Here, then, is an empirically based theoretical model of a functioning system, conceptualized on an intergroup level of analysis. Close study of this intergroup system leads Dubin, like Stogdill in the previous chapter, to heightened awareness that the large organizations whose interrelations he has studied are, in turn, parts of larger systems. Thus, external influences constantly impinge upon them, affecting their internal plans as well as the problems faced in collective encounters across group lines. Doubtless developments external to American union-management systems played a part in the stabilization of the contemporary modus vivendi. Dubin forecasts that external changes, especially developments enabling increased automation and the growing interdependence in international markets, will be the sources of future changes in the union-management system in this country.

EDITOR

4 LEADERSHIP IN UNION-MANAGEMENT RELATIONS AS AN INTERGROUP SYSTEM

by Robert Dubin

We will first consider union-management relations as a social system. Attention will then turn to management and union leaders to discover how leadership functions are carried out in such systems; particular emphasis will be placed on the system constraints affecting actions of leaders. The preponderance of this material, which is given more extended analysis elsewhere, will be drawn from the American experience (Dubin, 1958a).

Intergroup System

We emphasize three characteristics of a social system. (1) The participants have means for identifying who its members are, and therefore, the *boundaries* within which social relations take place. (2) Social relations within the system are given some coherence because they are guided by a *core of objectives* shared by system members. (3) These objectives are either attained or continuously sought through actions whose regularity of pattern can be labeled *institutionalized behavior*. Union-management relations meet these criteria of a social system.

The boundary of a given collective bargaining system is established with the interaction of the two basic units composing it—the union(s) and the employing organization whose workers are represented by the union. This boundary is clearly understood for any given collective bargaining relationship where management and union are included, and where they are excluded. This system boundary is recognized in union contracts as giving rise to a necessary relationship between a given company and the union of its employees (Dubin, 1949). Neither party is free, during the period of the contract, to bargain with any but the designated management or union. Thus, a union-management system, once established, has the special characteristic of being a necessary relationship for the parties to it, making it difficult to destroy the system, or even to substitute other parties for those who established it. For example, decertification proceedings seeking to eliminate a bargaining agent, or substitute another union as bargaining representative account for only a minor percentage of the case load of the National Labor Relations Board.

We will simply list several core objectives sought in union-management relations in order to demonstrate that some exist, entitling us to characterize this relationship as a social system. This list of core objectives of the system is not exhaustive, and we will not explicate the individual objectives since our concern is only to show that there are some.

(A) Continuity of an employment relationship—for management this centers on retaining a body of trained workers readily available for specialized productive tasks, while for the union a continuous employment relationship is a central feature of economic security for its members.

(B) Stability of an employment relationship—from management's standpoint this serves to minimize replacement and training costs (very considerable personnel expenses) and presumably increases productivity by enhancing morale and satisfaction with work; on the union side stability of employment guarantees long-term payoffs for working, including *continuity* of employment with a single employer, pensions, health and welfare benefits and supplementary unemployment benefits.

(C) Maintenance of markets for the products of an affluent society—results in management's interest in wages as purchasing power, and a similar union stance.

(D) Concern with future social goals—ranging for management from the survival of capitalism to the automation of production, and for unions from technological unemployment to the survival of unions as the labor force shifts from blue to white collars.

It will be noted that most of these core objectives are shared, but accepted for different reasons by the respective parties. This is not uncommon in social systems. The more usual search for shared social goals—shared by diverse groups for the *same* reason—has tended to turn analytical attention away from discovery of mechanisms of social adjustment in which a single broad objective may have support of several groups, each with its own special grounds for approval. Thus, one of the important contemporary analysts of social systems, Talcott Parsons, fails to give adequate attention to the role of core objectives, rationalized on separate grounds by the groups holding them. In the industrial relations literature, frequent attempts have been made to set forth common goals of the parties which are presumed to rest on identical interests. (See, for example, Bakke, 1946 and Twentieth Century Fund, Labor Committee publication, 1949.)

The third feature of a social system—that the behavior within it is institutionalized—is clearly evident in a collective bargaining relationship. Indeed, collective bargaining is one of the few social systems in which the institutionalized features of behavior are committed to writing and agreed to in advance by the parties. This is contained in the union contract that specifies the rights, duties, obligations, and benefits or payoffs of the parties. It is probably true that the union contract, as developed in the United States, is a close approximation to the Social Contract theory of social organization that was so popular in the seventeenth and eighteenth century intellectual environments. While treaties, commercial contracts, and similar written documents of accord between contending parties display features of a social contract, the union agreement tends to be much more detailed and specific, and to cover the full range of day-to-day interactions between the parties, as well as general goals and methods for their attainment. When we couple with the written contract the constant interaction between the parties and their representatives in day-to-day administration of union-management relations, particularly in handling worker complaints through the grievance procedure, we can readily comprehend the degree to which behavior in the union-management system is institutionalized. The functions of grievance procedures in industrial relations are discussed further in Dubin (1958b, Chapter 17).

The relationship between company and union is the interaction of two independent organizations which have their special logics and internal needs that are independent of the relationship itself. A company can certainly exist without a union representing its employees (although probably its policies towards workers would differ from those achieved under unionism). Worker organizations (including but not limited to unions, as for example, beneficial and fraternal organizations, cooperatives, and political parties) may also exist without reference to particular employers or relations with them. Worker organizations not engaged in collective bargaining will, of course, have goals different from those directed towards bargaining with employers.

The union-management relationship is first of all a system of intergroup relations. What happens in the relationship is shaped, in part, by what happens independently inside each organization. The collective bargaining system, when established, has important feedbacks on the two groups composing it. We may then summarize the union-management relationship as being contained in a social system in which the parties are clearly in recognition of each other and capable of distinguishing the members of the system from nonmembers. There is an obvious set of shared goals recognized by the parties, and a clear-cut institutionalization of their interaction behaviors.

The framework for analysis of leadership in a union-management relationship is then clear. We are primarily interested in predicting leadership behaviors that are determined by the environments of the separate organizations, and the collective bargaining environment of their relationship. Special attention will be directed to the constraints on leaders that are built into the structures and operations of business and labor organizations.

Leaders and Decisions

In the customary analyses of decision making, attention is focused on (1) the *range of choices* available to the decision

maker and (2) the *processes of choosing* among viable alternatives. Less analytical attention is given to the nonviable alternatives, and the conditions that rule them out of consideration.
(For a general bibliography on decision making, with special
reference to organizational decisions, see Wasserman and Silander, 1958.)

It is precisely the consideration of alternatives for decision
that *are not chosen* that leads directly to our examination of
the constraints on leadership behavior in collective bargaining.
It is from this analytical stance that we can discover the situational constraints operating on leaders of both sides. When we
can apprehend the alternatives for decision that are not available, we discover that which is removed from consideration by
situational factors.

Three major propositions, or predictions, about leadership behavior in collective bargaining are stated and analyzed. They
derive from a simple model of union-management relations, the
broad features of which have already been suggested.

The three propositions follow:

1. Leadership decisions are appropriate to the purposes of the
organization led, and the structure of the internal division of
labor for achieving these purposes.

2. Autonomy in the choice of leadership decisions decreases
as the complexity of the division of labor in the organization
increases.

3. In any system involving continuous relations between two
or more organizations, autonomy of leadership decision in any
one organization is decreased by the need to take into account
the limitations on leadership decisions in the other organizations.

Leaders and Organization Purpose

We start by viewing any formal organization as being organized around limited purposes with specified relationships among
its members for carrying out these purposes. A union, and a
company with which it bargains, both exhibit these characteristics.

Leaders of organizations occupy offices that are established parts of the organizational division of labor. Those who fill leadership positions have their behaviors defined within the limited purposes for which the organization exists. Furthermore, leadership behavior is specialized from, but linked to, the behaviors of other members so that what the leader does cannot be independent of the behaviors of nonleaders.

This leads directly to our first proposition. *The choice of leadership behavior is appropriate to the purposes of the organization led, and the structure of internal division of labor for achieving these purposes.* This first prediction tells us that the leader of an organization is not free to make unrestricted choices for his own behavior. The constraints operating on him come from the organization itself.

The general mission of an industrial or commercial organization is to produce goods or services. Executive behaviors in running such organizations involve the integration of men, machines, and materials (including financial resources) in order to produce the goods or services chosen as the field of endeavor. The nature of the goods or services to be produced for a market determines the product's design, its manufacturing processes, marketing structures, pricing policies, and a host of other related issues.

There may be general attributes of executives, and even general skills possessed by all good business executives (cf. Barnard, 1938). In any given business firm, however, there is a specific overlay of knowledge about the purposes of that organization, and the technical means necessary to achieve these purposes. Leadership positions in business organizations, therefore, require an "expertise" peculiar to the particular industry in which executive positions are held.

This specialization of knowledge is what Veblen (1933) has associated with the "trained incapacity" of the expert (including the executive as expert). Trained incapacity implies that knowing something extremely well precludes the possibility of knowing other things equally well. While Veblen pointed to trained incapacity as a limitation on the breadth of leadership knowledge, the other side of the coin is equally important. Expertise means deeper and more detailed knowledge in the area of specialization than is held by laymen. Thus, the trained incapacity of the expert is balanced by his trained capacity for expert behavior in his area of specialization.

For our purposes, the whole range of things for which business executives have a trained incapacity, either as a class of executives, or as leaders of specific industrial and commercial organizations, includes considerable areas of society important for other groups, including unions. Among leaders of business organizations, the very specialization of attention to the purposes of their organizations, and the development of unique skills and knowledge to achieve these purposes, exclude from attention viable alternatives for decision that might come into the purview of others with different kinds of specialized outlooks.

Of the factors of organization manipulated by business management in directing the affairs of their firms, the most costly, and the ones for which the balance sheet has to account, are materials and machines. Both involve fixed investments of capital which, when once made, have to be recaptured or depreciated in reasonable fashion. On the other hand, while the work force of a firm may represent considerable investment in its training and experience, the return on this investment is immediate in the productive output, and is paid for as the work is performed. Consequently, there is no future commitment to the employment of any given number in the firm's labor force, nor is there a need "to write off" or to recapture an investment made in the work force. Of the three general elements involved in the management of a firm, the work force (men) is the one element that is not carried on the accounting books and for which no future accounting need be made.*

We may characterize the emphasis on management of materials and machines as giving to top executives of business firms a "thing" orientation. A firm's balance sheet accurately reflects this thing orientation. What is typically incorporated in the balance sheet is an accounting for the assets and liabilities of the firm in terms of materials and machines.

When we examine the internal organization of a business firm, additional kinds of restraint on executive decisions come into

---

* There are minor exceptions, such as the need to account for future obligations to executives in the form of deferred-payment bonuses, and commitments to retirement programs and similar forms of company contributions to the welfare of its work force.

view. Each functional specialty within the business firm has to have its activities coordinated with those of others. This coordination is achieved through decisions which flow from establishing an order of preference for the various outcomes of business behavior. Once these preference schedules are established, decisions are made which maximize the achievement of given preferences by establishing the kind and level of operations for each functional specialty. These internal decisions not only are interrelated but have to bear some logical relationship with and consistency among them. If, for example, there is an anticipation of a sales decline, production schedules would not be adjusted upwardly, nor would inventories of raw materials normally be increased.

In general, the executive leader of a business firm is subject to two levels of constraints on his decisions. These decisions, first of all, must be relevant to the purposes of his particular firm. Secondly, these decisions must accommodate to the requirements of coordination and integration of specialized functional departments of the firm. Any factors, including union demands, that violate these constraints on executive decisions will be rejected, and if further pressed, will be combatted vigorously.

When we examine the constraints that act on union leadership, we discover that they can be characterized by the required orientation of union leaders to the solution of "people" problems. In a figurative sense, the only meaningful balance sheet that union leaders can draw up for their organizations is the balance sheet showing gains and losses for union members through collective bargaining, or through other activities of the union. It is significant, for example, that the formal accounting procedures of union organizations, accounting for monies received, are largely oriented towards protecting the organization against misappropriation. One in general does not (and certainly union members do not) measure the performance of a union by a "business-like" balance sheet.

Thus, union leaders are constrained as a principal component of their behavior to secure or maintain gains for union members through collective bargaining or collateral union activities. It becomes unseemly for union officers in any given bargaining situation to concern themselves with the management of materials or machines. For example, campaigns to improve productivity in which union leaders participate jointly with management are likely to jeopardize the leader's position with his membership, as well documented by Dymond (1947) and others. Similarly, union efforts to finance firms with which they bargain or to engage in product or market promotion of goods or services offered by the companies with which they bargain seldom catch on as permanent activities for union officials.* Where union interest in productivity has developed, it has been from the standpoint of "checking on" management moves to insure that they do not result in exploitation of workers (cf. Gomberg, 1948).

When we counterpose organizational goal of unions and constraint that this places on union leadership with the purposes of business organizations and their consequences for executive decisions, it becomes very apparent that there is a structural contradiction that most generally eventuates in conflict. Business executives, being "thing" oriented, give primary attention to machines and materials. Union officers, being "people" oriented, give primary attention to men. What is the specialized concern of one group of leaders lies at a secondary level for the other group.

This structural lack of coordination between the goals of union leaders and business executives is the central basis for conflict between their organizations. This contrasts with a Marxian view—that the control of the means of production and the antagonisms of goals between those who control and those who only produce is the root of social conflict. We would argue, for example, that disparity in outlook between executives and union officers appears in Communist Russia or Communist China as well as in capitalist countries of the West.

If our general argument is accurate, it follows that what may customarily be attributed to the ideological differences between management and union as grounds for conflict is rooted rather

---

* The United Mine Workers have, in the distant past, extended financial aid to at least one company; the Amalgamated Clothing Workers established banks, in part to help finance employers; the International Ladies Garment Workers Union has devoted substantial sums to promoting New York as an apparel center; and The Teamsters Union in recent years has lent money to a sympathetic truck trailer executive to permit him to retain control of his company.

in the technical differences between the goals of the two organizations and the consequences these goals have for the leaders of both kinds of organizations. Business leaders may appear to be indifferent to the fate of industrial workers, not because of genuine indifference, but because the organizational goals, the achievement of which is their responsibility, do not permit this consequence to be taken into account. Union leaders who appear to oppose technological advance and the improvement of production efficiency are not ideologically dedicated to the inefficient welfare state so much as they are compelled to emphasize people's welfare in their decisions by the goals of their own organization.

These differences between the organization goals of union and management contain within them one of the important seeds of accommodation between union and company. We have emphasized that the goals are complementary to each other, not necessarily contradictory to each other. We have further emphasized that what is foreground concern for management executives is background concern for union officers, and vice versa. When company officials become sympathetic toward the goals of unions and begin to understand union needs, they do not cease being "company men." What happens is that their emphasis on materials and machines is brought into a somewhat closer balance with a concern for men. Similarly, when union officers become assimilated to a managerial outlook, they may not thereby become "lackeys of management." From their standpoint, they bring into closer balance their own primary emphasis on men with the managerial concern about materials and machines.

It is this complementary balancing of opposing organizational objectives, rather than supplanting one set by the other, that provides the basis for the accommodations worked out through collective bargaining. In this sense, systems of collective bargaining evolve by meshing distinctive organization goals through agreements that permit their simultaneous (if not maximum) accomplishment.

Leaders and Organization Structure

A second proposition closely related to the first is: *Autonomy in the choice of leadership behavior decreases as the complexity of the division of labor in the organization increases.*

This prediction is based on the consequences of the webs of interdependence and linkage among parts of any organization. In general, the more specialized a department or function, the less capable it is of independent existence outside the organization of which it is a part. But this dependence, in turn, makes crucial for any specialized part the reciprocal behaviors of all other parts in relation to it. There is then imposed upon an intricately specialized organization a constant volume of internal demands to stabilize and routinize linkages among organization parts (cf. Dubin, 1959). This means that among other things, leadership decisions (1) will be made in the light of their organization consequences for all the organization units affected by the decision; and (2) will be policed by the feedback from affected units claiming inappropriateness, inefficiency, or ineptitude of the decision, or even covert sabotage.

Given the need to "run" a complex organization, autonomy in making leadership decisions will diminish at the top of the organization (quite aside from the question of the amount of knowledge and information there located) as downward delegation of functions increases. Indeed, it is this "iron law of partition" that leads to principles of decentralization in organization structure in the form of self-contained units. Each executive head of such self-contained units has more autonomy in decision making than he would have if he were a division head in a fully integrated organization.

Our basic proposition helps to explain one of the common features of collective bargaining. It has frequently been noted that the company bargainers tend to have less flexibility in making on-the-spot decisions, as contrasted with union leaders. Company negotiators tend constantly to insist that they must check back with the organization before final decisions on specific proposals can be accepted. On the other hand, union negotiators are often able to say, "We will (or will not) accept the proposal" without more than the perfunctory suggestion that "of course, the entire contract must be ratified by the membership." (It is seldom that the membership ever rejects a contract presented to it as "the best we could get" by the bargaining committee.)

This difference in flexibility is a product of the fact that the managerial division of labor is so extensive that many segments of the firm, and managers within these segments, need to be consulted before final decisions can be reached. This consultation entails determining the extent to which particular bargaining decisions will have consequences for each operating unit of the company.

From an organizational standpoint, the union has interests of a local character which may not be fully consonant with those of the national union. This distinction between local and national goals parallels the structural distinction between the local union as a unit and the national union of which the local is a part. This distinction between national and local union is the primary organizational specialization. Such differences in interests as may exist between local and national units of the union are likely to be less extensive than those among the various levels and specializations of the business firm. The union negotiators are, therefore, more likely to be able to make on-the-spot bargaining decisions committing the union to a particular agreement than can company bargainers.

There is another feature of organizational structure that has relevance for collective bargaining. The positions in management are graded positions with normal promotion and progression being from the bottom of the managerial structure to the top. This means that in the usual individual career, management officials tend to start somewhere near the bottom, and, with normal competence and availability when openings occur, gradually secure promotions to higher levels of management. Thus, at the lower levels of management there is both a closeness to the rank and file of workers in the company, and status striving to be higher within the managerial organization. Closeness to the work level generates a very strong awareness of the relatively slight differences in status that may exist. This is clearly evident in the problem many companies face in keeping salaries of first line supervision ahead of wages of their subordinates, the latter being advanced through collective bargaining. It is not uncommon for management to have to give a salary increase to foremen after bargaining with a union for production employees, in order to keep some differential in earnings favoring supervisors. The contact between lower management and workers may lead to a need to amplify whatever differences exist in order to maintain some status-conferring distinctions for the first lines of management.

At the same time, the status striving to move up in management enhances the striver's sensitivity to the real or imputed expectations of top management, especially in the realms of "proper managerial behavior and outlook" (see, for example, Whyte, 1956). This striving and its consequent sensitization to expectations of superiors may lead to attributions of top management attitudes that are more anti-union than the real opinions and attitudes actually held by top management. Indeed, in the absence of any concrete specification of where top management stands, or even where this specification is equivocal, there is a high probability that attributions of an anti-union stance will be made to higher management officials. This is true partly because it has been the historic position of management, partly because any equivocation about where management stands will be interpreted as disguised anti-unionism hidden from view on account of the legal requirement to bargain with unions, and partly because this stance accords with the status protection needs of lower management officials.

The lower level of the company organization is peopled by officials aware of the need to maintain distinctions between themselves and the rank and file, and who are uncommonly sensitive to expectations they have attributed to top management. Both factors may tend to make of lower managerial officials a group more anti-union than top management. This has particular relevance to the day-to-day bargaining situation between company and union where much of the relationship is carried on by middle and first line managers. The upward mobility of managerial officials, and the structure within which this occurs, may enhance the possibilities of conflict in day-to-day administration of the union contract because of the probability that lower management officials may have a more anti-union outlook than their superiors. This conclusion is countered by one study which suggests that at the lowest levels of collective bargaining there is collusion between foremen and union officers to make bargaining work even if it means exceeding the intent of the official agreement (Dalton, 1950).

On the union side, the structure of the organization is such that the structural imperatives playing on attitudes parallel those of the company organization, but are characterized by different causes. The lower reaches of union offices, up to and including the president or business agent of the local are usually elective. (So are higher union offices, but they tend to be career offices.) Furthermore, local union office generally is not a career avidly pursued by many members. There is a high turnover rate among local union officers which is perhaps the best single index of the fact that holding such positions is not viewed as a career opportunity by many workers. (This must be distinguished from the fact that higher union office is gained more readily if the office seeker has the "right" background, like holding local union office first, and working in the industry organized by the union—the union politician's equivalent of "having to be born in a log cabin" to secure favorable access to public office.) Consequently, local grievance men, bargaining committee members, elected officers and trustees, are likely to represent rank-and-file interests and may be generally indifferent to or even hostile to long range union interests (not to mention company interests). On the other hand, the career officials of the national union, including the international representatives who typically link the local with the national union, can more readily take a long range view of the union goals and the problems encountered in realizing them, and can even adopt a less belligerent attitude towards management than can the purely local, noncareer union officers. Furthermore, the career officials of the national union may have specialist knowledge that generates an understanding of company problems, and the requirements that must be satisfied on both sides, for mutual survival in collective bargaining, as amply documented in Wilensky's study (1956) of the bureaucratization of the national level of American labor unions.

We may then conclude that there is some probability that there will be a greater degree of hostility between lower ranking representatives of both sides than may be true for higher ranking officials. (This generalization undoubtedly has application to a much wider realm than union-management relations. For example, it is notable that the "sit-in" was developed by rank-and-file Negroes who did not seek direct aid and leadership from the official race organizations.) This generalization may account for the fact that there is always a problem of "managing" a national bargaining committee made up of local union representatives (as in coal and steel, for example) when company-wide or industry-wide bargaining is undertaken. The "managing" problem is to give the representatives the impression that they are active participants in the bargaining, while at the same time limiting the opportunity to bargain to a few representatives of the representatives. A similar problem exists for the company when any attempt is made to bring lower management into the bargaining situation, which may account for the relative rarity of this practice. (One of the rare examples of bringing lower management officials into actual negotiations is found in the pulp and paper industry. See Kerr and Randall, 1948.)

A secondary proposition related to the one with which we opened this section on leaders and organization is this: The nearer personal career development is related to progression "through the chairs" of an organization, the greater is the probability that persons early in their career will be psychologically oriented towards anticipating what they think their superiors expect of them. This prediction tells us that management officials in the early stages of their careers will be oriented towards anticipating an anti-union attitude on the part of their superiors and will behave in accord with this anticipation. Local union officials who do not see their tenancy in office as a step in their unfolding careers will not exhibit the same sensitivity to the anticipations of national union officers.

We may conclude then, that: (1) The more complex structure of the company organization makes rapid, on-the-spot decision making in collective bargaining difficult, and certainly less likely to be exhibited by that organization than by the union with which it deals. (2) The nature of working careers of management officials tends to make them anti-union in the early stages. (3) Local union officers are likely to be more belligerent towards the company than are national officers. (4) Finally, the structural features discussed in this section suggest that antagonism between the lowest ranks of representatives of company and union is probably greater than between the highest ranks.

Leaders and Intergroup Relations

Our third general proposition is this: *In any system involving continuous relations between two organizations, autonomy of leadership decisions in any one organization is decreased by the need to take into account the limitations on leadership decisions in the other organization.* Given the fact that union and company are bargaining in good faith and both anticipate continuity of the bargaining relationships, leaders on each side can pursue courses of action that are limited by the feasible alternatives with which the other side must operate.

This means that decisions of management officials take into account the fact that the action consequences shall not injure the union or the position of leaders in it. Any attempt, for example, to set aside union leadership as a channel of communication to union members may produce violent union reaction. This is so, not because it intrinsically threatens the content of the bargaining agreement. The reaction is grounded in the fact that short-circuiting union leadership may threaten the stability of the union organization. In a similar fashion a company bargaining offer which is its first and best offer, remaining unaltered through the course of negotiation, may also threaten leadership functions in the union which are traditionally defined as that of bargaining for a deal better than that which was first offered by the company. (This has been the pattern followed by General Electric in recent years. The company has made its first offer its best offer and then stood firm throughout the subsequent bargaining. Bitter attacks have been made on this practice by the Electrical Workers Union president, James B. Carey, who has charged that making the last offer first is not collective bargaining, in the traditional sense. We may interpret his ire as meaning that in the face of such a situation the union representatives have nothing to bargain about, and hence have been deprived of an important function by this management practice.) A good example would be the attempt of a company to recapture management rights on an exclusive basis—rights that had previously been incorporated in bargaining. Here the previous habituation of union leadership to bargaining on, and administering, the area covered by these management rights, is suddenly threatened by the managerial move to regain exclusive jurisdiction in these areas. The recent steel negotiation is a good example. Management attempted to take certain issues out of collective bargaining and reassume unilateral jurisdiction over them (cf. Dubin, 1960).

These are the three general illustrations of the way in which a unilateral decision from the side of management may have the consequence of seriously unstabilizing the union-management relationship. This occurs because accustomed functions performed in the union organization are either set aside or threatened. So long as the joint objective is to maintain viability of the collective bargaining relationship, decisions of the sort just illustrated which threatened the union as an organization are, for all practical purposes, foreclosed to management.

Viewed from the union side there are comparable illustrations. The union may, for example, pursue a policy of pushing all items of dispute to the highest levels of management for decision. This has the consequence of undercutting the established authority system in the managerial organization. It will inevitably engender strong opposition among the ranks of managers being by-passed by the union leaders. In making economic demands on management, the union is constrained by the recognition that any given management is vulnerable to charges by stockholders and other financial interests in the firm that it has reduced profits because it made extraordinary concessions to the union. This places a very real limitation on the extent to which a given union can push a management by its excessive demands. It is notable in this connection that the major arguments unions tend to use with individual managements are the arguments of industry or area practices with respect to these economic issues. Unions tend to justify their demands as being at the norm for the industry, the occupation, or the area, and to insist that each management at least approximate this norm.

On the management side, concessions can be made that are in line with the norms of wages or fringe benefits precisely because the norms themselves constitute a justification or rationalization that is independent of the profitability or earning ability of the company itself. This situation, of course, raises the interesting problem of leadership by individual companies in establishing new norms. An important part of overall union strategy is to select a company that has the potential of granting economic benefits in excess of existing norms, and seek to bargain first with such a company in the hope of setting the pattern for the industry. In autos, the union has recently rotated the leadership among the "Big Three." Where U.S. Steel used to occupy this position in the past, the companies have more recently moved to industry-wide bargaining, in part to do away with the "pattern setting" technique of the union.

We may then come back to the proposition. Leaders on each side in the bargaining situation are constrained to avoid certain courses of action that threaten the leadership positions of their counterparts. Such threats strain the system of intergroup relations by shifting attention to problems of tension within one of the groups composing the system. The evidence in collective bargaining in support of this conclusion is of two sorts. Where there is genuine interest in maintaining the bargaining relationships, studies indicate that leaders on both sides clearly take into account the limitations that their opposite numbers must contend with and minimize behaviors that produce embarrassment or problem-creating consequences for them (Slichter, 1941; Lester and Robie, 1948; Scanlon, 1948).

On the other hand, where there is genuine interest in destroying collective bargaining, the strategies and tactics employed typically are directed at maximizing the sources of instability of leadership in the opposing organization. For management to get out from under collective bargaining, its primary strategy is designed to weaken the union by destroying it as an organization, particularly by undermining leadership positions in the union. Where unions have been interested in eschewing collective bargaining, as in racketeering or in policing highly competitive industries, they too have engaged in activities which clearly undermine the leadership positions and consequently the stability of managerial organizations.*

* There is ample evidence in the McClellan Committee hearings of the recent past of the ways in which the union may undermine the management organization. See, *Investigation of improper activities in the labor or management field: Hearings before the select committee on improper activities in the labor or management field.* 85th and 86th Congresses, Parts 1–54, *passim.* Washington, D.C., Government Printing Office, 1957–1959.

We may then summarize the general prediction by pointing to the fact that two independent organizations engaged in a relationship which constitutes a system will limit decisions to those which maintain the stability of the participating groups. This conclusion, in principle, would appear to apply to any social system composed of independent groups, such as federations of private organizations, and organizations of independent nations. (In the union field, for example, the rise of the C.I.O. came as a consequence of the threat posed to craft unions by the organization of industrial unions. The A.F. of L. was torn apart as a federation by this genuine threat to some of its craft union constituents.)

Social Change

A central feature in the evolution of American collective bargaining has been the development of social systems that accommodated to the internal needs of the two principal organizations making up the system. Most of the inventiveness in collective bargaining has centered on satisfying this problem. Such inventions as union security, check-off of union dues, superseniority for union officials, exclusive bargaining rights, and the exclusive presentation of grievances by the union, have all been devices invented to support and sustain the union as an organization. Similarly, the retention of large areas of decision making by management under the general heading of managerial prerogatives has been important in sustaining the integrity of the managerial organization. Other features of collective bargaining have also contributed to sustaining the management organization: features such as the organization of grievance handling to accord with the authority structure of management; the determination and maintenance of industrial discipline by management; the choice of products, their volume of output, and their pricing as managerial decisions; and in general the vast control over the financial operations as well as the productive processes.

The history of American collective bargaining up to this point has largely been a process of inventing means for developing reliable systems of intergroup relations. Individual problems faced by the union and management organizations have largely been solved in favor of maintaining their separate identity and integrity at the same time developing systems by which their mutual interests can be mediated and effectively integrated.

Primarily, attention has been centered on solving the problems of building permanent systems of collective bargaining where these problems are largely those of the organizations involved. Thus the systems of collective bargaining as we now know them have evolved in the process of solving *internal* problems—internal to the organizations composing these systems.

As we now talk about mature collective bargaining, we really mean that the bargaining systems evolved are ones in which the separate organizations of union and management live together in a literal sense, neither one oriented towards destroying the other (cf. Lester, 1958). The systems have highly institutionalized aspects formalized in behaviors that are readily predictable. But this institutionalization of behavior has been focused entirely, or almost entirely, on internal problems. We may conclude that, in general, mature collective bargaining has solved problems internal to the units composing such systems.

The next decades will see two significant developments which are *external* to the collective bargaining systems, each of which will have important feedbacks upon them. The first is the general automation of industry and commerce. The second is the increasing industrialization of the backward areas of the world.

If mechanization is one of the central features of the first industrial revolution, then automation is the core of the second industrial revolution. Automation is basically a marriage of scientific knowledge with technology and engineering. The roots of automation are in the scientific institutions, where there have been developed communications systems, rapid data processing systems, and work transfer systems. It is obvious that automation will have and is already having its consequences for the skilled composition of the labor force, the number of workers needed, the hours of work employed, the pay levels at which employment is offered, and the ability of the economy to consume the products of automated output. This brief list only highlights some of the obvious concerns that now, and increasingly in the future, will face collective bargaining systems. This threat to collective bargaining is made all the more pointed by the fact that it in turn will not only change the subject matter of collective bargaining systems, but will also change the composition of the managerial group and the union group which compose the systems. This double-barreled influence external to the system is a kind of problem with which collective bargaining systems have, in general, little experience. They have in the past been attuned to solving internal problems of accommodation between the parties and have not really ever jointly attacked the issues of social change originating outside their own bargaining spheres.

A similar kind of external problem is generated by the increasing industrialization of the world at large. In its most obvious dimensions this poses problems like that of reciprocal trade relations between our country and newly industrializing areas. The competitive sphere for markets will be increasingly extended to international dimensions and this obviously will play back upon local economics. For the plywood industry in Oregon and the electronics industry on the East and West Coasts, for example, the problems of international competition begin to intrude themselves as central issues with which both management and labor must deal as collective bargaining problems, and also as industrial survival problems. It is not our point here to examine any of the detailed arrangements which will eventually evolve as world markets become truly internationalized. We simply want to point out that a second significant area of problem-generating issues lies outside the immediate realm of collective bargaining, and will increasingly intrude itself on bargaining systems.

Indeed, we would predict that the newer phases of intergroup relations known as American collective bargaining will see entirely new issues entering into the consideration of the parties, issues that are the product of *external* developments to which the parties must adjust for their mutual survival. Whether these major external social changes will tend to destroy collective bargaining systems, or merely to change them in significant ways, is a matter of social prophecy beyond the scope of this paper.

References

Bakke, E. W., 1946. *Mutual survival: The goals of unions and management.* New Haven, Conn., Labor and Management Center.

Barnard, C. I., 1938. *The functions of the executive.* Cambridge, Mass., Harvard University Press.

Dalton, M., 1950. Unofficial union-management relations. *Amer. sociol. Rev.,* 15, 611–619.

Dubin, R., 1949. Union-management cooperation and productivity. *Indust. Lab. Relat. Rev.,* 2, 195–209.

——, 1958a. *Working union-management relations: The sociology of industrial relations.* Englewood Cliffs, N.J., Prentice-Hall.

——, 1958b. *The world of work: Industrial society and human relations.* Englewood Cliffs, N.J., Prentice-Hall.

——, 1959. Stability of human organizations. In M. Haire (ed.), *Modern organization theory.* New York, Wiley.

——, 1960. A theory of conflict and power in union-management relations. *Indust. Lab. Relat. Rev.,* 13, 501–518.

Dymond, W. R., 1947. Union-management cooperation at the Toronto factory of Lever Brothers Limited. *Canad. J. Econ. pol. Sci.,* 13, 1–42.

Gomberg, W., 1948. *A trade union analysis of time study.* Chicago, Science Research Associates.

Kerr, C., and R. Randall, 1948. Case study no. 1. In *Causes of industrial peace.* Washington, D.C., National Planning Assoc.

Lester, R. A., 1958. *As unions mature.* Princeton, N.J., Princeton University Press.

Lester, R. A., and E. A. Robie, 1948. *Constructive labor relations: Experience in four firms.* Princeton, N.J., Industrial Relations Section, Princeton University.

Scanlon, J. M., 1948. Profit sharing under collective bargaining: Three case studies. *Indust. Lab. Relat. Rev.,* 2, 58–75.

Slichter, S. H., 1941. *Union policies and industrial management.* Washington, D.C., The Brookings Institution.

Twentieth Century Fund, Labor Committee, 1949. *Partners in production: A basis for labor-management understanding.* New York, The Fund.

Veblen, T., 1933. *The engineers and the price system.* New York, Viking Press.

Wasserman, P., and F. S. Silander, 1958. *Decision-making: An annotated bibliography.* Ithaca, N.Y., Cornell University Graduate School of Business and Public Administration.

Whyte, W. H., Jr., 1956. *The organization man.* New York, Simon and Schuster.

Wilensky, H. L., 1956. *Intellectuals in labor unions.* Glencoe, Ill., Free Press.

5

WITHIN contemporary union-management relationships, conceptualized by Dubin in the last chapter, the history of past conflicts is frequently a constant companion affecting both sides' views of the other and of the other's intent. This state of affairs is the chief concern of this chapter.

In the first part of the chapter, Robert Blake and Jane Mouton summarize research findings on intergroup competition between small groups of youth and adults, when the only alternatives are victory for one group and defeat for the other.

The second part has a more practical bent. It summarizes Blake's attempts as a management consultant to reduce group stereotyping and to alleviate intergroup disputes. The reports of what Blake prefers to call "behavioral science intervention" in intergroup conflicts raise important research problems related to the effectiveness of the steps described.

Among the problems for future research, it may be pointed out that a realistic assessment is needed of what factors determined the decision by the top policy authority to acquiesce to "behavioral science intervention," even when the policy board it had appointed expressed apprehensions, as noted in the chapter. A related problem concerns the representativeness of acquiescence by top policy makers to intervention in its policy-making prerogatives. It is well known that policy makers in any organization are inclined to be rather jealous of these prerogatives.

Finally, the formal and informal lines and the content of communication between the top authority and its policy board need to be assessed. Advances in research on such problems may well mark important breakthroughs for social science in the study of power relations in intergroup systems.

In summarizing their findings, Blake and Mouton employ individual pathology as a didactic analogy to dramatize the determinants of hostility on group and intergroup levels of interaction. They are critical of psychodynamic explanations of intergroup behavior, citing numerous instances of individual behavior bounded by the properties of an intergroup system.

EDITOR

5 THE INTERGROUP DYNAMICS OF WIN-LOSE CONFLICT AND PROBLEM-SOLVING COLLABORATION IN UNION-MANAGEMENT RELATIONS*

by Robert R. Blake and Jane S. Mouton

On many fronts one can hear crying, whining, and the gnashing of teeth when conversation centers on the apparently irresolvable conflict evident in present-day union and management relationships. Pleas are heard for more restrictive legislation in order to control the conflict which disrupts industrial life and for human relations committees to study the problem when it threatens continuity in production. Indeed, the same approach is being employed on the national level by the recent appointment of the President's Advisory Committee on Labor-Management Policy. Crying and teeth gnashing only aggravate the problem. Constrictive legislation can do little more than to drive the basic problem underground. Committees can recommend and advise, but, too frequently, the protagonists of a dispute do not consent to terminate hostilities simply because public pressure is brought upon them.

A fresh approach, which deals with and relieves causes of conflict rather than trying to treat the symptoms, has been under development during the past decade. What is the strategy of this approach? An analogy will provide perspective in viewing the constructive alternative. Psychiatric medicine seeks to relieve causes of personal difficulty in the effort to restore personal health by applying personality theory to individual situations of behavioral pathology. Treatment is dictated by theory. In a similar way, the approach described here applies

* Studies reported concerned with intergroup behavior were partially supported by Grant M-2447, Behavior of Group Representatives under Pressure, National Institute of Health, and by a grant from Esso Division, Humble Oil and Refining Company.

systematic theory of intergroup relations to concrete situations of intergroup disturbances. The focus is on searching out the causes of the pathology and treating them directly, rather than trying to control the symptoms of pathology by legislation, by taking the defeatist attitude of crying and whining, or by convening committees to study the problem.

The strategy of our work is based on a two-pronged approach. One prong involves developing a comprehensive theory of intergroup warfare and collaboration, validated through experimental work. The other prong is the application of this comprehensive theory in concrete situations with the aim of shifting union-management warfare to conditions of mutual respect and problem solving. We want to survey both theory and application and to evaluate its more sweeping implications for the future of union-management relations as we now see them.

EXPERIMENTAL STUDIES OF INTERGROUP CONFLICT AND COOPERATION

Intergroup Pathology and Health

The first questions are, "What are the causes of intergroup pathology, as seen in symptoms involving discord and conflict? What are the causes of intergroup health, as revealed through cooperative problem solving that leads to concord?" Intergroup pathology is to be found whenever there is a move away from objectivity between groups which jointly shoulder responsibility for solving problems shared in common. But, what circumstances cause such pathology, and once pathology has appeared, how can it be treated so that the intergroup system can be restored to a state of improved health?

After reviewing the outlines of a theory of intergroup pathology and health we want to describe its utility for restoring intergroup health in actual disturbed union and management situations.

Strategy of Experimental Investigation

The prototype experiment was designed and executed by Sherif. Two autonomous groups of children were brought into a situation of competition from which there was no realistic possibility of escape (Sherif and Sherif, 1953). In-group and intergroup phenomena generated by the competitive circumstances first were studied, and then conditions that were effective and those that were ineffective in reducing competitive tensions and conflict between groups were identified.

Our work has been concerned with the same basic problem, but it has been conducted with adults drawn from industrial organizations. Each of the thirty experiments we have conducted, which proceed through a series of phases extending over a two-week period, has dealt with a different systematic problem. The first phase in each has consisted of ten to eighteen hours of interaction during which time groups develop goals, norms of conduct and performance, and power relations among members. During the second phase, conditions were created so that the groups were thrown into competition; each developed its own solution to some basic issue with which all members were familiar. The third phase began when one group had won by creating the better solution, and the other group had lost by producing a poorer one. Fourth and fifth phases have dealt with reduction of conflict and the restoration of intergroup problem solving.

While these are the broad outlines, the specific tactics for each experiment were dictated by concrete needs to round out the details of a more comprehensive theory of intergroup relations directly useful in untangling ticklish problems of union-management relations. The experiments have been carried out over several years and have involved approximately one thousand subjects as members of more than one hundred and fifty groups which were matched on a paired basis, in size, personal characteristics of members, and other relevant dimensions. Each of the studies was repeated whenever necessary to verify the conclusions drawn.

Rationale for Studying the Win-Lose Design

A word of rationale for designing the experiments as described above will help place our work in perspective. We could have taken the route of designing experiments in which groups could agree on a joint solution through the process of *compromise*. Some say this type of design provides a closer approximation to actual existing union-management relations than does the win-lose design. In a sense we agree. However, rather than studying situations of give-and-take, where intergroup pathology either is absent or else is hidden from view, we have preferred to create strong victory-defeat conditions under which win-lose pathology is thrown into bold relief. The latter condition is what produces strikes and lockouts and demands for coercive legislation. Beyond this key reason, however, we are led to doubt that the absence of open conflict is equivalent with constructive intergroup problem solving. Indeed, many union-management situations that look "healthy" are, under closer examination, better characterized as win-lose situations held in equilibrium by an uneasy truce. The conditions for conflict are there, but neither side feels strong enough to fire the opening volley. Thus, we think the win-lose design to be critical for developing a theory of intergroup relations useful for unraveling factors producing industrial conflicts.

In addition, there is widespread evidence that union and management do approach many outstanding issues from a win-lose point of view. A shift away from the idea of complete and total victory is made only when the chips are down and economic and social realities intrude to blur the situation, and sometimes not even then, to wit, a 119-day steel strike of the recent past. Often, though, as new issues and realities invade the scene, the compulsion of compromise enters. It does not obliterate the desire to win, but drives it underground, with each group pledging itself to a stronger position which will lead to total victory in the next round. The prevalence of win-lose, fixed position taking, which generates acrimony and makes problem redefinition or give-and-take compromise more difficult has led, on the one hand, to the development of federal, state, and private mediation services, and, on the other hand, to the building into contracts of arbitration clauses as a mechanism for ultimate resolution to be invoked when an impasse has become insurmountable. Yet, mediation signals weakness and arbitration speaks of failure. Intervention by the government is an unattractive court of last resort.

The realism between the experiments concerning the win-lose dynamics and situations of industrial conflict is to be found whenever a union and a management approach bargaining, grievance handling, complaints or other situations with fixed positions and with the intention not to compromise but to win. Typical areas of win-lose position taking in present-day union-management relations deal with contracting of work, work flexibility, and so on.

Intergroup Win-Lose Dynamics

Details of individual experiments have been reported elsewhere. The outstanding generalizations from them that have been found most central for understanding situations of union-management pathology and for suggesting necessary steps to develop more healthy interdependence in their problem-solving relations will be summarized here.

At the point where competition emerges, the fundamental significance of the win-lose dynamic appears. When the goal "to win" is accepted by a group, it has spontaneous motivating power to mobilize team effort and to give it character. The consequences for intergroup life, when the goal taken by each is "to win" over the other, are substantial.

Rises in Cohesion with Competition

Under the circumstances described, a variety of measurable phenomena of high predictability come into prominence. One is an upward shift in cohesion among group members. The rule is, when an adversary approaches, members close ranks to defend against defeat. Spirits go up. Former disagreements are put aside. Members "pitch in." They pull together toward the common goal of victory (Blake and Mouton, 1960a). The heavier turnout of members at union meetings during periods of tension is but typical of the phenomenon being described.

Exciting though it is to march together toward victory, the urge "to win" is primitive and basic. Here is a first sign of group pathology. Disagreement, the raw material of creative thinking which can lead to the re-examination and enrichment of the position of one's group, tends to be snuffed out. Failure to go along after a certain point can arouse insidious group pressures toward conformity and, in the extreme, may even lead to expulsion of members who resist the tide.

Refinement and Consolidation of In-group Power Structures

The presence of a "pecking order" among group members is well known. Some voices carry more weight than others in defining group direction and character. In our groups, prior to competition, power relations tend to be loose, rather poorly worked out. With neither time nor performance pressures, pecking relations tend to be fuzzy and unclear.

What happens when clear, sharp competition comes forth? Stakes are involved. Personal reputations merge with group reputation. Some members, who are better able to talk than others, or for whom the thought of victory carries particular relish, begin to exercise more weight than previously had been characteristic of them. In the extreme, the result can be essentially a complete "taking over" by one or two persons. Others who are less able and aggressive and more dependent, fall in line. To avoid being responsible for defeat, still others "bite their tongues" and are less vocal.

What are the results? There definitely is group accomplishment. A more differentiated pecking order is established. But, if those who control the major lines of group effort fail to exercise their influence in ways that recognize "legitimate" rights of others, the seeds for civil war are there to germinate. Later on, defeat is the fertile soil that nourishes growth and development of dissension and discord. In-group pathology can erupt too, like Vesuvius, almost without announcement. By and large, people do not know how to cope with in-group pathology. Barriers to future in-group cooperation, which are extremely resistant to change, may have been created unwittingly by the impelling forward surge toward victory.

Intergroup Comparison: Elevating Own Position, De-evaluating the Adversary's

After group positions have taken shape and after they are exchanged between contending groups, members quickly develop attitudes toward both solutions. Judgments concerning the quality of competing positions are colored by membership considerations. The direction of distortion is for one's own position to be judged superior to the other, almost without regard for quality differences between them that do exist, as can be shown by use of objective criteria. Group members strongly identify with their own position, they rationalize, or justify the comparison, and downgrade the competitor's product (Blake and Mouton, forthcoming *b*).

The indication of intergroup pathology is that win-lose conflict disrupts realistic judgment; it tends to obliterate objectivity. Yet, objectivity is a primary condition of intergroup problem solving. When win-lose attitudes can increase subjectivity to such a degree that realistic appraisal is diminished, then the conditions of future cooperation are effectively eliminated.

Belittling the Adversary: Paper Bombs as Substitutes for Bullets

After studying the two solutions, groups interact through representatives to determine victor and vanquished. But before the final decision, a phase of interaction is provided for the purpose of clarifying similarities and differences. During the clarification stage, questions are formulated by each group to be answered by the other.

By studying the questions from a behavioral science point of view, the underlying motivation they carry becomes quite evident. Are they intended to clarify? For the most part, they are not. They are couched to belittle the competitor's proposal, to cast doubt on its validity, and to demonstrate its inferiority in relation to the position of one's own group (Blake and Mouton, 1961b). "Throw-aways," "handouts," full page newspaper advertisements, and company organs used to belittle the adversary and to express "self-righteousness" are all examples of hostile messages which purport to "clarify" the issues but which, all too frequently, produce no more than an incendiary effect.

What is the pathology? Rather than reducing the conflict and increasing objectivity, intergroup contact for purposes of clarification has the opposite effect: conflict is intensified and heightened subjectivity promoted; suspicion of the "motivation of the others" is increased.

Negative Stereotypes Regarding the Competitor

As groups interact over a period of time, under conditions in which the activities are competitive and mutually frustrating, members develop negative attitudes and express hostility toward members of the other group in the form of stereotypes (Avigdor, 1952; Harvey, 1954; Haire, 1955; Sherif and Sherif, 1953, 1956).

Do stereotypes help clear the air? No, they do not. They have a provocative effect, because, by their nature, they are saturated with negative emotions. The consequence of provocation is counterprovocation with the intensification of conflict and with a further erosion of mutual respect and common confidence in the intentions of the other.

Let us take a recent example of how negative stereotypes occurred in the last General Electric strike. When conflict was at its peak, negative thrusts by each group against the other filled the airwaves. The union called management's approach "bargaining by ultimatum." Management accused the union of wanting "auction type" bargaining. Acrimony was increased by such "labeling." By blurring the real issues and focusing attention on "labels" rather than on the existing problems, stereotyping added a further difficulty to problem solving, beyond the issues which were in disagreement (*U.S. News and World Report*, 1960).

Cognitive Distortions

As has been shown, group members develop negative feelings and emotions toward their adversary. Is this the sole source of the problem or is there something beyond? Does competition affect one's capacity to think, to understand, and to comprehend? The answer is "yes," and the effect on mental functions is insidious. How is this demonstrated?

At the time when all members indicate subjective certainty that they have achieved intellectual understanding of the adversary's position, an objective knowledge test covering positions of contending groups is introduced. The analysis of such test results is enlightening for showing how win-lose attitudes contaminate objective thinking and for pointing out something of the character of the resulting distortions.

Shared agreements minimized, differences highlighted. Areas of literal agreement are not attended to very well, but areas of actual differences are highlighted. Items missed most frequently are identical items that are contained in both proposals. While group members correctly recognize that such items belong in their own group's position, they fail to see they also were contained in the position of their adversary as well. Communalities in positions tend to be overlooked when groups stand in a competitive relationship to one another and consequently barriers to agreement are thus created (Blake and Mouton, forthcoming c). You cannot very well agree to what you do not understand. We have recently seen a management summary of a set of union demands that reveal the insidious phenomena being discussed. The summary, entitled *Differences between Union and Management Bargaining Positions,* listed 62 items. It failed to acknowledge 182 areas of agreement in the two positions. Would you expect such a document to aid policy makers, who had not even studied the original document, to gain realistic perspective for bargaining?

Knowledge of own position greater than knowledge of adversary's position. In comparison, items which are distinctive, that is, which are contained only in the position of one group or the other, but not in both, are much more frequently recognized correctly. But even then group members perceive elements distinctive to their own position better than they identify items distinctive by being contained only in the adversary's position (Blake and Mouton, 1961c).

What is the pathology here? These conclusions demonstrate that our mental outlook is affected by the desire "to win." One generalization is that there is an underattention to areas of agreement which are shared in common and an overattention to areas of disagreement which increase difficulties of cooperation in attaining a final result. Objectivity of cognition is distorted, and barriers to common understanding are erected by a win-lose mentality.

Without exploring the motivation for these distortions in greater detail, it can be said that cognitive "blind spots" are not entirely due to greater familiarity with one's own position. Differences in familiarity are a factor, to be sure. Beyond familiarity, differences described can only be accounted for in terms of group membership, feelings of personal ownership, group identification and defensiveness under the threat of defeat.

Loyalty of Representatives

When representatives from competing groups meet to decide the winner and the loser, what is the character of their deliberations? *Deadlock* is the most likely result. When a representative, through exercising impartiality, and taking an objective point of view, stands to lose for his group, loyalty pressures often are sufficient to overwhelm logic. Even though the representative operates under the intellectual compulsion to exercise objectivity in judgment, he rarely does so (Blake and Mouton, 1961d). As Stephen Decatur, in 1816 said, "Our country! In her intercourse with foreign nations, may she always be in the right; but our country, right or wrong!" The motive "to win" produces behavior which is incomprehensible when viewed from the standpoint of the psychophysics of comparative judgments only. If problem solving between groups is to lead to mutually satisfactory solutions, objectivity in seeking resolutions to difficulties is desperately needed to substitute for considerations based on loyalty (Blake, 1959).

Hero-Traitor Dynamics

Underlying the pressures on the representative to stand by his group through "thick and thin," and "for better or worse," is the traitor threat. A traitor is a group member in good standing, who contacts the adversary, but who capitulates to the enemy's position and loses for his group. On the other hand, the hero is a person who wins for his group by devastating his adversary and bringing victory. Deadlock, though it does not carry with it the elevation in status accorded a hero, at least is one way to avoid the traitor trap.

In the background of intergroup contact under win-lose conditions, there often lurk the shadows of hero-traitor dynamics. To be a hero is its own reward. Yet, the behavior required to be heroic can be at variance with the actions called for by objectivity and problem solving. On the other hand, and equally unfortunately, behavior based on objective problem-solving requirements may be withheld to avoid the traitor trap (Blake and Mouton, 1960*b*).

Reactions to the Judge

Since the winner is difficult to determine through representatives, for reasons given above, an impartial judge is called on to make the decision in circumstances paralleling arbitration. Not being vested with membership interests, he is able to do so, usually without too much hesitation or hedging. He renders his verdict. One group wins; the other loses.

How is the impartial judge perceived? Prior to his verdict, both groups agree he is intelligent, fair, honest, thoughtful, unprejudiced, unbiased, tactful, and capable. After the verdict, the picture shifts dramatically. Those awarded victory are reinforced in their positive perceptions of him. His verdict "proves" that he was a "good" judge. This is not so in the defeated group. The judge's ability to render a competent verdict now is questioned. He is still seen as intelligent and as basically honest. But he now is perceived by members of the losing group to be unfair, thoughtless, biased, and tactless. The reaction in the defeated group is, "It was not we who had the inferior proposition and were wrong. It was the judge who failed to comprehend."

On the one hand, the pathology is in the inability to accept neutral judgment as valid judgment. The illness is one of erecting rationalizations which protect the position in spite of the defeat (Blake and Mouton, 1960b). A third, and equally negative consideration, is that arbitration too frequently results in warring factions absolving themselves of responsibility to work together and thus "throwing away" the privilege of acting with reason.

Two Effects of Victory and Defeat

There are still other differences between groups after the verdict is rendered. Victory or defeat has predictable outcomes which influence the conditions of successive contact between the groups.

Leadership consolidation versus leadership replacement. In the winning groups, those who led it to victory are congratulated. Their positions are strengthened and enhanced and those who followed become even more dependent on them for future direction and guidance. In defeated groups, in-group fighting and splintering into factions often occur, as members seek to place blame for failure. Former leaders are replaced, because their ability and integrity are in question (Blake and Mouton, 1960b). Feeling unfairly attacked by their own group, they may fight back, and, if unsuccessful, pout and sulk and eventually withdraw active interest.

Group mentality. The group mentality, "bad" though the concept is said to be, is dramatically different in the winning and losing groups. This is evidenced not only in the reactions to the judge and to the representatives, but also in the "atmosphere" of the group. Members of victorious groups feel the glow of victory. The dominant theme is complacency stemming from success. There is a "fat and happy" atmosphere with members coasting and resting on their laurels rather than working. On the other hand, in the defeated groups, the atmosphere is "lean and hungry" and filled with tension that must be discharged. Members describe their interactions as "digging" activities focused on ferreting out fallacies of operation that led to failure. A recent example of a defeated group was discussed in the following way by the *Wall Street Journal* shortly after November 4, 1960, "The Republican Party, scarcely stopping to lick its wounds after a narrow national defeat, today enters a period of protracted, intense and possibly disruptive civil war."

Without elaborating on details, it can be said that victory can promote a pathology of complacency which fails to come to grips with the problems of the future and which is no less disturbing to intergroup health than the destructive in-group fighting which too often is associated with defeat (Blake and Mouton, 1961*b*).

Summary

The sequence of the above phenomena is derived from intergroup competition situations in which the win-lose assumption prevails. Knowledge of these experimentally based conclusions concerning significant dynamics of a competitive relationship is fundamental to understanding union and management conflicts and for shifting it towards a relationship of collaboration based on mutual respect, trust, and problem solving, as will be discussed later on.

Generating Collaboration After Conflict

Two broad orientations toward problems of replacing intergroup conflict with cooperation have been evaluated according to systematic techniques. One way seeks to relieve the conflict between groups by reducing negative stereotypes through eliminating the boundaries that separate people into groups. The other, and the more realistic for many situations, recognizes the

inevitability of people being segregated into functional groupings and focuses on devising ways in which to protect group
identification and membership and yet to promote intergroup
cooperation.

Collaboration Based on Breaking Down Old Group Lines and Producing a Single Group

Several procedures have been evaluated with children (Sherif
and Sherif, 1956) and with adults (Blake and Mouton, 1961a),
with the objective of promoting cooperation between group members who have been locked in a prior history of intergroup win-
lose competition. The source of motivation to cooperate in
these investigations is not in the personal commitment of group
members themselves, but is external to the groups. The goal
appears to avoid the pathology created by conflicting relations
between groups by eliminating the boundaries that separate
people and by reducing symptoms of intergroup competition.

The exercise of authority. In spite of efforts of persons in
higher authority to do away with hostility between groups,
through breaking up group lines by emphasizing individual
rather than group competition and by preaching the "benefits"
of cooperation, preferences still follow group boundaries. Stereotypes derogatory to the former adversary continue to be prominent and to persist (Sherif and Sherif, 1953).

Forced contact between members from contending groups.
Neutral contact situations, where members of conflicting groups
are thrown together for work and play types of activities not
organized around competitive goals, seem to have little or no
significant effect in reducing intergroup friction. If anything,
these situations are utilized by members of both groups as opportunities for extending hostility and conflict. Once developed,
group lines defining borders of conflict are extremely difficult to
erase (Sherif and Sherif, 1956).

*Interaction between group members induced by common
goals.* A series of common or *superordinate goals* calling for interaction between group members in order to achieve a mutually

desired goal, which cannot be obtained through the skills and resources of either group by itself but only through the combined efforts of both groups, can result in conflict being replaced by collaboration as each individual contributes his share to the total effort. A "common enemy" may reduce friction between two groups by uniting them into a single entity, but it does so at the expense of producing friction between other groups. If the goal is of sufficiently strong motivating power, such as threats to survival and security, or a highly desired aim, group boundaries may tend to disappear as the common goal becomes the focus of organization and joint effort (Sherif and Sherif, 1956).

Utility for reducing industrial conflict. The approaches to intergroup collaboration described above, which eliminate group lines as the basis for reducing conflict, are essentially contradictory to the legal definition of the appropriate relations between union and management. The groups cannot be united into one against the will of the working man, nor, because of human realities of interdependence, can they exist in parallel with little or no interaction between them. Yet, conditions of conflicting contact where groups pull in opposite directions, each trying to achieve its aims at the expense of the other, can become pathological in varying degrees. The components have to blend in order to produce a total end result which meets management's legitimate goals of efficiency and productivity, on the one hand, and the union members' needs for security, dignity, and personal welfare on the other.

Many times, in industrial life, collaboration has arisen against a background of competition because of the necessity of company survival. The common goal of survival will serve to impel cooperation to the degree that real problems of survival penetrate the intellectual life of both sides. In a thriving, growing economy, survival is frequently insured, however. Since it is a need which is more or less satisfied, it does not furnish a compelling motivation as the basis for cooperation. Furthermore, many goals of the two groups are essentially distinctive, i.e., not shared by both, once the survival question no longer is of functional significance. We draw the conclusion that cooperation is an alternative to competition only when there is a shared internal motivation to solve both *common* and *distinctive* problems, while respecting the maintenance of legitimate group boundaries. This approach to cooperative problem solving is formulated below.

Background Conditions for Replacing a Win-Lose Approach with a Collaborative Orientation Based on Shared Internal Motivation to Solve both Common and Distinctive Problems while Retaining Group Boundaries

If cooperation between groups is the shared goal, because both groups stand to gain more through this approach to relations between themselves than they stand to achieve by competing in order to "win," a different route is taken in order to shift away from conflict.

The first difference between a win-lose approach and a collaboration orientation to another group is in a mental attitude which says "cooperation is feasible," rather than "warfare is inevitable." But the pressing question remains: "How can mental attitudes be shifted from a win-lose to a collaborative orientation?" The approaches to be described have been employed successfully in four union-management warfare situations, sufficient to establish that groups locked in conflict with one another can re-establish a collaborative relationship. The first step in achieving this result is for people themselves to examine the consequences of win-lose warfare against the background of the anticipated consequences of collaboration.

Training in theory and in the recognition of phenomena associated with win-lose conflict. Deep-lying human attitudes are not changed by an expert's telling how "it should be," or even pointing the way. Yet a first step toward changing attitudes can be taken if one can understand his own reactions toward warfare through experiencing them in the direct "heat" of conflict, and then talking about them in a systematic manner. In order to correct faulty reactions, conditions need to be created under which direct experience and the resulting abstractions regarding it bear a more valid relationship to one another. A laboratory training program—in which participants experience directly, through the involvement of their own actions, thinking, and emotions, the conditions that arouse intergroup hostility and conflict, and compare these experiences with the conditions necessary to bring about collaboration—is a first step in shifting mental attitudes towards cooperation through comprehension of systematic theory and through valid, personal recognition of phenomena associated with win-lose conflict (Blake and Mouton, 1961a).

Norm-setting conferences for achieving unanimity of attitudes. A second step consists of group norm setting where the aim is to achieve uniformity in opinion and attitude with respect to the orientation to intergroup relations to which participants are committed. If a shift is to be made, it cannot be done by changing individuals in isolation from the social framework in which they operate; to do so would be to increase the traitor threat. In addition, no one person in the group, even the highest ranking one, can with assurance of success compel a group to shift from warfare to cooperation by edict. Therefore, in order to consolidate attitudes as the basis for future action, norm-setting conferences are used, in which actual participants talk through their own attitudes, reservations, doubts, hopes, and so on, concerning cooperation as an orientation to a former adversary. Once a group as a whole has a shared perception of such a goal and a commitment to it, energies of many individuals can be released and focused in the same direction. People can move with assurance of the support of others (Blake and Mouton, forthcoming *a*).

Behavioral science intervention concerning ongoing organization. The third approach for translating theoretical concepts into concrete behavior is through the use of a behavioral scientist to intervene in ongoing activities of interaction between groups. Against a background of intense conflict which is *real* to the persons involved, even laboratory type of "learning through experience" can be washed away and lose its significance in the intense heat of battle. It is at these points that the outsider can step in and "freeze" a problem situation long enough to recast it into theoretical terms so that alternative ways of behaving can be examined before a precipitous, incendiary win-lose event occurs. If there is heavy tension, then it is all the more important that alternatives be explored *before* an action is taken; yet it is often very difficult to resist slipping into "second nature" habits and modes of thinking that group members may have become accustomed to over twenty or thirty years. It is at these critical points that a behavioral scientist can help by recasting an ongoing situation into theoretical terms (Blake and Mouton, forthcoming *a*).

Another way of formulating the concept of intervention type participation in organizational activities is possible by comparing it with the typical sociological orientation. A sociologist, under similar circumstances, might attend meetings and engage in problem-solving conferences—but as an observer making copious notes on details concerning person-to-person interactions, and so on. However, he would seek to avoid influencing the actual problem-solving sequence itself, to shift the conclusion in one direction or another according to theoretical considerations. That is, he would remain passive as regards the activity, though he would be active in measuring it.

By comparison, the behavioral science interventionist takes a direct role in the interactions, not from the point of view of suggestions concerning the content being discussed, but rather from the standpoint of presenting theoretical alternatives for examining the relationships likely to arise from different courses of action.

Leveling conferences—the introduction of intergroup therapy
When other approaches to erasing conflict fail, a final opportunity remains through the use of a leveling conference. What is involved?

Rather than convening for an accusation and counteraccusation session, the warring factions explore with one another the attitudes, feelings, and emotions that undergird disrespect, distrust, and the motivation to frustrate and destroy. Amazing though it is, once leveling starts, the tension in the situation is reduced. People are telling one another the very attitudes they ordinarily withhold—the underlying ones which "explain" the mutually destructive surface actions.

With leveling started, usually through a behavioral science intervention, the way is opened for much more extensive joint exploration of history leading to the present situation. An historical review, say over a decade, offers the advantages of placing present conflict in perspective, providing diagnostic cues to account for the present dilemma, and offering suggestions for the kinds of altered thinking necessary to achieve success against a background of failure.

Each of the four techniques outlined above is useful for translating theoretical concepts concerning intergroup conflict and collaboration into concrete action at the point where pathology needs to be replaced with a problem-solving approach.

Mental Reorientations Basic to Intergroup Cooperation

Three basic mental attitudes which greatly facilitate a cooperative orientation toward another group with which one's own group has been in conflict are given below. The critical question that can be asked of each is, "How does avoidance of this orientation aid in reducing intergroup pathology?"

Avoiding the win-lose trap. Just as the "win-lose" orientation can be elicited more or less spontaneously as a basic condition of competitiveness, a fundamental key to collaboration is based on avoiding impulsiveness that leads into win-lose pitfalls, through sensitivity to "win-lose" signals and cues that elicit conflict. This means that each action and every assumption underlying a reaction that feels "natural" must be deliberately screened for win-lose dynamics in order to avoid the pathology associated with it.

Recognition of signals of warfare is not easy, and inhibition of attacking reactions is equally arduous. It is very difficult for participants, in the actual incipient warfare setting, to refrain from operating according to rules of mutual recrimination, even though they have the intellectual comprehension of negative consequences of warfare and the commitment to cooperation as a condition of establishing a mature relationship. A participant-observer, with a behavioral science orientation, may need to intervene in the situation many times in order to "freeze" an impulsive action or "barb" long enough to examine alternative ways of proceeding that are *not* provocative.

Avoiding the psychodynamic fallacy. In the failure to recognize intergroup dynamics, incorrect, personality-based ascription of motivation for warfare often is given. This is the psychodynamic fallacy, and it occurs when the motivation for behavior of a person is *incorrectly* attributed to factors "within him" rather than to group or intergroup dynamics acting on him. For example, a pathological condition may be contained in the statement, "He is a hostile, aggressive person," if the reference is to the attack by an adversary on one's own representative. With awareness of how dynamics of intergroup conflict act in a more or less standardized manner on *any* representative, the more valid interpretation is to attribute the behavior to distortions in judgment in the direction of devaluating and belittling the adversary, as demonstrated earlier. Such an altered interpretation can serve to reduce the "hot" emotion of wanting to attack a "destructive" person. Similarly when union officers are viewed by management as *representatives,* committed to a fixed position under win-lose conditions, with the traitor threat behind their intractableness, then proper emphasis can be placed on the conditions surrounding the behavior that "cause" resistant actions to appear. By such a correct orientation, the psychodynamic fallacy can be effectively avoided. A change in attitude and action can be achieved, not by hoping for replacement or defeat of an aggressive union officer, who is mistakenly seen as an "unreasonable" person, but by working towards changing the conditions that, in fact, do account for the behavior.

Avoiding the self-fulfilling prophecy. Another dynamic, the self-fulfilling prophecy, also operates to cause one to misplace motivation and to assess intent incorrectly by failing to recognize intergroup factors in the situation. The self-fulfilling prophecy is a prophecy made by oneself and which, in experience, is fulfilled—not because it was an accurate prediction, but because the person who made the prophecy altered his own actions in such a way that his expectations are met in the behavior of the other. Furthermore, when his expectations are met, he misperceives the event and is unaware of how his own behavior exerted an influence on the behavior of another.

Recognition of the way in which the self-fulfilling prophecy operates is particularly significant in situations where intergroup conflict has ruled the day, and where negative stereotypes are rampant. One is most likely to react automatically towards a member of an adversary group in terms of negative stereotypes which are a reflection of competitive relationships. Members of one group, though espousing that they want to cooperate, in fact, often give off signals of conflict. When their attacking, conflicting cues are *correctly* read and reacted to by another group, this only "proves" that the second group was unwilling to cooperate. The pathology thus produced can be avoided by both understanding the dynamics of the self-fulfilling prophecy and also by being aware of the way in which automatic assumptions, particularly derogatory stereotypes, are conditioned by the nature of the intergroup relations.

Procedural Steps Leading toward Intergroup Cooperation

Theory relating to intergroup conflict is indispensable, but insufficient. Leveling is helpful, but it stops far short of producing the concrete conditions for collaboration.

Concrete and practical procedures which facilitate collaboration are needed in order to accomplish it. Each of the validated procedural steps formulated below that aid intergroup cooperation are pointed towards avoiding some pathology of intergroup conflict.

Intergroup therapy. The rationale underlying intergroup therapy is that groups may hold perceptions and stereotypes of one another which are distorted, negative, or so hidden that they prevent functional relationships from arising between them. Only after basic problems of relationship have been eliminated is effective interaction possible. Intergroup therapy is an extension of leveling conferences as described above.

Contending groups are brought together as groups. In private, each discusses and seeks to agree on its perception and attitudes toward the other and its perceptions of itself as well. Then *representatives* of both groups talk together in the presence of other group members from both sides who are obligated to remain silent. During this phase, representatives are responsible for accurate communication of the picture that each group has constructed of the other and of itself. They are free to ask questions for clarification of the other group's point of view, but ground rules prevent them from giving rationalizations, justifications, etc. The reason for using representatives is that communication remains more orderly, and there is an increased responsibility to provide an accurate version of the situation. Members of both groups then discuss *in private* the way they perceive each other, in order to develop an understanding of the discrepancies between their own view of themselves and the description of them by the other side. Finally, again working through representatives, each group helps the other to appreciate bases of differences, to correct *invalid* perceptions, and to consider alternative explanations of past behavior. Fundamental value conflicts not based on distortions also can be identified and examined, then suggestions can be developed for ways of working on problems which can result in solutions other than basic value conflicts.

Problem definition based on facts defined under conditions of interdependence. Facts, as the basis for solving problems that separate groups, are a substitute to one's own group's formulation of the facts from its own point of view alone. Facts that are interdependently agreed upon serve to diminish greatly, sometimes to eliminate entirely, the perceptual and attitudinal selectivity produced by viewing a situation solely from one's own point of view.

Many times, a disagreement between two groups comes about because the problem is defined independently by both sides, each in terms of their own in-group perceptions. This is likely to mean that solutions proposed by members from different groups meet their own criteria of what the problem is and, thus, share little in common. When problem identification is achieved by *joint* action on the part of the groups involved and where it is based on shared fact finding rather than on in-group perceptions, a substantial foundation is provided for obtaining mutually satisfactory resolutions of differences.

Range of alternatives versus fixed position taking. When it is not feasible for groups to develop the solutions together, then

presenting a range of alternatives as possible ways to resolve the
difficulty by each group is conducive to obtaining better end-
products than both groups presenting only their most preferred
position to the other, failing to consider alternatives, or keeping
them hidden.

For a group that has a fixed position, which it considers the
best and only position, to approach an opposing group is like
hurling a challenge to one's adversary.   There are several reasons why.   Locking attitudes and commitments to the "one best
way" that is "our" way flows almost inevitably from a fixed
position.   Members become wedded to their position, and the
stage is set for cognitive distortions, inability to comprehend
communalities and all of the biases in judgment demonstrated
above.   The point is that by initially settling on one's position
as a basis from which to work, sides are drawn more sharply,
and necessary flexibility and tentativeness of the kind that come
from starting with a number of alternatives as a provisional
basis for interaction are lost.

In addition to the negative attitudes that are likely to arise,
it also is probable that a solution which is proposed by only
one group to a problem separating two groups is not likely to be
as superior in quality as a solution that emerges from their joint
deliberations.   When the stated aim is to develop several alternatives, an added push should be given toward seeking for
better ways to solve a problem rather than being tempted to
seize upon the first that appears feasible.   Final positions that
emerge from the interaction and pooled thinking of people with
different points of view are likely to be superior in quality to
the one position produced by either group in isolation, as can
be judged in terms of meeting the common and distinctive needs
of both groups.

Procedural Steps Facilitating Intergroup Problem Solving

Three procedural steps which can aid intergroup problem
solving also have been evaluated experimentally and tested in
actual union-management conflict situations.

Seeking communalities along with tackling differences. When groups have one or a series of preferred positions, the appropriate point of departure is to establish clearly points of *similarity* in the proposals. Testing for comprehension and intent underlying the proposal from another group is critical in arriving at a mutually acceptable solution. Because of the insidious and relatively "silent" nature of the cognitive distortions under conditions of intergroup conflict, the importance of this step can hardly be overestimated. Group members feel subjective certainty of comprehension, so that the biases owing to membership affiliation, perspective, and experience constitute built-in "blindnesses" which are difficult to overcome. It is easy to skip this step of seeking communalities and to seize immediately upon differences between positions. But then, differences tend to be magnified into insurmountable barriers rather than to be perceived within the perspective of similarities. Often areas of agreement between groups are much greater than appear on first glance or even on a second or third look.

Avoiding the traitor threat through increased participation of members in the problem-solving process. Possibly one of the greatest barriers to intergroup cooperation through representative interaction stems from the traitor threat, which involves loss of status and rejection of "disloyal" persons who go against their group position even though there is an objective, logical, factually based rationale for their doing so. When appropriate emphasis is placed on avoiding the motivating power of the hero-traitor dynamic, experimentally validated procedures can be employed to reduce obstacles to problem solving that are anchored to the plight of the representative.

A representative speaks as one voice for a group and thus gives the appearance of unanimity among the in-group. Rarely is this the case. Involvement of more people in problem identification, in suggesting alternatives for solutions, and in testing their feasibility permits divergences in opinions to be aired more fully and brings a greater number of points of view to bear on solving the problem. The wider the involvement in the actual problem-solving sequence itself, the greater the commitment to a solution once it is obtained. The use of representatives is in part based on the notion of the expediency of concentrating effort in a few and thus avoiding "unnecessary" expense and time. But, the longer decision time required by spreading participation can lead to quicker acceptance and greater commitment.

Keeping the group with the representatives versus representatives diverging from group positions. Although it may be impossible to involve an entire group, or even a sizable portion, in the problem-solving procedure, more frequent contact between representatives and constituent groups, as agreements are being formed, also can be employed to avoid the traitor threat. The reason is that a representative can keep his group changing with him as he shifts a position. This means that a "package" which has been bargained in private is not withheld for presentation until all details are ironed out smoothly. The "holding until done" procedure has the earmarks of presenting the conclusions reached without providing the rationale on which the conclusions are based. Not having been through the steps of thinking through implications and examining a variety of alternatives, constituent groups may have little basis for realistically evaluating the product except in terms of degree of difference from an original position. Advance thinking by cross-checking with members *before* changes in position are made means that the group is moving with the representatives rather than the representatives moving *away* from the original position or disposition of the group.

Summary

Once systematic theory of intergroup phenomena has been established through laboratory training programs, norm-setting conferences, and the aid of a behavioral science interventionist, the differences, particularly in the behavior of representatives, under conditions of collaboration are dramatic. The replacement of symptoms of intergroup pathology by successful intergroup cooperation in achieving common and distinctive needs of two groups can be achieved by a mental attitude conducive to collaboration and by employing procedures which are designed to avoid the pitfalls of win-lose conflict. Intergroup leveling sessions can serve to "clear the air." Both the psychodynamic fallacy, which incorrectly assesses motivation as due exclusively to "personality," and the self-fulfilling prophecy, which blinds one to the silent reverberations of his own stereotypical behavior as the basis for action, aid in breaking the mental assumptions underlying win-lose conflict. Factually based mutual problem identification, fluidity in initial stages of proposing solutions, rather than fixed position taking, free and frequent interchange between representatives and their constituent groups, and focus on communalities as well as differences as the basis for achieving agreement are but a few of the ways that have been experimentally demonstrated to increase the likelihood of arriving at mutually acceptable solutions under conditions of collaboration between groups.

APPLICATIONS OF SYSTEMATIC GENERALIZATIONS CONCERNING INTERGROUP CONFLICT AND COLLABORATIONS IN ACTUAL SETTINGS OF LABOR-MANAGEMENT CONFLICT

Now we present a brief résumé of critical steps actually employed in changing union-management relations from conflict toward collaboration. Four examples are involved. In one of the examples there was *unilateral* motivation for collaboration. Management had committed itself to achieving cooperative relationships, but the union remained adamant, oriented toward win-lose competition with the clear-cut image of victory in mind. In two other situations, cooperation was the objective of both management and the union groups who had been through past episodes of conflict. The final example is one representing motivation toward increased collaboration against a short history of successful cooperation, following an earlier period of warfare. In each of these companies, the management recognized that continuation of win-lose bargaining and warfare with the respective unions was not the most sound way to proceed. Rather there was interest in converting conflict into cooperation.

Our story begins with the managements of these companies turning to a behavioral science approach in the hope they would find something of value. First steps in each setting were about

the same. They involved, as the prerequisite for change, laboratory training concerning behavioral science theory with the
direct experience of intergroup experiments followed by study
of theories by all management. After the training phase had
been completed, behavioral science intervention into the ongoing activities of converting to collaboration was available to
slow down precipitous actions that were likely to lead to warfare,
long enough for examination of alternatives dictated by systematic theory of intergroup conflict and cooperation.

The Lakeside Company: Unilateral Motivation
for Cooperation

Several thousand people are employed at the Lakeside Company, which is an integrated manufacturing center. Through a
series of complicated chemical, electrical, and mechanical operations, raw materials are converted into a host of finished products. Union-management relations at Lakeside can be characterized as a state of continuous win-lose conflict, over the past
ten or twelve years. At the time when behavioral science theory
of intergroup conflict and collaboration was first introduced, it
can be said that both union and management felt defeated in
their past relationship, but each on a different issue.

We pick up the story at the point where at least part of
management was seeking for ways to establish collaborative relations with the union. At the same time, the union was stepping
up preparations for warfare, with the clear-cut goal of victory
in mind during the next round of contract negotiations.

The first question to be examined is, "What happens when
one group which is dedicated to battle meets an 'adversary'
which no longer acts like one?" This is the Lakeside story.
The sequence of significant turning points, of win-lose dynamics
in the union, and of steps toward cooperation in management,
will be presented for the critical period during which cooperation emerged against the background of conflict.

Management's Preparation for Collaboration

Preparation for collaboration on the part of management involved three critical actions.

The first step: experience human phenomena and then talk systematically about them afterwards. The initial step at Lakeside was taken several years ago when the decision was made to engage in a laboratory training program with the curriculum focused on problems of intergroup conflict and collaboration. The critical intervention here was by the behavioral scientist, whose advice was sought regarding how to improve union-management relations. A training program was recommended in which participants experience the phenomena as the basis for systematic generalizations regarding conflict, rather than simply "telling" management about theory and experimental results through traditional lecture methods and discussion techniques or suggesting concrete steps that management might take to accomplish the goal of improved relationships.

All members of management participated in such a training program. The union was invited to take part in the training, but it refused. The union said, "This is just another management manipulation intended to 'soften us up,' to 'brainwash,' and to get us so they can beat us in the next round. No soap."

The second step: behavioral science intervention. The second step was for a behavioral scientist, who had specialized in theory of intergroup warfare and cooperation, to become a participant-observer-intervener in the ongoing activities of the company itself. The interventions of the behavioral scientist were particularly powerful for two reasons. One was that he possessed necessary background knowledge of systematic and procedural alternatives for viewing the intergroup situation and for planning constructive action. Secondly, he was not identified with particular solutions for the content issues under examination and, therefore, he was uninvolved in the win-lose dynamic.

The behavioral science interventions were made with the management bargaining team. The simple reason is that similar access was unavailable to the union. At first this one-sided relationship seemed unfortunate. However, it provided a more severe test of the possibility of shifting from competition to collaboration when access is available to only one of the warring factions. Intervention with one side is probably the most realistic situation from the standpoint of many real life warfare situations, for the reason that if one side trusts an outsider, the outsider becomes suspect in the eyes of the other and, therefore, interventions with the second group are unacceptable.

The third step: norm-setting conferences. In spite of an "intellectual" commitment to seek cooperation with the union, it was clear that the management group was still divided among itself on this issue.

There were two contrasting attitudes. On the one extreme, there were people whose dominant feeling was, "All-out warfare is the way to straighten the union out and to 'clean it up.' This is the only way to go. *Make* them be responsible." The other point of view said the opposite: "Collaborate, learn how to solve problems together; accept the present union and its officers. From a legal point of view, they and we are equal. There can be no denial of that. If you accept union officers as equals, they will respond as equals. The problem is one of generating common respect and mutual trust and that can only be done if *we* behave toward them with respect and trust."

There was a deep internal split within the management organization. It could not be resolved by mere edict from above. No one person in the management branch could, with assurance of success, compel the group to shift its mental attitudes from warfare to cooperation. The contending factions needed to be brought together to thrash through their own positions and to find common ground. The critical intervention at this point focused the issue on the problem of divergent attitudes and on the necessity of obtaining unanimity of attitude if at all possible. The procedure followed involved the use of norm-setting conferences as described earlier.

The purpose of these norm-setting conferences was to obtain convictions and concrete proposals for action in response to the question, "What kind of relations do we want to develop between the union and ourselves?" All members of management participated in a series of such norm-setting conferences concerning the union, each a day and one half in length.

Many recommendations emerged from these deliberations. The outstanding one to which all agreed was, "Treat the union and its officers with dignity and respect." Many members of management did a complete "flip-flop" from attitudes regarding the validity of engaging in warfare to accepting intergroup cooperation as the only possible way to proceed over the long term.

This initial "talking through" constituted one of the more important events that has happened at the Lakeside Company regarding labor and management relations in the last several years. The "unlocking" of attitudes and emotions in these norm-setting conferences released the organization to initiate a sequence of events that, in aftermath, has created essentially sound conditions of collaboration. Management had to develop uniformity of attitude at the emotional level *before* any steps toward collaboration could be accomplished. The norm-setting conferences did this.

Union Prepares for Battle

What was the union doing while management was engaged in the steps described above? In the best tradition of win-lose conflict, the union was preparing for the coming battle it envisaged with management. A bird's-eye view of the events in the union will set the stage for understanding the initial contact between union and management.

The Lakeside union officers recently had won a representational battle, but only by the skin of their teeth, and had also squeaked through an intra-union election battle. Even though "victorious" according to the number of votes the union officers received, they felt morally defeated by the reduction in support that they had suffered over a previous landslide.

Re-establishment of group integration in the union after moral defeat. The union needed a clear-cut, well-defined goal to permit its members to close ranks and to work together as a team. In parallel with the reactions in defeated groups studied under experimental conditions, the officers examined union history, in an effort to avoid the kinds of mistakes that it had made in previous bargaining. One mistake the union felt it had made was in not spending sufficient time developing its own positions prior to negotiations. The union spent approximately six months developing new proposals to serve as the agenda during the next round of negotiations. The belligerent and aggressive tone was indicated by the items in the bargaining agenda. It contained many proposals that management would find very difficult even to listen to, to say nothing of accepting them.

"We are out to win"—rise in cohesion with competition. In composing its positions, the union officers and many members had entered into a spirit of a new competition. Even though the whistle had not blown, this group was literally itching to begin a new win-lose battle. By the time the proposals were completed, the union was strong; it was tough, and it was disciplined. Having come to an agreement to prepare strong and defiant proposals, the union members closed ranks. The predicted rise in cohesion, within a group that has the clear-cut goal of winning over its adversary, was conspicuous to those who "knew what was going on."

Union's Reaction to Its Own Proposal: Elevating Own Position

Union officers in their "informal" contacts with management indicated their evaluations of their own document in a spontaneous way. The gist of their reaction was, "Put together, these proposals are *much* better than the old contract. They tie down many more points where management has misconstrued the intention of our previous agreements. It is simple, and it can be understood." Having "sweated through" the production of many pages of proposals, the union officers found their "own" product much superior to the previous contract for which they felt little or no ownership. Now, the union had fixed positions.

The union signals competition to management. When the proposals were handed to management with a flippant "Study them, and when you are ready to talk seriously, let us know," a dramatic restructuring of management's attitudes also took place. Even against the laboratory training and norm-setting conferences from which there emerged the conviction to "treat the union officers with dignity and respect," the deeper lying win-lose orientation to the union resurged in full strength.

Management's Initial Reactions to the Union's Proposal: Emergence of Win-Lose Dynamics

What were the initial reactions of management to the union's proposals? A brief study of the differences between the union demands and the existing contract was made. Differences were many and deep. As the gulf between the existing contract and the union proposals apparently was wider than it had ever been, several members of the Company President's Policy Committee threw up their hands saying, "This proves what an impossible union we have to deal with. Everyone will recognize the absurdity of the positions proposed by the union." Negative stereotypes quickly came to the fore as members of management read through the union proposals. Management found great delight in pointing out errors of grammar, punctuation, and spelling which served to justify their negative attitudes toward the union. The "demands" were considered outrageous and unreasonable. They must be rejected immediately. Management's judgements of the document, and their attitudes toward the union as a group for having prepared such a monstrous proposal, were bitter and destructive reactions.

Meet attack with counterattack: "Throw the proposals back in their faces." The dominant attitude in management was, "Let's have a meeting with the union, take these proposals, and push them back in their faces. We will take whatever consequences come our way, but we can't work with this kind of an impossible union." There was a situation of readiness for bitter conflict. In spite of behavioral science laboratory training and norm-setting conferences which led to verbal intentions to "treat the union with dignity and respect," the intense, long-standing emotional attitudes of a decade had taken over and were in full sway.

The first step in the attack was to grab the offensive away from the union. This was accomplished by creating such conditions that union officers would be under maximum pressure and frustration at not being able to meet with management and then by developing a communications program which would "go directly to the people and convince them of union viciousness and of management's good intentions."

Confronting management with the self-fulfilling prophecy. A behavioral science intervention was called for because management was disregarding the predictable consequences of its actions. It was rushing headlong into disaster. Members of management knew, in an intellectual sense, that their spontaneous reactions of pushing the proposals "back in the faces of the union" would only intensify the incipient conflict already present. Management was headed directly for establishing its battle lines in order to take over an entrenched enemy and force him to capitulate.

The intervention took the following form.

Wait a minute. This is flying off the handle; it is going into orbit. Examine what is going on and what the consequences would be of throwing the proposals "back in their faces." You are reacting to the competition urge, to the win-lose signals from the union. A counter-attack will only produce more intense and open warfare. You will be invoking the self-fulfilling prophecy. By your own behavior, you will provoke the very fighting you want to avoid. You can't hope to receive cooperation from the union when you are in uniform for battle. This would mean the end of face-to-face communications and the reopening, on public level, of intergroup hostility. What would be the gain? Could management, with the background of its action, look towards cooperation ever, or would the lines of communication be so obliterated that no further efforts at cooperation could even be anticipated? The mandate from the norm-setting conference was "treat the union officers with dignity and respect." Is it either dignified or respectful to throw the proposals back in their faces?

These remarks were enough to shatter the impulse for thoughtless action and to reset management's orientation. Rather than rushing headlong into warfare, management continued to explore its own attitudes. The Company President's Policy Committee was confronted with the fact that it was reacting to the situation with feeling and emotion rather than with thought and logic; thus headlong action was diverted at least for the moment. The intervention turned the tide. Several members of the

Company President's Policy Committee began to think, "Is there such a possibility?" Gradually, the feeling arose that there was a possibility of constructive collaboration if only management could be "smart enough" to find the conditions under which to shift the union thinking away from win-lose hostility toward problem solving. Others also began to show a bit of doubt in their initial convictions of certainty that no problem solving would be possible. Negative attitudes began to dissipate slightly. Finally, the decision was made. In spite of the provocative action of "hurling a 'paper bomb' at management," efforts to establish a spirit of cooperation with the union would be taken.

"Seek for Similarities in Positions"

There were still serious reservations about whether collaboration was feasible. One reason for viewing the situation as nearly hopeless was that in their own emphasis on differences, management had grossly exaggerated the magnitude of the issues separating the two groups.

Since there seemed to be no explicit awareness of the basic tendency to ignore communalities in the competing positions, another intervention was needed. In order to break the faulty perspective which had been created by exaggerated emphasis on perceived differences alone, the Company President's Policy Committee was confronted with another proposition. It should evaluate not only differences, but also the similarities existing between the contract and the union's proposals.

The intervention produced a reduction in feelings of antagonism by management toward the union's proposals. The meeting broke up with the decision to prepare a summary document to evaluate similarities as well as differences. In the next meeting, against this more valid perspective, management members still felt that the differences separating their own positions and those proposed by the union were so large as to be fundamental blocks to acceptance. But they also sensed that points in dispute were not as great as had been believed previously. The end result of this intervention and the reappraisal of similarities as well as differences was an increased readiness on the part of management to talk with the union on a more give-and-take exploration of similarities and differences rather than in terms of win-lose dynamics. Instead of arranging a meeting with the union as an offensive maneuver, the approach to the initial bargaining session was planned in a spirit of collaboration.

The sequence above provides a good indication of a fundamental difficulty in shifting from win-lose warfare to cooperative problem solving. The "hot" emotions of win-lose competition tend to submerge the cold eye of analytical examination.

Penetrating the Union's First Proposals

Following the study of the proposals by management, the two groups got together to discuss them. At this point the approach for examining the proposals provided a basis for avoiding the re-emergence of conflict.

Testing for understanding and intention. The management committee felt, with an inner degree of positiveness, that they understood the demands set forth by the union "completely." They were ready to launch into a discussion centered on getting justifications from the union for what it had demanded. At this point, a behavioral science intervention was made. It appeared that searching for justification would be interpreted by the union as an attack, and, in the spirit of the union's orientation, provoke a counterattack. In this case, the win-lose process would begin again. To avoid such an impasse, management made the decision to listen to the union read and explain their proposals in order to insure that they were understood. The goal was to understand the problems *underlying* each proposal as well as to analyze the intention behind the words, as viewed by the union.

The union agreed to explain its proposals, line-by-line while management listened. For the first time in at least a decade, real efforts to talk, to be heard, and to listen with understanding were being made.

Re-emergence of win-lose conflict. In spite of management's decision to listen for intentions, when union proposals were seen to be extreme, management could not keep from trying to demonstrate to the union its "unreasonableness." As items were approached, management started asking questions in an attacking way to get justification, or to "prove" to the union that its demands were unsound. The atmosphere underwent a dramatic transformation from tentative collaboration to fixed position taking, to denial and counterattack. For example, after the question was put to the union by management, "How in the hell can you justify demanding this?" the tension in the situation rose climactically. Both groups were on the launching platform waiting for the countdown. If someone had pushed the button, warfare would have been under way. In the post mortem, following this session, management was tense and antagonistic. It seemed that the time for a critical intervention had occurred, but before the behavioral scientist intervened, a member of management stepped in to call attention to the behavior. It was the first instance in which a member of management himself took responsibility for testing a present course of action against the behavioral science theory which could promote a more constructive alternative for action. The strategy worked. Management backed away from demanding statements of justification and returned to listening in order to comprehend the union's intentions.

Further Progress in Bargaining: Solving Problems Rather than Forcing Capitulation

After completing the reading phases, bargaining started in earnest, but by this time, a sounder foundation for collaboration had been established. The critical steps were those involved in the initial stages. Again, emotional reactions took over as efforts towards intellectual comprehension began to disappear. Again, behavioral science intervention seemed to prevent intergroup interactions from running headlong into conflict. As management acted in a cooperative way, the union began to respond in kind. This is not to say that the path was a smooth one, nor that conflict did not erupt from time to time. On each occasion when a win-lose trap was sprung, it was either averted or overcome.

One example of the types of difficulties which arose occurred as a central issue of a rather complex nature, with a number of subparts, qualifying phases and so on, came under discussion. After preliminary interaction, a sharp cleavage appeared with respect to the economic aspects of the item under consideration. A flip into conflict resulted, with the union pushing for a resolution which would mean a bigger bite from the profit picture. Management "dug in" and established its position, with the attitude being that no more issues could be discussed until this one had been cleared up. Furthermore, the implication was that the only way it could be resolved was for the union to accept management's position.

Management held a strategy planning caucus. During this time, a behavioral science intervention served to point out the likely consequences of fixed position taking. In addition, it was emphasized that there were many other items in the total package which appeared to contain substantial areas of agreement. Management recognized the validity of reviewing the areas of agreement with the union as a different tack for talking through the issue of discord.

After the caucus a member of management reviewed the areas of agreement as management saw them, and the step was well received. After a brief union caucus, the union spokesman summarized what the union understood the areas of agreement to be. His phrasing was essentially the same as that by management. Spirits rose. Both union and management members were able to tackle the remaining area of disagreement in a more factual, problem-solving atmosphere, and the issue subsequently was resolved in a mutually satisfactory manner.

Summary

The interventions depicted above set the stage for long term collaboration at Lakeside. Once the critical hurdles of establishing a posture of cooperation and of achieving some degree of successful problem resolution on a joint basis rather than win-lose victory and defeat had been reached, a more healthy union and management relationship based on mutual respect and understanding was effected. This is not to say that pathological elements of win-lose conflict did not emerge as highly important issues arose for resolution. They did, and they required the utmost skill and determination on the part of management and the union to pursue vigorously the route of collaboration. This particular situation, however, demonstrates that it *is* possible to generate collaboration between two groups when each stands to gain more by cooperation than by conflict, even though there has been a long, intense history of tension and conflict in the background.

Mutual Motivation for Collaboration

Three examples from two different companies of different ways in which joint problem solving has proceeded, once both the union and management have accepted cooperation rather than conflict as the basis for their relationship, are described below.

The Seashore and the Hilltop Companies are, in many respects, similar to Lakeside. The same type of chemical manufacturing operations are involved, and the history of relationships between the union and management in both cases have been characterized by tension and strike, though not of such bitterness as at Lakeside. Only the management in these two companies had experienced the sequence of intergroup conflict and collaboration activities under laboratory training conditions, and each had the resources of a behavioral science interventionist available to intrude into problem solving during crisis periods.

The Seashore Company: Background of Conflict

The motivation for collaboration at Seashore came about because of an impasse that had been reached in negotiations. The positions of the two groups appeared 180 degrees apart on many issues that were significant to both. The differences became frozen and no one could see the possibility of either group shifting. After several weeks of fixed position taking, with both management and the union representatives attempting to extract capitulation to its own point of view from the other in any way possible, and with vituperative accusations and counter-

accusations filling the air, it was finally accepted that only hopeless deadlock could result.

Without the lessons of laboratory learning there would have
been only one recourse—to go outside to use external offices of
mediation or arbitration in an effort to solve the differences
between them. But management was not willing to "give up"
in this manner. With the aid of behavioral scientist intervention,
management developed the following proposal in order to work
in a more cooperative way.

Re-examining Problem Areas

The bargaining groups would work together to identify the
problem area. Committees would be set up, each composed of
three members of management and four from the union, one
for each problem area. Each committee's goal was to gather
facts and to propose a series of preferred solutions consistent
with the facts, to be presented to the bargaining committee in
the form of recommended actions. The possibilities in this proposal for breaking through the hopeless impasse that had been
reached included joint problem definition, focusing on a range
of solutions, increasing the base of participation, and, on the
part of management, attempting to demonstrate willingness to
collaborate through the imbalance in number on the committee
membership. If it came to voting, management could not "win."

Creating unanimity across in-group lines. The proposal was
accepted by the union. Problem areas emerged through joint
definition and eventually ten committees as described above
were formed. As they began to interact, win-lose conflict immediately re-emerged in each committee. The subunits of union
and management "squared off," in line with their larger group
affiliations. Positions became rigid. Problem-solving actions and
progress went out the window.

When this point was reached, the groups did not admit defeat, but rather they stepped away to take a fresh look at the
situation, making conscious and deliberate efforts to become
fact-oriented, rather than jumping at solutions based on an in-
group point of view only. By working through each subissue

to the point of mutual satisfaction, former group lines and loyalties tended to disappear. As another point of contention was reached, the cycle of the two subgroups drawing apart before they could pull together began again, only on each new occasion the stage of apartness was lessened in duration and intensity.

By the time three weeks had elapsed, when they reported back to the parent bargaining committee, they spoke with a single voice.

The impressive point here is in the way in which members of the subcommittees drew together with unanimity, not speaking of group loyalties, but rather speaking through focusing on the problem confronting them, the facts surrounding it, and the most appropriate solutions as they saw them. The ten subgroup recommendations were all accepted by the negotiating group as a basis for further interaction. Whereas three weeks before management and the union had been frozen in hopeless deadlock, the key had now been turned. The door had been opened for mutually satisfactory resolutions of problems. The creative thinking from the subgroups was sufficient to unfreeze the parent negotiating body, and as a result the way had been pointed toward more constructive cooperative actions between the two groups, without the use of external offices such as mediation or arbitration.

The Hilltop Company: Background of Conflict

The management in the Hilltop Company had taken a posture of collaboration at the outset of negotiations. The union adopted the same attitude very quickly thereafter. Thus, both groups were oriented to collaboration against a background of conflict, due to the union's acceptance, at face value, that management's intentions were straightforward and positive.

Management, having learned the lesson of intergroup collaboration and the pitfalls of intergroup competition, oriented itself to relating to the union in such a way as to avoid win-lose traps. It remains somewhat of a puzzle as to why the union responded so quickly to a management "promise," unsupported by actual performance evidence, but the fact is that it did. Quickly thereafter the following events took place.

Crossgroup problem identification. The bargaining sessions for a new contract took place in a sixteen-man unit, eight from management and eight from the union. The basic strategy involved establishing a number of subgroups, each consisting of two union and two management representatives, to investigate and to establish the facts behind each of the identified problem areas. Negotiators were better able to agree on the facts per se, since they did not have to examine the implications of these facts simultaneously in terms of solutions to which they pointed.

In due course the joint subgroups reported the facts as they had agreed upon them to the total union and management bargaining team. At this point a fascinating result was to be observed, for in many cases, the "facts," as developed and agreed on in the subgroups, were conspicuously different than the "facts" that the parent management and union had thought to lie behind the problems *before* the subgroup investigations had taken place. The more or less uniform reaction in the parent committees was that the definitions of facts by subgroup investigations had produced higher quality understandings than had been possible based on the "facts" originally perceived to be correct by each group analyzing the problem area separately and from its own point of view alone. Thus a strong foundation had been achieved for avoiding win-lose position taking on an in-group basis.

Searching for alternative solutions. Given mutually acceptable statements of fact within each problem area, the situation was ripe for the next step of seaching for solutions which would meet the common needs of both union and management as well as the needs unique to each. The total parent group of sixteen was divided into two subgroups of eight, with each group of eight composed of four from management and four from the union. Each group of eight, working independently of the other, used the facts as previously agreed upon as the basis for searching out solutions, though, of course, as new facts became evident they also were included in the basic approach. Rather than a management proposal being presented and countered with an alternative proposal (the typical approach that leads too commonly to win-lose competition), each eight-man group explored the widest possible spectrum of alternate solutions in a tentative way prior to placing evaluations of utility on any of them. The next step involved evaluating each suggested solution as to its adequacy for satisfying the common needs shared by both groups and the needs unique to each. This led more or less naturally to a priority ordering of suggested solutions in terms of overall adequacy as well as to further revisions and refinements of the better solutions by incorporating desirable elements of inferior solutions into them.

Evaluation and cross-checking of solutions. In the final stage, the two eight-man subgroups reunited into the total parent bargaining group of sixteen to compare the quality of the solutions by one group with the solutions that had been produced by the other. Since the octets were crossgroup in composition rather than being octets of management *or* the union they were able to evaluate solutions more objectively and, when necessary, to further modify the most highly agreed on suggested solutions as the basis for formalized agreements.

The sequential procedure for problem solving between groups described here proved outstandingly successful as a basis for statesmanlike union-management problem solving.

The Hilltop Company: Background of Collaboration

After the series of successful cooperative steps had been taken at Hilltop, a new slate of officers was elected with a shift in the composition of the union executive board as follows: four of the eight incumbents were returned to office and four members were defeated. This turnover in personnel provided the opportunity to study the evolution of relations between the same management team and a different team of union officers, against the background of trust and mutual respect that had been achieved between the management team and the old union executive group. Based on experiences of the previous union administration and on the learnings from Seashore which had been concerned with conditions necessary for mutual collaboration, a proposal formed up quickly in the minds of the union executive group. A significant aspect here is that this plan was the *first* innovative step proposed by a *union* group. It should be recalled that in each example only management had been trained. In this case, however, management had "taught" the union, in a sense, through its own attitudes towards innovation in the round of negotiations that recently had been completed. The proposal was for management and the union to collaborate in the following way in order to develop a bargaining agenda.

Problem identification at the grass roots level. The proposed procedure for *developing* an agenda began at the "grass roots." The actual work-group units were to be involved in problem identification. First, each of the twenty-odd work groups would be convened for perhaps a period of a half day or longer, if more time proved necessary. The union representative and the supervisor would be present in the deliberations. In addition, the president of the union and the personnel department head, who were the respective chairmen of the union and management bargaining teams, would be included. Each of the work groups would be asked to discuss outstanding problems confronting the union and management, not only concerning the particular work group, but also to identify problems confronting bargainable employees in general and management "in general." This step literally meant that the total union membership and all members of management who were in direct contact with them would be involved in the initial phase, for the first time in the series of application efforts being described here.

Evaluating and testing appropriateness of problems. On completion of the discussions, the following steps would be taken. Items would be sorted out, selecting first those items subject to correction by actions of the supervisor or by interaction and mutual accord between the union representative and the immediate supervisor of the work group. Problems not subject to resolution by this means would be given further study. Those that were appropriate would be presented to management for immediate correction under the terms of the existing contract. Others, for which there was no existing contract agreement, would serve as the agenda for bargaining. In this way, management and the union, at all levels, would be in closer agreement regarding the issues needing bargaining resolutions.

By this method, as proposed by the union, more would be accomplished than just negotiating a new contract. The clearing up of areas of difficulty not dealt with by union *or* management is probably of equal significance to developing a bargaining agenda through joint effort.

Continuing contact with the membership. Then, the proposal continued, as the bargaining progressed it would be feasible to return to these "grass root" groups to have small group discussions of agreements being achieved and of the outstanding problems remaining for resolution. In this way, continuing involvement in union-management affairs of bargainable personnel and of part time supervision would be insured.

Potential significance of involvement. By this proposal the front line supervisor is linked into the sequence of activities that eventually culminate with a contract. He is not a placid bystander, as is often true of one who sees things going on, but is more than likely to have a resistive, negative attitude toward agreements finally achieved at higher levels, since he has no opportunity to be involved. The involvement by both the union membership and the lower levels of management in problem identification, and later on in discussing agreements as they are reached, should serve to increase day-by-day collaboration at the point where it should be strongest: the level where problems are likely to arise in contract interpretation.

The procedure described here has been accepted by management, and it is now being implemented. First steps have already been taken and the indications are that this cooperative sequence between union and management will, indeed, lead to a new era in effective relationships.

It should be pointed out, however, that application of the approach has not been without its difficulties. The major stumbling block has been the part time supervisor. Many times he has felt threatened by the approach, apparently through fear that it would reflect negatively on his own supervision. In a number of cases the fear has proven justified, with the result that a new training program in effective supervision is being conducted at the present time. In all other respects the approach is working extremely well. Its most important feature is that it is uncovering problems which have been bothersome for years, but which no one knew how to bring to a level of problem solving.

Yet a more significant generalization appears from these application efforts. The generalization is that, too frequently, bargaining begins only after each group has: (1) defined the problem based on its own point of view, and (2) developed a fixed position, again based on its own point of view, as the basis for solution.

In several of the application examples described here, management and the union have learned to work *together* at the level of defining the problem, and then in searching out mutually agreeable solutions.

We attach utmost importance to the generalization that the bargaining relationship should begin with problem definition, *not* with the exchange of proposals and counterproposals, as is all too frequently the strategy of bargaining at the present time.

Overview

For years we have been approaching discord and disturbances between union and management primarily from the standpoint of legislative control. We think this basis for containing the conflict has about run its course, and that a new approach is indispensible for increasing union and management statesmanship in problem solving. This new approach will not come from high level union and management advisory committees, or from human relations committees; nor will it come from other "mechanical" strategies.

The new approach is rooted in behavioral science theory. It seeks to treat symptoms of intergroup pathology in an analogous way to the one that has been found so fruitful in the medical approach to the treatment of illness. The orientation is based on recognizing union and management disputes as symptoms of pathology in the problem-solving area, diagnosing the causes that produce the symptoms, and treating the causes directly, rather than dealing only with symptoms.

The steps are straightforward. On the one hand, the development of a comprehensive body of theory concerning the circumstances of intergroup conflict and cooperation is required. Needed on the other hand is the invention of methods which permit such theory to be immediately useful to the protagonists in an intergroup dispute as a basis for cutting through their conflicts and coming to an awareness of the conditions that promote cooperation. The final step is that of guiding the transformations from theory and intelligent insight to concrete steps of cooperation.

The broad outlines of a basic theory already are available, as has been summarized in the first part of this discussion. Applications of the theory and the strategy for using it in concrete situations of conflict is of demonstrated utility in replacing intergroup pathology with health, as exemplified in the second part. The next advances are ones of refinement.

Our conclusion is that behavioral science experimentation, concept formation, generalization, and application offer important suggestions regarding the conditions under which warring relationships can be reduced and replaced by cooperative conditions of interaction between groups.

References

Avigdor, R., 1952. The development of stereotypes as a result of group interaction. Doctorate dissertation, New York University.

Blake, R. R., 1959. Psychology and the crisis of statesmanship. *Amer. Psychologist*, 14, 87–94.

Blake, R. R., and Jane S. Mouton, 1960a. The story behind intergroup conflict. *Petroleum Refiner*, 39, 181–185.

——, 1960b. Why problem solving between groups sometimes fails. *Petroleum Refiner*, 39, 269–273.

——, 1961a. Applied group dynamics. Houston, Texas, Gulf Publishing Co.

——, 1961b. Reactions to intergroup competition under win-lose conditions. *Management Science*, June.

——, 1961c. Comprehension of own and outgroup positions under intergroup competition. *J. Conflict Resolution*, in press.

——, 1961d. Loyalty of representatives during intergroup competition. *Sociometry*, in press.

——, forthcoming a. Developing and maintaining corporate health through organic management. *Group Psychother.*, to appear.

Blake, R. R., and Jane S. Mouton, forthcoming *b*. Distortions in judgment related to intergroup competition. Submitted to *J. abnorm. soc. Psychol.*

——, forthcoming *c*. Comprehension of points of communality in competing solutions. Submitted to *Sociometry*.

Haire, M., 1955. Role perceptions in labor-management relations: an experimental approach. *Indust. labor relat. Rev.*, 8, 204–216.

Harvey, O. J., 1954. An experimental investigation of negative and positive relationships between small informal groups through judgmental indices. Doctorate dissertation. University of Oklahoma.

Sherif, M., and Carolyn W. Sherif, 1953. *Groups in harmony and tension.* New York, Harper.

——, 1956. *An outline of social psychology.* Revised edition. New York, Harper.

U.S. News and World Report, 1960. Bargaining test: who is boss—union or employer? Oct. 17, 85–87.

Wall Street Journal, 1960. GOP vs. GOP. Nov. 10, 26, #93, 1.

6

THE INTERPENETRATION of group and intergroup processes, so strikingly evident in the last two chapters, is not unique to labor-management relations. "Constraints" upon leaders and representatives from within their own organizations and from their stances in an intergroup system are also evident in Negro-white relations in the United States. In this chapter, Lewis M. Killian concentrates his analysis upon Negro leadership within the relatively stable system of segregation in the South prior to 1954 and the developing trends since that date.

Changes in Negro leadership in less than a decade have been extensive, particularly in urban areas where, in many cases, entirely different individuals have come to the fore. Through an institutional analysis, Killian presents these changes as products of events external to particular Negro or white groups in the South. As Klineberg also notes in Chapter 7, reactions of other nations to segregation in the United States became increasingly important to policy makers in the larger setting. The Supreme Court decision of 1954, declaring that "separate but equal" arrangements could not be equal, established new anchorages for Negro citizens, in terms of which "accommodating" leadership became unacceptable.

The social movements in the South, familiar to most newspaper readers, are further clarified by the researches of Killian and his associates. Continued investigations will provide invaluable data for understanding movements and countermovements and processes of social change. The framework for study provided by Killian's analysis will accommodate more detailed study of interaction within groups and between representatives, as well as further research on the contributions of particular individuals. Such data will be needed for an analysis integrating all relevant levels of interaction, which should be the aim of the social sciences, as S. Stansfeld Sargent reminds us in his discussion following Killian's chapter.

EDITOR

6 LEADERSHIP IN THE DESEGREGATION CRISIS: AN INSTITUTIONAL ANALYSIS

by Lewis M. Killian

It is obvious that the 1954 school desegregation decision of the United States Supreme Court precipitated a political and social crisis of such gravity that it is overshadowed only by the threat of nuclear war. What may not be so evident is that the decision and the ensuing crisis have confronted the social scientist with both a tremendous opportunity and an awesome challenge. The South has been transformed into one vast laboratory of social change, intergroup conflict, and collective behavior. The opportunities for first-hand, on-the-spot study of the dynamics of social change are manifold, but the risks involved in exploiting these opportunities are formidable.

The temptation is great for the social scientist to retreat into the security of the laboratory, with its sound-proof walls of objectivity, methodological rigor, and disdain for social problems. If social scientists succumb to this temptation and leave the analysis of this crisis to the historian and the journalist, they must live with the knowledge that they, who claim pre-eminence as students of society, have allowed momentous social changes to slip by without using them as a source of data.

But the opportunities for research found in this crisis are a challenge not only to the courage of the social scientist but also to the validity of his theory and the sophistication of his research. While the crisis in "race relations" is novel and dramatic for this century, "race relations" is hardly a new area of research. Before 1954 the volume of research on intergroup differences, on patterns of intergroup relations, and on prejudice was impressive. But it is questionable whether the contribution of this literature to the understanding of what has gone on in the South since 1954 is as impressive as its volume. It is even more doubtful whether the methods of research and the modes of analysis developed in the twenty-five years or so before 1954 are suitable for the study of the present crisis.

In retrospect, the first half of this century appears as Myrdal predicted it would—as a peaceful interregnum in race relations (Myrdal, 1944, p. 1014). After the uncertainty and the turmoil of Reconstruction and the gradual restoration of white supremacy in the South, there followed a period of accommodation. With the "separate but equal" doctrine, established and sustained by the Supreme Court, providing the foundation, a great superstructure of state and local laws effectively enforced an inferior status on the Negro. The combination of informal norms, state laws, and federal neutrality served to prevent rapid change in the status system and to preclude the emergence of dramatic and critical conflicts such as have become annual occurrences since 1954. As frustrating and repressive as it might have been to the Negro, the situation was relatively well structured. Although the system was under constant challenge, and exceptions became increasingly frequent after 1945, segregation was "the law of the land" in those local areas that chose to make it so. "Gradualism" was the only practical strategy, since neither the desire nor the resources were present for collective defiance of a legally sustained status quo.

Social science research in the field of race relations subtly reflected the influence of this situation. By and large it has been concerned with, first, the causes of the existing situation, and, second, the impact of the existing status system on the minority group, particularly the Negroes. Herbert Blumer has characterized a large proportion of race relations research as "inventory knowledge," consisting of "accounts of various minority groups, characterizations of discriminatory relationships, and reports on the distribution of attitudes" (1958, p. 431). Furthermore, the roots of race relations have been assumed to be prejudiced attitudes of individuals; studies of change have largely concentrated on the variables related to change in individual attitudes. Blumer terms this the "prejudice-discrimination axis" in research, and says, "It rests on a belief that the nature of the relations between racial groups results from the feelings and attitudes which these groups have toward each other. These feelings and attitudes are the chief objects to be studied in endeavoring to understand race relations" (p. 420).

There have been exceptions to these dominant trends, in a small number of "action research studies" and in studies of the effect of institutional sanctions on attitudes and behavior in situations of race relations. Even these studies have assumed that institutional policy was largely, if not entirely, a creature of the white dominant groups, and that changes would be initiated by white leaders.

In short, the minority, and particularly the Negro minority, has not been thought of as a really dynamic element in race relations, which does not simply adjust to a situation over which it has little control but challenges the situation and initiates change. Studies of Negro leadership were confined to the analysis of the phenomenon of "accommodating leadership" or of the exotic leaders of essentially separatist movements, such as Marcus Garvey or Father Divine. Even the most militant of Negro social scientists, such as W. E. B. DuBois and Oliver Cox, decried the unwillingness of Negro leaders to challenge the status quo radically. Perhaps this implicit assessment of the role of the Negro minority in race relations, particularly in the South, was valid before 1954. It is certain that it does not provide a fruitful approach to the study of race relations since 1954. Accommodation has given way to struggle, stability to change, adjustment to challenge. It is not gradual change that characterizes this era, but change in one critical situation after another.

In these crises, moreover, the initiative comes from the Negro. By and large, it is Negro leaders who determine when the stage shall be set for each crisis and what the specific issue shall be; it is the dominant group that reacts, resisting or adjusting. Traditional studies of Negro adjustment to segregation, and of the attitudes of individual white subjects, contribute little to the understanding of what is going on in the current integration controversy. The finding that, in one way or another, nearly every Negro resents segregation and finds it a psychological handicap does not explain why in many communities the visible face of race relations remains unchanged, while in others the vigor of the Negro protest has led to open conflict and sometimes to the abandonment of long-standing patterns of social relations. Recent studies of white attitudes towards desegregation, such as those done by Tumin (1958) and by Killian and Haer (1958), show only a small minority of whites at the extreme end of the "resistance scale"; there appears to be no correlation between the distribution of individual attitudes and the adamance of community resistance to change.

What is called for in the present situation is an approach which emphasizes collective behavior, not individual attitudes. The case being analyzed is a powerful, aggressive social movement in conflict with a determined resistance movement, not the adjustment of a minority group to the restrictions imposed by a dominant group. In particular, organization and leadership should be of central importance. Because of its dynamic and germinal function, Negro leadership will be emphasized in the present analysis. The same sort of analysis could be applied to white leadership, and some beginnings have been made.

But when one turns to the not inconsiderable body of research on leadership in search of a theoretical framework for the analysis of this specific case, the results are again disappointing. What does the "leadership research" of the past twenty-five years contribute to the explanation of the emergence of a Martin Luther King and of his less famous counterparts, or of the revolt of Negro college students against both white dominance and the conservatism of their own elders? It seems to me that the contribution can be summed up in the broad and crude generalization that leadership varies with the situation.

Even those situational studies which have provided an antidote to the unrestrained search for universal leadership traits have fallen largely within the realm of small-group analysis, often resting upon highly controlled laboratory situations. The microcosmic situations, the relatively specific tasks, and the direct interaction found in the experimental "leaderless group," the small military unit, or even the factory, are not necessarily comparable to their counterparts in a regional society caught in the throes of social change. "The situation" in the integration crisis encompasses such variables as a complex and evolving body of laws, the amorphous values and aspirations of dispersed masses of people, the indirect nature of much of the interaction of these people, and the continuous process of action-reaction both within and between the collectivities involved. Here, indeed, are to be found magnificent opportunities for advancing our knowledge of both intergroup relations and leadership, but the challenge to our methods is as great as the opportunity.

But the danger in being daunted by the complexities of a dynamic sociocultural setting has been pinpointed by Sherif and Koslin (1960) in their warning, "In social psychology, constriction of the research perspective to the arrangements of the immediate location in which attitudinal responses are obtained, or in which interaction categories and spoken words of the respondents are recorded, amounts to neglect of some of the crucial independent variables operative in the situation, whether or not these variables are immediately apparent within the confines of the immediate situation at the moment" (pp. 1–2).

With equal cogency, Sherif has reminded sociologists that it is their task to analyze and describe the stimulus conditions in which the behavior that the social psychologist studies takes place. Adhering to the role of the sociologist, I have labeled my analysis of Negro leadership in the integration crisis an "institutional analysis." Without discounting the importance of the study of the characteristics of individual leaders or of their behavior in interaction with followers, other leaders, and antagonists, I will confine my efforts to an analysis of the stimulus situation in its broadest aspects, to the social forces which define the limits within which these leaders function.

Changes in Negro Leadership

Even though social science research on Negro leadership has been and still is sparse, ample evidence is available that there has been a change, particularly in the South, since the 1954 desegregation decision. Fortunately, several intensive analyses of such leadership on both local and national levels were made shortly before the time of the decision, and they provide empirical support for the somewhat impressionistic overview of Negro leadership before the decision, which the general literature on race relations supports.

During the era of accommodation before the present crisis, Negro leadership even on the national level could hardly be described as dramatic or "revolutionary," to use Guy Johnson's classification (1937, p. 63). After the death of Booker T. Washington and the departure of W. E. B. DuBois from the NAACP, no figure of comparable national standing arose. A Negro journalist, Julius J. Adams, writing in 1949, was even harsher than this in his evaluation of Negro leadership. He declared, "There has not been a really great leader among Negroes since the untimely death of Frederick Douglass in 1895," and he contended that when Washington died in 1915 there ended "the reign of the last person who might have been entitled to be called 'a leader of the Negro'" (1949, p. 12). Guy Johnson had made the same observation in 1937, saying, "Booker T. Washington is the only Negro leader who has ever had anything like a race-wide following" (1937, p. 59). In his opinion, the differentiation of Negroes into social and economic classes so much like those of white society led to such a lack of cohesion that a truly race-wide leadership was impossible. He predicted that only the development of a radical movement in open conflict with the old order could lead to the emergence of another race-wide leader (p. 60).

E. F. Frazier disagreed with Johnson as to the causes of the paucity of first-rate Negro leaders. He contended that the differentiation of the Negro population resulted in the development of "functional" leadership, composed of leaders judged both by the outlook of the groups they represented and their stand on the integration of the Negro into particular spheres of American life. He classified these functional leaders in five types: religious, social welfare, political, labor, and intellectual. He predicted that the increasing integration of the Negro into American life would tend to perpetuate this sort of functional leadership, represented by such leaders as A. Clayton Powell, A. Phillip Randolph, Walter White, Roy Wilkins, and Thurgood Marshall (Frazier, 1957, pp. 548–549).

National Negro leadership during this period prior to 1954 was located outside the South. If Negro leadership outside the South was "functional," fragmented, and difficult to identify, leadership in the South was invisible, particularly to the white community. There were Negro leaders in local communities, but one of their salient characteristics was that they operated behind the scene. The other was that they were what Myrdal characterized as "accommodating leaders," depending for their leadership on their ability to get along with, and gain favors from, white influentials (Myrdal, 1944, pp. 720–733). For a long time it was a commonplace assumption that such leaders were ministers, undertakers, and educators. The gradual growth of the Negro middle class and the development of Negro voting during the forties changed this situation, however, if it had ever really existed.

Floyd Hunter, studying the power structure of the Negro subcommunity in "Regional City" in 1950–1951 found that representatives of these occupations did not dominate top leadership positions (1952, p. 117). In this metropolitan community businessmen and representatives of other professions overshadowed these types in influence. William G. Carleton (1958), in a study conducted in Jacksonville, Florida, after the Supreme Court decision of 1954, identified another type of leader—also identified by Hunter, the Negro politician. In the growing urban centers of the South where Negro voting has become accepted, the leader who can influence the Negro vote has been able to demand the attention of the white politician. But Carleton's theme is that even the Negro politician is changing, although the transition is still in progress.

In an article with the expressive title, " 'Good Jelly's' Last Stand," David Halberstam (1961) describes one of the "old-style" Negro politicians in Nashville. In Halberstam's words: "Very simply, he controls the votes of a large number of unbelievably poor people, and for a minimum of service, protection, and financial reward, he delivers these same votes without the slightest concern for ideology" (pp. 40–41). But both this author and Carleton are convinced that the growth of the Negro middle class has caused the days of "Good Jelly" and his ilk to be numbered. Carleton states, "The Negro leader is now answerable to the Negro middle-class community and he must deliver public advantages to the Negro community if he is to retain his leadership" (1958, p. 422).

While these Negro politicians represent a new subtype of Negro leadership, they are still variants of the old, accommodating type. Hunter concluded, "Under the existing patterns of segregation and social exclusion operative in the general community of Regional City, Negro leaders, as well as followers, have to adapt themselves to the situation" (1952, p. 138). They were not able to influence community policy directly, and they still operated "in the shadows" in that Hunter found that the top power leaders in the white community had a vague and inaccurate conception of Negro leadership as he found it to exist (p. 141). The type of politician whom Carleton (1958) found to be successful was what he called the "practical politician," not the idealistic "protest" leader. He said, "The practical politician brings concrete benefits to the Negro community but makes ideological concessions. The idealist solidifies ideological consciousness, but in consequence his ability to bring benefits to his community is often impaired" (p. 428).

These various subtypes of accommodating leaders continue to exist, sometimes vying with each other for pre-eminence. It may be that the most conservative of the accommodating leaders will persist for some time in the smaller towns of the South, where the Negro middle class continues to be small and voting is limited. But it is evident that, with the acceleration of the Desegregation Movement, a distinctly new type of Negro leader is emerging in the South—the protest leader who challenges segregation and the white power structure openly and directly. Martin Luther King is the outstanding example of this type of leader, but many lesser leaders of the same type have appeared and continue to appear throughout the South. King is remarkable not only for the militancy of his protest leadership but also for the fact that he, a southern Negro leader, has come closer than anyone since Booker T. Washington to achieving national leadership. Certainly he and his philosophy of nonviolent resistance have set the tone for the current phase of the Desegregation Movement. This is the "new leadership" which demands the attention of the social scientist.

In 1957, following the emergence of leadership of this sort during a bus boycott in a Florida city, Killian and Smith (1960) investigated the changes in leadership that had occurred. Panels of white and Negro leaders who were, or might have been, involved in the controversy and negotiations over the bus boycott, or who were known to have represented points of liaison between the white and Negro communities before the crisis, were interviewed. The purpose was to determine whether a group of new leaders had indeed emerged or whether the old, invisible leaders had merely become apparent. It was concluded that a complete change of leadership had taken place, and that this change was perceived not only by the Negro influentials themselves but also by the white leaders. The new leaders were clearly of the "protest" type; none of them was ranked by either Negroes or whites as being acceptable to white leaders as spokesmen for the Negro community. The old leaders, as defined by both whites and Negroes, were regarded by both groups as men who had been best able to deal effectively with white leaders.

Continued observation indicated that this change was not an ephemeral one. Interviews with the old leaders revealed that many of them felt betrayed and even bitter, and that they had lost confidence in their ability to influence the Negro community or to speak in its behalf. It was not that the new leaders were particularly successful in gaining concessions from the white community; the boycott which they had led had failed in its main objective of desegregating the city busses. Killian and Smith concluded, "The new leaders are becoming permanent leaders not because of the attractiveness of their personalities or their skill at organizing, but rather because they adhere rigorously to the *form* of militant leadership which is becoming the trend for Negroes throughout the United States" (1960, p. 257).

Subsequently, a challenge to these new leaders did arise, but it did not come from the old, accommodating leaders. As happened in so many southern communities during the winter and spring of 1960, the leaders of the student "sit-ins" took the initiative and compelled the adult leaders to back them up. This constituted an accentuation, not a reversal, of the trend towards militant leadership. Louis Lomax (1960) said of it, "This revolt, swelling under the ground for the past two decades, means the end of the traditional Negro leadership class." What are the broad, situational factors which have created such a rapid and abrupt change in the form of Negro leadership in the South, between 1950 and 1960?

The Situation Before 1954

The dominant feature of the situation before 1954 was that segregation seemed firmly entrenched as an institution. True, segregation laws were largely confined to the South, and some areas outside the South even had civil rights laws which prohibited it, at least in theory. But the right of the white dominant group to maintain segregation so long as the "separate but equal" fiction was adhered to had the blessing of the Constitution. Although Myrdal found the "American dilemma" easy to detect, the notion that segregation might some day be publicly defined as a violation of fundamental American values appears to have been a well-kept secret among white Americans. The Supreme Court ingeniously avoided accepting the question of segregation per se as a constitutional issue.

The major religious denominations accepted the status quo without comment. To be classified as a "southern liberal" it was necessary only to decry the existence of inequalities within the "separate but equal" framework without challenging the principle of segregation itself. Even the Southern Regional Council, biracial and unsegregated from its inception in 1945, accepted segregation as a legal fact and made no mention of desegregation as part of its program for the improvement of the condition of all citizens within the region.

Despite the objections of Negroes to "Jim Crow" and the persistence of the NAACP in trying to whittle away the legal basis, the possibility that the entire institutional basis might be overthrown seems to have had a remote and dreamlike quality to Negroes. It is doubtful that the great majority of Negroes even recognized the portents of a change in the thinking of the Supreme Court as that body gradually narrowed the requirements of the "equal" test, notably in the Sweatt and McLaurin cases. Almost on the eve of the decision Charles H. Thompson, editor of the *Journal of Negro Education,* expressed concern at the lack of preparation for action following a ruling that segregation was unconstitutional, saying, "Unfortunately there has developed among the majority of people concerned an attitude of 'wait and see'" (Thompson, 1954, pp. 107–108).

There is little wonder, therefore, that Negro leaders in the South accepted segregation and the inferior social status which it symbolized as an enduring institutional feature of their situation. Openly challenging the system was not only risky from the legal and personal standpoint; it jeopardized any chances the leader might have to gain concessions for the Negro community through playing the role of the accommodating leader. Further-more, the fact that the law supported the system of segregation, from the municipal to the federal level, gave him a certain im-munity from criticism for compromising with the system. Myrdal (1944) even went so far as to claim that the Negro leader who was too militant was feared in the southern Negro community because he might invoke reprisals against the whole community (pp. 770–771).

Hence the leadership in the fight against the principle of segre-gation came from outside the South. This does not mean that there was not cooperation from within the South, in the form of plaintiffs in school suits. The nature of the tactics at this time dictated that this was the only kind of cooperation that was essen-tial. Strategy was devised in the legal offices of the NAACP in New York; the battle was fought in courtrooms, particularly in the Supreme Court Building in Washington. As long as the few plaintiffs needed for the critical test cases could be found, neither outstanding Southern leadership nor active mass support were required. As was true of the Abolition Movement, the leadership in the Movement for the overthrow of legally sus-tained segregation was a "leadership in exile" for Negroes in the South.

The Situation After the Desegregation Decision

The day after the Supreme Court issued its historic decision, the sun rose over America as usual; millions of Negroes awak-ened and went to their same jobs on the same segregated busses; the children in Prince Edward and Clarendon Counties went to the same segregated schools. Practices were not changed; only a legal principle had been changed. A former justice of the Supreme Court predicted that a half-century of litigation would result from the change. Yet the fact that the legal principle had been changed meant that the social stimulus situation for both whites and Negroes in the South was now different, and the importance of this difference cannot be overemphasized.

First, the fact was most obvious that one phase of the De-segregation Movement, the rather orderly legal campaign to get the Supreme Court to reverse Plessey versus Ferguson, was over. The task then for Negro leaders was to insure that the new principle would be implemented. It is apparent now that this is a much more arduous and complicated task than the earlier one was. Second, the Negro leader in the South could no longer rely so heavily on the law as a justification for lack of militancy. The white dominant group had not been ordered to desegregate, but the Negro minority had been given a legal basis for demanding that they do so. Failure to insist upon a right that has been declared to exist is quite a different matter from failure to demand a right that doesn't exist.

Most important, the issue in Negro-white relations had been publicly redefined in unmistakable terms. That Negroes might have a constitutional right to demand the end of state-imposed segregation was no longer a theory or a dream. In the eyes of Negroes themselves, it was now a fact: the question was now when and how segregation would be ended. Many white people, particularly in the South, did not agree that such a constitutional right had been established, as their denunciations of the Supreme Court and its ruling showed. But no matter how reluctantly, they recognized that the powers of the federal judiciary were now arrayed against segregation instead of in favor of it. Desegregation was no longer an imaginary threat to be invoked as an argument against such changes as extending voting rights to Negroes. It was now a real and deadly threat to the traditional status system.

The immediate reaction, or lack of reaction, of large numbers of Negroes to the decision gave no clue to these changes in the situation. Many white people sought reassurance in the argument that it was only a few Negroes, "agitators" and "outsiders," who opposed segregation, and that the vast majority of Negroes in the South were unchanged. In interviews with white and Negro leaders in ten Florida counties in the summer of 1954, Killian and others (1954) found that 54 per cent of the white leaders believed that most of the Negroes in their community disagreed with the desegregation decision of the previous May. It was found that only 4.1 per cent of the Negro leaders interviewed in these same counties felt that the decision was wrong, and only 6 per cent felt that most of the Negroes in their communities disagreed with the decision. Subsequent events in this and other southern states indicated that while there might not be large numbers of Negroes who were willing to be pioneers in claiming their newly defined rights, the temper of the masses had indeed changed.

Developments After the 1954 Decision

For over a year after the 1954 decision, and for months after the April, 1955, "implementation" ruling, active Negro leadership remained primarily in the hands of the NAACP. Local chapters in the South did become more active partners of the national leaders in attempting to exploit the new legal situation. But the strategy was essentially that recommended by the NAACP lawyers—bringing suits against segregated facilities in as many communities as possible. Such a strategy was inherently "gradualist," for legal battles are typically long ones and the somewhat enigmatic formula, "with all deliberate speed," held out to the resistance the hope of even longer delay. Moreover, this strategy placed a low premium on dynamic leadership and mass support in the South. What was needed instead were shrewd strategists and a few courageous individuals willing to serve as plaintiffs in test cases. Thurgood Marshall was the hero of the day, but he was the leader of a shrewd, well-disciplined task force, not of a large, inspired army. This is not to imply, however, that the old, accommodating mode of leadership could still function effectively in the new situation.

Interviews with Negro leaders in Florida at this time indicated that they were already feeling pressure from their own people to affirm to the white community their desire for rapid implementation of the desegregation decision. At the same time, white people who had felt secure in a paternalistic relationship with Negro accommodating leaders for years no longer felt the same confidence in them. The complaint that "communication between the races had broken down" was already becoming common. Ostensibly, the philosophy of "gradualism" had received its deathblow among Negroes, yet the leadership that the NAACP was providing in its legalistic approach was implicitly gradualist. A vacuum existed in which a new type of leadership could arise.

The first clear manifestation of the altered temper of the Negroes of the South came in the Montgomery bus boycott of December 1955. This collective protest was unplanned and lacked the shrewd strategy of a carefully selected test case, but it depended on and consisted of the personal action of thousands of Negroes. L. D. Reddick (1959) describes the reaction of the Negro community to the precipitating incident as "massive," and says of it

The Montgomery bus boycott was like the bursting of a huge dam. Pent-up fears and resentments, latent hopes and aspirations came to the surface. The torrent exposed real race relations and revealed the true mood of Southern Negroes, usually hidden underneath a daily masquerade of self-effacing courtesy (p. 112).

The significant factor here is not the accumulation of grievances; fears and resentments had existed for a long time. Turner and Killian (1957) have pointed out that frustration and deprivation are not sufficient conditions for the development of collective action of a revolutionary type: "there must also be a belief in better conditions which can be brought about through collective action." One of the sources from which such a belief may be derived is a situation in which "as conditions are improving for a group . . . the members . . . develop an image of an even better state of affairs, as their early gains give them hope" (p. 31). The legal victory in the school desegregation cases was just such an early gain which gave the group hope for success through collective action.

Reddick (1959) also reveals that this protest was not only not planned by the NAACP but that for the first two months of the boycott the NAACP "would not touch it" because it did not demand the end of segregated bus seating, but only seating on a "first come, first served" basis (p. 113). Only later was the demand for desegregated seating specified and only later was legal pressure brought in on the side of the Negro protest.

But the leadership of the NAACP was not needed in this movement, for it produced its own leader of a new type—Martin Luther King, Jr. He did not start the boycott and he was not the only leader who emerged in it, but he became the outstanding leader and the model of a new type of leadership among Negroes not only in the South but throughout the nation. The nature of the movement itself was such as to create a heroic type of leader, for this mass movement dramatized the Negro protest in a way that a complex and slow-moving legal battle never could. It contained the elements to make it irresistible to the press; that a leader of national reputation would be created was inevitable.

Why it happened to be King, Reddick, his biographer, finds it difficult to explain. He accounts for it in part by King's personal appearance and skill as an orator. Equally important, he thinks, was the novelty of King's philosophy of nonviolent resistance (Reddick, 1959, p. 131). Certainly his effective promulgation of this philosophy among his many followers in Montgomery, to the point that it became the hallmark of the movement, established a new factor in the situational limits within which Negro leaders would operate in the future. It made the Montgomery bus boycott one of the most significant events in the new phase of race relations.

The next major event in the development of the new situation in race relations came at Little Rock, in the Fall of 1957. This crisis differed from the one in Montgomery, in that the NAACP did provide the leadership, and no mass action on the side of the Negroes was involved. The same sort of defiance of powerful forces, including the police powers of the state and the lawless violence of the mob, was displayed by the nine Negro students and their adult sponsors. What was most significant in this case, however, were the tactics of the resistance, the consequences of the use of these tactics, and the resulting change in the balance of power between the Desegregation Movement and the Segregation Countermovement.

In his experimental research on intergroup relations, group structure and group norms, Sherif concluded, "The behavior within the groups themselves could not be analyzed apart from the trends in intergroup relations, once the groups came into contact. The impact of conflicting intergroup relations changed the power structure within the groups . . ." (Sherif and Koslin, 1960, pp. 14–15). Turner and Killian have emphasized the constant interplay between the tactics of a social movement and the tactics of the opposition (1957, pp. 361–384).

In Little Rock, the sending of troops by the President of the United States demonstrated that apparently reckless defiance of the forces of the resistance could have very practical results: the forcing of the commitment of the powers of the federal executive on the side of the Negro protest. In addition, the power of persistent defiance of apparently overwhelming odds to arouse an indignant, nation-wide public and to boost Negro morale even higher was affirmed again. Kenneth Clark (1958) made the following observations after conducting interviews in Little Rock following the entrance of federal troops:

In general, it appears that the Negro community in Little Rock has become more unified as a consequence of these recent tensions. . . . The Negro community may be characterized as fearless, determined, and stolid. There is a relentless refusal to move backwards. This stolidity is supported by a strong feeling that they are on the right side of this issue, that history is on their side, that international and national imperatives make the position of the pro-segregationists untenable. The Negro community does not seem to be in a mood for further compromises or temporizing of their right to attend non-segregated schools (p. 5).

There was no marked increase in the pace of desegregation following Little Rock, but the validity of Clark's observations of the effect of the crisis on the mood of Negroes was confirmed by the occurrence of the next critical event—the "sit-ins" of the Spring of 1960. Here again it was the tactics of the resistance plus the untemporizing mood of the minority group that produced another significant change in the tactics of the desegregation movement.

The NAACP strategy of litigation had evoked a highly effective counterstrategy—the Pupil Placement law. While this strategy was opposed by some white leaders because it permitted some desegregation, its effectiveness as a delaying device was attested by the fact that this type of desegregation came to be labeled "token integration." Some Negroes felt the desegregation movement had "stalled." Charles H. Thompson (1960) said of the wave of sit-ins:

First and most important is that fact that it has pushed the desegregation struggle off "dead center" where it seems to have been resting for the past two or three years. We have been winning court battles but apparently losing the propaganda war (p. 107).

At the same time Thompson pointed out this latest instance of the use of nonviolent resistance, and even civil disobedience, took the students' elders by surprise, and he felt that the NAACP "high command" would have advised against the move at the time.

In an unpublished paper, Charles U. Smith, a sociologist at one of the universities whose students participated in the sit-in movement, has sought to analyze the reasons why the time was "ripe" for such a movement. One important reason, he concluded, was that by 1960, six years after desegregation rulings, "The Negro was able to appreciate the full significance of the interposition declarations, pupil assignment laws, residential requirements, achievement score requrements, health requirements, school closings, and massive resistance techniques which have effectively kept segregation despite the Court's ruling" (Smith, unpublished).

In short, the demonstrations of 1960 were a forcible reminder even to the "new" Negro leaders that the mood of their followers was such that the movement would not be permitted to slacken its pace. If the leaders of the moment did not produce tangible examples of progress, even more militant leaders would arise. The students and the Congress on Racial Equality, a previously little known organization, demonstrated that they could not only seize the leadership but could compel the NAACP and adult Negro leaders in general to support them, even when their legal position was tenuous and their methods drastic. Finally, the sit-ins demonstrated even more clearly than did the Montgomery bus boycott that use of the nonviolent resistance technique could throw the white community into a paroxysm of fear, guilt and self-defeating violent tactics.

Operational Limits on Negro Leadership

As a result of this sequence of events, we may say that the sociocultural setting in which the Negro leader functions incorporates severe limits on his freedom of action. While local variations in the size, the characteristics, and the organization of the Negro population, as well as in the responsiveness of the white power structure to pressure from the national level, cause a differential in the rate of development, a definite trend toward a new form of Negro leadership has developed.

As has already been pointed out, one important limit is the suspicion of white leaders with whom the old accommodating leaders used to deal, the fear that Negroes can no longer be trusted to "stay in their place." Secondly, there is abundant evidence that there is an increasing and spreading unwillingness of Negro communities in the South to accept the accommodating leader as their emissary. As a consequence of these two variables, communication of the traditional type has indeed broken down.

The third limit is that, in addition to rejecting accommodating leadership, Negroes demand of protest leaders constant progress. The combination of long-standing discontent and a new-found belief in the possibility of change produces a constant state of tension and aggressiveness in the Negro community. But this discontent is vague and diffuse, not specific; the masses do not define the issues around which action shall revolve. This the leader must do.

In research in a southeastern city, Grigg and Killian found widespread dissatisfaction among Negroes about job opportunities for their children, recreational facilities, health services, police protection, and educational facilities (Killian, 1961). There was less dissatisfaction about educational facilities, however, than about other aspects of the community. In a study, in the same city, of the Negro's sensitivitiy to various forms of discrimination, it was found that the Negro's rank order of preference for change was as follows: improvement in job opportunities and pay; equal treatment by the police and in the courts; the end of segregation in public transportation and at sports events; the end of segregation in public schools; increasing freedom to vote; and finally, freedom to visit in white homes, to swim in the same places with whites, and to eat in the same restaurants. Yet, shortly after the study was completed, a crisis arose in this same city over segregated lunch counters.

Hence, it was postulated that the concentration of the attack of militant leaders on specific forms of segregation, such as segregated lunch counters, beaches, and golf courses, even though there is no clear evidence of a popular demand for giving them high priority, rests upon strategic considerations. Grigg and Killian suggest:

Improvement of employment opportunities, equalization of pay, and opening the higher levels of employment to Negroes is a long and arduous task. . . . When gains are made, they are likely to come slowly and gradually, not dramatically. In contrast, a court suit to gain admittance to a publicly supported school, park or golf course is a tactic with a history of success in bringing quite concrete and evident results. Similarly, sit-ins and other types of demonstrations dramatize the Negro protest, whether the results be desegregated lunch-counters or martyrdom for the participants. These are things around which dissatisfied people may rally, even though they may not personally intend to make use of the desegregated facilities (Killian, 1961).

It is suggested, then, that the Negro leader is not only under pressure to propose and initiate action but also to select issues. Many years ago Walter Lippmann (1922) commented on this function of the leader. He remarked in *Public Opinion*, "There would be nothing in the feeling of the mass that fatally determined the choice of any particular policy. All that the feeling of the mass demands is that policy as it is developed and exposed shall be, if not logically, then by analogy and association, connected with the original feeling" (p. 185).

Certain other situational factors serve to give the advantage to the more militant leader. One is the tendency of Negroes and white liberals to lionize the leader who displays aggressiveness and courage in defying the white power structure in his community. The prestige rewards are great. The leader of the largely unsuccessful Tallahassee bus boycott, one of King's early imitators, achieved a measure of national prominence among Negroes as a result of his activities. One of his lieutenants, another minister, received a call to a much larger church in another southern state shortly after the boycott ended. During the summer of 1960 some of the student leaders in the sit-ins were afforded the opportunity of appearing before the Platform Committee of the Democratic Party and perhaps influenced the platform that was presented at the National Convention. Even more important is the nation-wide and even world-wide press coverage that such a leader is likely to receive, particularly if his tactics are met by illegal violence or police brutality.

Finally, there is little to lose and much to gain strategically by drastic but nonviolent resistance, although the personal risk to life and liberty is great. If Negroes cannot gain the concessions they seek through massive, nonviolent protest, they may still provoke the opposition into using such extreme tactics that sympathy is aroused in influential segments of the local white community or, as in Little Rock, the federal executive intervenes in their behalf.

Negro leaders who may have serious misgivings concerning the tensions and violence which such militancy entails, and would prefer a more peaceful means of insuring that change takes place, are well aware of the existence of these pressures or limitations. In a number of cities in Florida, including some which have had serious crises, official or unoffical biracial committees have been established to act in the manner of mediation boards. It has been the experience of Negroes on such committees, as reported to the writer, that no matter how much respect they command in the Negro community, the extent to which they can prevent crises by negotiation is severely restricted. As the Sherifs point out,

> The leadership role usually carries with it a primary or more weighty responsibility in contacts or dealings with other groups and their leaders. But in such contacts or dealings he must still operate within the permissible latitude of the norms of his group, unless secrecy is possible. This is one of the reasons why the notion of solving all intergroup tensions by bringing prominent citizens around a conference table has limitations (Sherif and Sherif, 1953, p. 45).

From the outset, Negro leaders realize that they must combat the suspicion among their followers that they have "sold out" to the white community and are permitting themselves to be used to preserve the status quo. But even if they overcome this suspicion, they must constantly be able to advance proof that they are either gaining some concessions from the white community or making progress towards some gains through their negotiations. The change need not necessarily be directly related to desegregation; even these leaders have some latitude in defining issues for the Negro group. But as soon as it appears that no change at all can be expected as a result of the efforts of such a group, other leaders begin to channel the discontent of the masses toward the creation of a new crisis. W. K. Williams, who analyzed the background of the Jacksonville riot of August, 1960, observed: "The 'sit-ins' are more a form of protest and public statement by Southern Negroes than they are a focal point of Negro objectives. Behind them are the struggles for improved educational opportunities, better housing, employment and the like" (1960, p. 5).

The difficulty that Negro negotiators encounter in promoting peaceful change is increased by the fact that their white counterparts operate under similar pressures—suspicion in the white community that *their* real purpose is simply to promote desegregation, and reluctance of key white leaders to make any concessions to what they perceive as Negro "pressure."

This "institutional" analysis of the sociocultural setting in which Negro leadership in the South functions today obviously falls short of the standards of a rigorous empiricism. Some of the support for the theoretical analysis is derived from carefully designed empirical studies; much is admittedly based on historical analysis of unique cases, on personal documents, and on insights gained from intimate but uncontrolled observation of the social movement in its natural state.

But sociologists will fail miserably in their task of describing stimulus conditions in their broadest aspect if they limit themselves to the techniques of the small group laboratory experiment and the time-consuming and often irrelevant attitude survey. Not only will they have failed to pay their debt to the society which supports them, but they will have failed to provide the social psychologist with the knowledge from the sociological level which he requires for the design of meaningful experiments on his own level. In conclusion, let us consider some of the questions which may be raised on the levels of small-group study and personality analysis.

Needed Research on the Social Psychological Level

The framework in which the Negro leader must function and interact with both his fellow Negro leaders and white leaders has been analyzed. One impression that emerges from the observation of the new Negro leaders in action is that many of them are inexperienced in the role of leader, and that nearly all are inexperienced in exercising leadership in this sort of situation.

For instance, a case study of the Tallahassee bus boycott by Killian and Smith (1957) revealed that for the first ten days of the boycott the leaders were not even clear what their demands, as publicly announced, really meant. Further investigation showed that these demands were merely a word-for-word repetition of the original demands of the Montgomery Improvement Association, which had ultimately been clarified and revised by King and his lieutenants. King's own account of the development of the Montgomery protest reveals that the goals and the tactics of that movement were the products of a complex and sometimes halting process of interaction between the leaders, not a blueprint laid down by a master strategist (King, 1958).

In the usually abortive negotiations between white and Negro leaders, both groups may suffer from a lack of experience in this sort of setting. Neither white nor Negro leaders in the South are accustomed to dealing with each other in a situation in which both speak from a position of power. Members of biracial committees which have at least been able to survive have reported to the author that it takes weeks or even months of meetings before the members are able to establish sufficient rapport to enable them to give concerted attention to the specific problems confronting their communities. In other instances, biracial negotiating groups adjourned after one meeting because the white and Negro members reached an initial impasse over the general issue of segregation.

The interaction process itself in the face-to-face encounters between Negro and white leaders, and between various types of leaders within both groups, requires careful analysis. Naturalistic study of this process is possible through interviews with various participants or, better yet, through participant-observation by social scientists serving as consultants. It would be worthwhile to conduct more carefully controlled studies of the problems of communication and interaction with discussion groups of experimental subjects not actually involved in leadership roles in the desegregation crisis, but representing different points of view. In designing such studies, the sociocultural setting in which Negro leadership has to operate should be taken into account. This institutional analysis of leadership has explicitly rejected the proposition that recent changes in the nature of Negro leadership occurred simply on the basis of the personality of the individuals involved. This is in line with the main current in the developing body of theory of leadership. Launor Carter (1953) stated it well when he said, "Since leadership is related to the determination of group goals, it becomes apparent that the leader is seldom a free agent. . . ." C. M. Gilbert, in his excellent analysis of authoritarian leadership entitled *The Psychology of Dictatorship* (1950) gives, as his main thesis, the proposition that "authoritarian leadership, like any other, reflects the nature of the culture in which it emerges." He adds, however,

> It must not be assumed . . . that the dictator is merely the passive tool of cultural forces. On the contrary, we must recognize that social interaction implies a two-way process, in which cultural mores help to determine the nature of political leadership, and the latter in turn influences the development of the cultural pattern (p. 33).

This approach must certainly be applied to the analysis of Negro leadership in the present crisis. While the sociocultural framework sets limits within which the leader must operate, defining the bounds of the role of the Negro leader today, there can be variations within the boundaries of this role. Furthermore, it is specific individuals with their unique personalities who initally create and play the role. Many of the new leaders among southern Negroes are indeed "new" in the sense that they were not influential in the Negro community before 1954 or 1955. This was true of King, who was only twenty-seven years old at the time of the Montgomery crisis.

Killian and Smith (1960) established in their study of leadership in Tallahassee that there was an almost total replacement of the Negro leadership in that city during the bus boycott. Yet some "old leaders" have adapted to the new role. As Gouldner (1950) has suggested, a radical situationist approach cannot account for this selection process. He states: "To find, or allege, individuals to be adaptable to the extent suggested by the situationists—that is, almost infinitely plastic—can be anticipated only under very limited psychological and, therefore, cultural conditions" (p. 28).

The analysis of the sociocultural limits of Negro leadership today was introduced with the suggestion that the South today constitutes a fruitful laboratory for the sociologist who seeks fresh, first-hand data on social change, intergroup conflict and collective behavior. It also constitutes a potential laboratory and source of hypotheses for the social psychologist. For both, however, the challenge to both courage and ingenuity is as great as the opportunity.

References

Adams, J. J., 1949. *The challenge.* New York, Wendell Malliet.
Blumer, H. 1958. Research on race relations. *Internat. soc. Sci. Bull.,* 10.
Carleton, W. G., 1958. Negro politics in Florida: Another middle-class revolution in the making. *South Atlantic Quart.,* 57, 419–432.
Carter, L. F., 1953. Leadership and small group behavior. In M. O. Wilson and M. Sherif (eds.), *Group relations at the crossroads.* New York, Harper, 262–265.
Clark, K. B., 1958. Observations on Little Rock. *New South.* Atlanta, Ga., Southern Regional Council, June, 3–8.
Frazier, E. F., 1957. *The Negro in the United States.* New York, Macmillan.
Gilbert, G. M., 1950. *Psychology of dictatorship.* New York, Ronald Press.
Gouldner, A. W., 1950. *Studies in leadership.* New York, Harper.
Halberstam, D., 1961. "Good-Jelly's" last stand. *The Reporter,* Jan. 19, 40–41.
Hunter, F., 1952. *Community power structure.* Chapel Hill, University of North Carolina Press.
Johnson, G. B., 1937. Negro racial movements and leadership in the United States. *Amer. J. Sociol.,* 43, 63.
Killian, L. M., 1961. Community satisfaction and race relations in a Florida city. *Research Reports in Social Science.* Tallahassee, Florida, Institute for Social Research, Florida State University, 3, No. 2, April.
Killian, L. M., et al., 1954. *Amicus Curiae* brief of the Attorney General, State of Florida, in the Case of Brown v. Board of Education of Topeka, Kansas, in the Supreme Court of the U.S., October Term, 1954, Appendix A.
Killian, L. M., and J. L. Haer, 1958. Variables related to attitudes regarding school desegregation among white southerners. *Sociometry,* 21, 159–164.
Killian, L. M., and C. U. Smith, 1957. The Tallahassee bus protest movement. Field Report No. 5, Anti-Defamation League, 515 Madison Ave., New York, 22.
——, 1960. Negro protest leaders in a southern community. *Soc. Forces,* 38, 253–257.
King, M. L., 1958. *Stride toward freedom.* New York, Harper.
Lippmann, W., 1922. *Public opinion.* New York, Penguin Books.

Lomax, L., 1960. The Negro revolt against "the Negro leaders." *Harper's Magazine*, June, 41–48.

Myrdal, G., 1944. *An American dilemma.* New York, Harper.

Reddick, L. D., 1959. *Crusader without violence.* New York, Harper.

Sherif, M., and B. L. Koslin, 1960. The "institutional" vs. "behavioral" controversy in social science with special reference to political science. (Multilithed.) Norman, Okla., Institute of Group Relations, The University of Oklahoma.

Sherif, M., and Carolyn W. Sherif, 1953. *Groups in harmony and tension.* New York, Harper.

Smith, C. U. The sit-in demonstrations in Tallahassee, Florida. Unpublished.

Thompson, C. H., 1954. *J. Negro Education,* 23, Spring issue, 107–108.

——, 1960. Desegregation pushed off dead center. *J. Negro Education,* 29, 107–111.

Tumin, M., 1958. Readiness and resistance to desegregation: A social portrait of the hard core. *Soc. Forces,* 36.

Turner, R. H., and L. M. Killian, 1957. *Collective behavior.* Englewood Cliffs, N.J., Prentice-Hall.

PROBLEMS OF ATTITUDE, PERSONALITY, AND INSTITUTIONAL ANALYSIS (WITH SPECIAL REFERENCE TO LEWIS M. KILLIAN'S CHAPTER)

by S. Stansfeld Sargent

It seems much more difficult to discuss an intelligent, relevant, well-documented paper with which one essentially agrees than to fire verbal broadsides against the opposite kind of production. However, I must remember that "discuss" does not mean "contradict" or "demolish"; it connotes something more constructive. So my comments may take the direction of approving, disapproving, differing slightly, or even saying "It's right as far as it goes, but it doesn't go nearly far enough."

At the outset I commend Dr. Killian for his forthright support of institutional analysis rather than attitude study in handling a crisis produced by social change. I should like to comment, however, that the method chosen depends primarily on the question asked. For example, attitude studies have played and still play the major role in answering the question *how people feel* about discrimination and segregation, when that is the burning question. Another approach became of great significance a little later—personality study—to answer the question what segregation does to the Negro child. (This culminated, of course, in the document prepared by the social scientists in 1952, which prepared the way for the Supreme Court decision two years later.) Dr. Killian's concern is with the forces promoting and impeding desegregation here and now, which highlights institutional analysis, though I shall try to indicate that it may be aided also by the study of personality dynamics.

To refresh myself on current trends in research on desegregation, I turned to the latest issue of the *Joint Newsletter on Intergroup Relations* (January, 1961) put out by the Society for Psychological Study of Social Issues and the Society for the Study of Social Problems, and to the most recent *Journal of Social Issues,* devoted to "Desegregation Research in North and South" (1959, 15, No. 4). I would say that, generally speaking, most of the research could be called attitude studies; but they certainly differ from the attitude studies of a generation ago. They involve more depth, and are often couched in dynamic terms such as wishes, fears, hostility, or self-images and mutual perceptions. Furthermore, many of the studies invoke new types of conceptualization. For example, after describing the three parties to conflict in "Southville," one investigator notes:

. . . the most important causal factors are exogenous; they are controlled from the outside. The "nine men in Washington," as the Supreme Court is frequently called south of the Potomac, and the Federal Court system start series of events of crucial importance for the community. Moves to implement the court orders are made by the local Negro community and to some extent by the integrationists, and counter-moves are made by the segregationists. But this is not like a real local controversy where the parties know each other and can predict each other's behavior (Galtung, 1959, p. 39).

Also, of the studies which could be called *institutional,* a number involve attitudinal and personality variables. Thus, my small survey indicates that current research is neither clearly attitudinal nor purely institutional, which I suspect is good and reflects an awareness of the complexity of our subject matter.

Dr. Killian is unhappy about social scientists becoming so engrossed in their laboratories and experiments that they leave the lively and controversial material to journalists and others. I would go even further and suggest that their concern for exact methodology verges into downright timidity. Ralph Linton, the anthropologist, sometimes poked fun at psychologists who never dare to say anything unless they can find at least eight or ten others who said it first—and who can then be neatly listed in the footnotes and bibliography. Furthermore, the social scientist's rigidity often leads him to neglect, if not actually to disapprove of, journalists who plunge in and cope with thorny issues and problems. They have paid little attention, for example, to Croswell Bowen's excellent case studies of young American criminals, including the leader of a fascist group, published in the paperback *They Went Wrong*. The writings of Albert Deutsch, Lucy Freeman, Margaret Halsey, Lillian Smith, and others dealing with mental health and ethnic prejudice, have not received the notice they deserve from social scientists. (Recently, Calvin Hall's articles in *Contemporary Psychology* on "Paperbacks in the Classroom" have been bringing such books to the attention of psychologists.)

Fortunately, however, the picture is not all black. Due to the leadership of men like Lewin and Sherif, social psychological research has become more realistic and vital. Their experiments, in real life situations, on issues of both theoretical and practical importance, have become models to inspire succeeding generations of students. Nor are case studies entirely lacking; one thinks of Cantril and Sherif's study of Father Divine, of Keith Sward's book on Henry Ford, of Lindner's *Fifty Minute Hour*, and Greenwald's research on call girls. Then there are the studies of evanescent social phenomena such as Cantril's *Invasion from Mars* and Johnson's "Phantom Anesthetist of Mattoon."

But these are not enough in a world that so badly needs the focused energies of trained investigators. I have sometimes daydreamed of a medium—a newspaper or magazine, entitled *Hunches and Hypotheses* (or perhaps even *Brainstorming*)— where creative but inhibited social scientists could share their potentially fruitful ideas with less inhibited writers and researchers and with students, who might, we hope, have greater flexibility than their mentors. In fact, such a medium could go in both directions; the journalists and popularizers could also give their suggestions for topics needing more substantial research than they are trained or willing to undertake.

I wish Dr. Killian could have said more about the lack of leadership on the part of southern white people. Is it because the educated and progressive white community leaders have been frightened into conformity by the White Citizens Councils and other fanatical movements? Or is it, perhaps, because the whites favoring desegregation have failed to organize and plan, to use tactics as clever as those of the opposition? I remember how Lillian Smith, years ago, argued that the key figure in the battle against prejudice and discrimination was the southern white woman, because of her high status. Apparently the Congress on Racial Equality understands this, even as southern white liberals do not. *Look* magazine, for January 3, 1961, pictured a native-born southern white girl, a student at Sophie Newcomb College in New Orleans, who has joined CORE many times in its sit-in demonstrations against segregation.

Difficulties encountered by white and Negro leaders in getting together were mentioned by Dr. Killian. I believe we can learn something here from group therapy and studies of intergroup relations. Several years ago Gordon Allport reported on the value of catharsis, particularly the talking out of pent-up hostility and other negative feelings, in clearing the air so that constructive action can proceed. Perhaps the leaders of white and Negro delegations can learn to accept the expression of suspicion and even hostility as a necessary first step toward cooperation.

Now for a few thoughts on personality dynamics, which Dr. Killian implies are not particularly relevant to the present situation. First of all, I agree heartily that some psychologists have been naive in assuming that a given attitude leads to or causes a given type of behavior—just as, for example, prejudice is supposed to lead, inevitably, to discrimination. K. B. Clark (1953) and others have indicated that prejudice does not prevent a person from adjusting to a changed social situation, such as desegregated schools. Actually, one of the great contributions of social psychology, drawing upon sociology and cultural anthropology, is to correct the assumption that personality *causes* behavior— that a particular personality trait leads necessarily to a particular kind of social behavior. One great value of such concepts as social norms, reference groups and social roles is to correct psychological and psychiatric preoccupation with personality dynamics.

On the other hand, may we not, as social scientists, make just as great an error in failing to consider the influence of personality variables? Let me put it this way: assuming the change in Negro leadership in the present crisis is not to be explained via personality dynamics, what about the emergence of particular leaders or types of leaders? How shall we explain why

Martin Luther King rather than twenty-nine others has become the outstanding Negro leader, if not through understanding his attitudes, values, motives, and abilities—in a word, his personality?

When Dr. Killian speaks of an "aggressive social movement" or a "collective protest," is he not talking of the motives and frustrations of thousands of Negroes? Feelings toward the older types of leader have changed from favorable to unfavorable, and positive, enthusiastic feelings for new leaders have developed. These are personality trends which could have been studied by depth interviews and projective techniques; in fact the change might have been predicted if such studies had been undertaken at the right time. In addition, important cognitive ingredients are present, such as a belief in better conditions, as Dr. Killian insists.

This brings me to my conclusion: Unless we support a complete social or cultural determinism, do we not need to strive for an integrated, balanced approach such as Dr. Stogdill outlines in his chapter? Ultimately we must have a sophisticated social psychological theory which encompasses all the interoperating forces—whether they are legal and political coercion, propaganda and education, social norms, perceptions, and social roles, or attitudes, motives, feelings, and other aspects of personality dynamics. Sometimes one of these is more salient, sometimes another or several others, but all of them (and other variables not mentioned) may be significant.

Dr. Killian is a fine researcher and a courageous person who is contributing tremendously in a stormy sector; there is no reason for him to be defensive because he is in an area full of uncontrolled variables. Nor should the psychiatrist who ventures into the same domain, as the Group for Advancement of Psychiatry has done with its pamphlet on emotional aspects of desegregation. And by the same token, of course, neither should the specialist—any specialist—be cocksure. It is difficult for any one person, or even a whole group, to fit together the many varicolored pieces into a meaningful whole. But *someone* has to do it, *sometime*, if we are to survive and progress! So let us keep working toward it as the ultimate goal for scientists and researchers, and an inspiration for practitioners as well.

References

Clark, K. B., 1953. Desegregation: An appraisal of the evidence. *J. soc. Issues*, 9, No. 4.

Galtung, J., 1959. A model for studying images of participants in a conflict: Southville. *J. soc. Issues*, 1959, 15, No. 4.

7

THE TEMPORAL and spatial dimensions of the world shrink each year as modern communication, transportation, industrialization, and commerce bring separate nations into closer interdependence, and as modern means of mass destruction pose their awful questions to all. Otto Klineberg sees this heightened interdependence as a source of challenge to the traditional conceptions of what constitutes the "internal affairs" of a country. Chapter 7 discusses this challenge as it relates to treatment of ethnic, "racial," and national groups within national boundaries, hence the coupling of "intergroup" and "international" relations in his title.

Following several examples of international issues raised by discriminatory arrangements within various nations, Klineberg explores related problems of research, with emphasis upon problems raised by prevailing images of ethnic and national groups in the United States and, conversely, images of Americans held in other countries. Implicit in this discussion is the considerable body of research on prejudice and social distance in the United States, summarized elsewhere by Klineberg and many other authors.

Research prior to World War II documents in detail the acceptance of racist doctrine by the overwhelming majority of citizens in all regions, with varying intensity and varying consistency. The ensuing stereotypes of out-groups tend to persist even as discriminatory practices are questioned and as change is initiated, prompted to an important extent by "the desire of the United States to face the dark-skinned peoples of the world with 'clean hands,'" in Klineberg's words.

Along with further research on problems wrought by discriminatory practices and stereotyped conceptions manifested in behavior at home and abroad, Klineberg urges study of the extent of adherence to racist doctrine, including signs of its adoption by some who have been its victims. Such research, he notes, may fruitfully be linked to research on leadership in established and newly developing movements and nations.

EDITOR

173

7 INTERGROUP RELATIONS AND INTERNATIONAL RELATIONS

by Otto Klineberg

The Background

There is a widespread view, incorporated in the Charter of the United Nations, that what happens inside the boundaries of a particular nation is the concern of that nation alone, and is therefore not a legitimate field of action or even of inquiry by the international community. This view is undoubtedly justified for many internal phenomena, but at least in the special case of the relations between ethnic or "racial" groups, it cannot possibly be defended.

Even the most cursory glance at the current *inter*national situation shows the impact of *intra*national events. South Africa has withdrawn from the British Commonwealth as a direct consequence of the practice and philosophy of *apartheid;* its position in the United Nations and the specialized agencies of the United Nations has become exceedingly precarious; its relations with India and with the new African states have been strained to the breaking point; the resentment which has developed among Africans in general threatens the peace of the whole continent. Slightly more indirectly, it has been suggested (Strausz-Hupé, et al., 1956) that the attitude of India towards the United States has been adversely affected by our unwillingness in past United Nations votes to join the chorus of condemnation of South African policies. (Our position has recently changed in this respect.)

It would not be difficult to multiply examples of such interpenetration. Portuguese actions in Angola not only affect its relations with other African communities but also with the

174

United States and every other country that has taken a stand against the Portuguese position. Relations between India and Pakistan are influenced by the way in which Hindus and Muslims interact *within* each of these countries. French troubles in Algeria have an impact not only on the attitudes of the Arab states but on all nations that have taken sides in this continuing controversy. The emergence of the new African nationalism frequently reveals a racial orientation that can be traced directly to preceding experience with prejudice and discrimination. The very existence of an Afro-Asian bloc appears to depend not so much on political alignments as on a feeling of identification among all peoples and nations who are not "white."

The historical fact of "colonialism" is of course crucial as an explanation of many of these phenomena. Although most of the powers previously responsible for the colonization of so much of Africa and Asia have recently been engaged in reversing the process, granting independence at a rate which some critics have even regarded as too precipitate, the *effects* of that process are not so easily reversible. This is not the place to enter into a discussion of the merits and demerits of the colonial system as such. The "white man's burden" of the British and the "mission civilizatrice" of the French undoubtedly aroused a great deal of true ethical idealism, but they also served as a convenient rationalization for exploitation and abuse of the darker-skinned peoples of the world. For our purposes the important point is that colonialism was almost invariably accompanied by racialism, i.e., by a conviction of the inherent superiority of the whites, and by the treatment of other groups based on the assumption of their inferiority. It is this aspect of the heritage of colonialism which continues to play an important part in international relations, and affects the attitudes of the newly emerging nations.

As far as the United States is concerned, colonialism as such has played a relatively minor role in our history, but since our alliances have usually been with those nations that have been identified with the colonizing process, we have frequently been placed in the same category. In addition, our own treatment of minorities has given support to those who have placed us in the camp of the racialists, and has certainly affected our relations with many other nations. The whole history of our immigration laws, especially the various Oriental Exclusion Acts, undoubtedly contributed to the worsening of our relations with Japan, and must bear some of the responsibility for preparing the way for World War II. As Roger Baldwin has expressed it (in MacIver, 1949): "Of all major countries in the world the United States has by law most deliberately insulted all Asiatic peoples by declaring them unfit for immigration and for citizenship." During a period of twenty years, he adds, from 1924 to 1945, "we served notice on over half of mankind that they were not racially qualified to associate with us" (p. 83). Further: "It was this very Exclusion Act which after 1924 so largely contributed to the defeat of the liberals in Japanese politics as to make possible the rise of the militarists" (p. 86). In Baldwin's judgment, this did more to break the bonds of friendship with the American people and set Japan on the road to anti-Americanism than any other factor.

The treatment of the Negro in the United States has also had very definite international repercussions. With regard to our relations with Latin America, Berle has written: "To say that racial discrimination damages the Good Neighbor policy is a masterpiece of understatement . . . the habit of race discrimination practiced in considerable parts of the United States is the greatest single danger to the foreign relations of the United States . . ." (in MacIver, 1949, pp. 91–92).

Our inability to arrive at a complete solution of this problem has placed us at a considerable disadvantage in the competition with the USSR to gain the friendship and cooperation of many of the new nations. The fact that the Soviet Union has been guilty of its own variety of "colonialism" in relation to the Baltic States, Hungary, and other areas has not had the same impact because it has mainly involved Europeans, and has therefore not been interpreted in "racial" terms.

This summary, inadequate though it undoubtedly is, perhaps gives sufficient indication of the impossibility of separating intergroup from international relations and suggests the need for a reinterpretation of the United Nations' position regarding what constitutes the "internal" or "domestic" affairs of a nation.

Some Psychological Aspects

We turn now to a discussion of a series of problems which are more directly psychological in nature and in connection with which the techniques of psychological investigation either have been, or could be, applied. In some of these areas substantial research data have already been collected; in others, the best that we can do at present is to indicate the nature of the problems in the hope that they will soon receive the research attention which, in the judgment of the writer, they richly deserve.

The Generality of Attitudes

Direct evidence of the connection between intergroup and international relations at the psychological level is furnished by a series of investigations which have indicated that those individuals who show prejudice or hostility or social distance against minority groups in their own country tend also to show similar reactions to "foreigners" (Adorno et al., 1950). One is reminded of the *New Yorker* cartoon in which a man in a bar, after a few drinks too many, states in a loud voice, "I hate everybody, irrespective of race, creed, color or national origin." Such an association of hostilities occurs with sufficient frequency in the populations studied to be regarded as a demonstrated tendency, even though it clearly does not hold for all individuals.

The question arises as to whether it will hold for all groups. One apparent exception is the American South, where in the past an insistence on keeping the Negro in his (inferior) place was accompanied by a definitely *international* viewpoint. This was reflected over a long period by the readiness on the part of southern congressmen and senators to vote in favor of foreign aid, support the British during World War II before the United States had entered the war, etc., while maintaining the traditional southern attitude toward Negroes at home. This suggests that cultural patterns of behavior in a particular region may override the "personality" aspects of generalized prejudice or hostility demonstrated elsewhere. Dr. Alfred Hero, who has been engaged in an investigation of such attitudes in the South, suggests, however, that this pattern has changed, and that southern leaders are now more likely to take an isolationist position (personal communication). This may be due to the fact that the pressure to remove all disabilities in the case of American Negroes has been increased by the situation created by the Cold War, and one consequence may be the tendency for many southerners to withdraw as far as possible from the international scene. The fact remains that cultural norms require further exploration in connection with the whole issue of the generality of attitudes.

The experimental studies (Sherif et al., 1961) of the development of hostility between two groups in a boys' camp showed how such hostility could be resolved by the technique of presenting "superordinate goals" (the present author prefers the term "common goals") shared by the two groups, and in which a satisfactory solution of the problem requires cooperation between them. Although the research design was shaped by concern with intergroup relations, the conclusions appear to be applicable to international relations as well. The task of setting up such superordinate goals for the participants in the current Cold War is not simple, and one can only express the hope that it will not require something like an "Invasion from Mars" to bring the two sides closer together.

The Foreign Image of the United States

Reference has already been made to the fact that the domestic "racial" situation in the United States has a definite impact on the image of the United States held by nationals of other countries. The status of the United States as "the leader of the free world" and the champion of democracy has made Americans particularly vulnerable to the charge that they do not practice what they preach. This situation has presented difficult problems to the various information agencies charged with the task of "projecting" America to the rest of the world, and has embarrassed the individual American traveler who is so often asked to explain a prejudice for which he himself may have little or no sympathy. A common, and on the whole the most acceptable, procedure has been to admit—and deplore—the existence of the problem, and to point to the undeniable progress that has been made toward its solution as evidence of America's good intentions in this respect and of a genuine desire to achieve a more complete democracy. The Supreme Court decision of May 17, 1954, declaring the enforced segregation of Negro school children to be unconstitutional, provided a wonderful demonstration—or so it seemed—of the fact that the United States, by perfectly legal and democratic means, could produce a revolutionary transformation of society in the desired direction. The present author was in his office at UNESCO in Paris on the morning of May 18, and the telephone rang all that day with congratulations from nationals of other countries who wished to express gratification that their confidence in the United States had been so brilliantly justified.

On the whole the foreign press reacted to this event in a predictable manner. Dr. John A. Davis, of the Council on Race and Caste in World Affairs, has made a study of "Foreign Reactions to Civil Rights and Race Relations in America" (unpublished), which deals mainly with European reactions. The friendly press in countries like France, the United Kingdom, Italy, and Norway, hailed it as a great victory for democracy; more fulsome praise was expressed by the Dutch, possibly smarting still from American criticism in connection with the Indonesian struggle; and outright scepticism was expressed by the communist press, in the USSR and elsewhere, which predicted that discrimination and segregation would continue in spite of legal decisions to the contrary. As is well known, the actual results have been somewhere between these two extremes; there has been progress, but there has also been resistance; there have been bright spots like Washington and St. Louis, and setbacks like those represented by Little Rock and New Orleans.

Unfortunately, Dr. Davis did not continue his valuable study long enough to include much of the aftermath of the desegregation decision of 1954. On several occasions during 1958, the present author conducted a small content analysis, much too inadequate and unrepresentative to deserve publication, of French and English newspaper comment on the American race situation. A conservative estimate would be that for every reference to progress made in the United States there were at least ten accounts of difficulties and disturbances. (In Norway he was informed that everyone knew the name of the Governor of Arkansas, and almost nobody that of the United States Secretary of State.) The reports were factual, not distorted (as they often are in the USSR), but they were highly selective in a negative direction. This was evidently done without any real malice, although one cannot rule out the possibility that for the nationals of weaker nations some satisfaction was experienced from the exposure of the American giant's feet of clay. More probably the foreign press and the American news agencies were in agreement that riots and arrests make more interesting reading than the news that Negro children now attend integrated schools in rural Florida or Virginia.

All of this represents a very real problem with regard to the foreign image of the United States. There is a challenge to journalists and psychologists alike as to how to make good news in this field at least as interesting as bad news. There is, of course, no question of hiding anything, or of creating a favorable image which is not in accord with the facts. The task is rather one of presenting a balanced picture, with all the errors and flaws acknowledged, but placed in proper perspective against the background of the undeniable progress that has been made. The difficulties are themselves, in many cases, an indication that a change is occurring; they represent the price that is being paid for progress. The ugliness is there, and it would, in the judgment of the author, be unethical to use the psychological techniques of propaganda to project an image of America which would not take the ugliness into account, but it is surely not unethical to aid in finding methods of presenting the whole, true story.

Americans Abroad

A great deal has been read and written about the effect of Americans abroad on the image of the United States, and on the attitudes toward the United States which develop in foreign countries as a consequence. The only aspect of the complicated problem of the effect of such contacts on international relations which concerns us at this point refers to acts and statements by these Americans with regard to racial and ethnic groups. Since many Americans maintain a belief in Western superiority, the probability that some of the travelers will reveal this belief is not inconsiderable. As far as ordinary tourists are concerned, there is perhaps little that can be done except to remind them, as President Eisenhower once did, that they are informal ambassadors of the United States, and that they have a corresponding responsibility to represent their country in a manner which will not bring discredit upon it.

The problem is different with regard to official representatives abroad, whether at various levels of the diplomatic service or as members of transatlantic missions, etc. In their case, those responsible for personnel selection would seem to have not only the right but the duty to inquire into their "racial" attitudes and to send abroad in such capacities only those who are as nearly as possible above reproach in this respect. How this can best be done is a problem of considerable complexity. Direct questions regarding such attitudes will usually elicit the "desirable" answers, which may or may not be the true ones. Psychologists may be of help here, if their cooperation is requested, in the process of devising indirect methods of obtaining the necessary information. Experience with the F-scale (Adorno et al., 1950) has suggested the possibility of determining the ethnocentric attitudes of respondents without asking any questions which relate specifically to ethnic groups. This technique is not completely dependable in the case of every individual, but, taken together with other indications, it may be of real value. Obviously it will be difficult to apply the F-scale to all applicants for overseas assignments, particularly at the upper echelons, but it may be quite practical to include in the personal interviews which usually precede such assignments at least some of the items from the F-scale which have been found to have diagnostic value. More psychological research will probably be needed before such a technique can be confidently applied. The first and most important step is to recognize the importance of this issue in the selection of personnel; the succeeding task of developing the necessary tools should not be insurmountable.

The special problem of Negro-Americans abroad, especially when they visit or are sent to African countries, will be discussed below.

Africans and Asians in the United States

Americans who go abroad may carry their ethnic prejudice with them; Africans and Asians who come to this country, whether as diplomatic representatives or university students, run the risk of encountering such prejudice here. This issue has caused great concern to many Americans in governmental circles as well as elsewhere, especially when incidents of discrimination—in housing, restaurants and hotels, private clubs, etc.— are reported in connection with foreign ambassadors or members of official delegations, and in several cases formal apologies have had to be offered by the State Department or by governors of the states involved. The coverage of such incidents in the mass media has been extensive, but one cannot help wondering about the frequency of similar occurrences in the case of university students and other visitors who do not have the official status to make their experiences quite so newsworthy. In this connection the present author will not soon forget his sense of shock when, on a recent visit to Paris, one of his colleagues there, a non-American known for his friendship for the United States, spoke of his plans to call a conference of African students and added: "I don't want to have such a conference in the United States because African students always leave with anti-American attitudes after their experiences there."

This is undoubtedly an exaggeration, but to what extent? In this connection psychologists could make an important contribution by devoting some of their energy to discovering just what effect a sojourn in an American university has on African and Asian students. The number of such students continues to grow; the investment, in funds supplied by governmental and private agencies, and in time and energy on the part of educators and administrators, is very great, but we know much too little about the effect of this extensive program. Such studies should also reveal the nature and frequency of unpleasant experiences, the sources of annoyance and irritation, as well as the areas of enjoyment and satisfaction, and give the needed guidance to those who are seeking to bring about some improvement in the overall situation.

A special problem arises with regard to the contacts and relationships between Africans and American Negroes. The naive expectation that such contacts would invariably be friendly because of the identity of racial origins has frequently, but not always, been realized. A certain degree of ambivalence has also entered, due to a variety of causes: the critical attitude of many Africans who think that by this time American Negroes should have obtained a greater degree of freedom and "independence"; the feeling on the part of many American Negroes that Africans are less "civilized"; the unwillingness of many proud Africans to become identified with a group which in the United States still retains some of the characteristics of second-class citizens; the African judgment that American Negroes are on the whole more white than Negro, etc. Here is a rich field for research into the complex pattern of the relationships involved.

An important start on such research has been made by Harold Isaacs (1961), of the Massachusetts Institute of Technology, who has interviewed many American Negroes with regard to their attitudes toward Africans, including a number of American Negroes who have gone, either permanently or for a visit, to Africa. All the ambivalences to which reference was made above are revealed in these interviews. The experiences of American Negro travelers and expatriates has frequently been a mixture of pride and disillusionment, of acceptance and rejection, of identification and withdrawal. One can only express the hope that more research on this important area will soon be forthcoming.

The Impact of the International Situation

We spoke earlier of the impact of our domestic situation on our relations with other countries, particularly those in Africa and Asia. The reverse phenomenon also deserves attention, viz., the effect of the international situation on intergroup relations within the United States. We have already referred to this aspect of the problem in connection with the apparent increase in isolationism among many southern whites. For the country as a whole there is good reason to believe that the Cold War and the desire on the part of the United States to face the darker-skinned peoples of the world with "clean hands," have heightened the country's awareness of the need to come to grips with the Negro problem. Statements by government officials are filled with references to this need *because* of the international situation. Newspaper accounts of the New Orleans resistance to desegregation have referred to the rioting women as "traitors to their country." Whether the international implications were in the minds of the Supreme Court judges who unanimously ruled against such segregation is difficult to determine, but in general a good case could be made for the proposition that our international commitments have hastened the process of the more complete acquisition of civil rights for Negroes.

At the same time it seems highly probable that the international situation has increased the determination as well as the impatience of Negroes in seeking and obtaining those rights. They have been able to point to one further argument for quicker action; in addition to ethical and religious considerations, and the loss of valuable manpower as the result of discrimination, there is also the fact that our position in the world demands it.

One especially intriguing aspect of the effect of the international situation relates to the changes which have occurred in the "self-image" of the American Negro as the result of the emergence of the new African states. Although there is as yet little solid research to which one can point in this area, it seems highly probable that whereas in the past African origins symbolized to American Negroes colonialism, slavery, and "barbarism," now the sight of African statesmen speaking to respectful audiences in the United Nations, visiting Washington and other world capitols as honored guests, receiving the courteous attention of world powers competing for their support and friendship —all of this must have a profound effect on what it means to be a Negro. Typifying this change is an experience reported to the author by an African student now in this country. When he was here previously, ten years ago, he was asked to speak to an American Negro group in New York City. He appeared in the flowing robes of his country and was severely criticized for the fact that he, a "civilized," Westernized intellectual, should continue to emphasize his identification with native Africa. Ten years later he received a similar invitation, and this time he appeared in Western dress. He was asked why he had not worn the clothes typical of his newly liberated and independent country! As has already been noted, there are ambivalences in the relations between Africans and American Negroes, and the change in self-image is probably not a simple one, nor does it always go in the same direction. Again we can only hope that clinical and social psychologists may turn some of their research interests in this direction.

"Racialism in Reverse"

This term has been used for the phenomenon of anti-white prejudice on the part of colored peoples. Its use suggests that racialism is an invention of the whites, and it may be argued that it is a misnomer, since groups of all kinds have throughout history shown in varying degrees a "dislike of the unlike." The fact remains that prejudice which takes a specifically "racial" form, i.e., which becomes attached to differences in inherited physical characteristics, has been more frequently associated with the attitudes of whites who have occupied a position of dominance over darker-skinned subject peoples. It may therefore not be inappropriate to use the expression "racialism in reverse" for recent developments in the opposite direction.

The phenomenon has taken many forms. Reference has already been made to the existence of an Afro-Asian bloc which to some extent has an "anti-white" or at the very least a "distinct from white" orientation. The notion of "negritude" in the writings of intellectuals in Haiti, Martinique, and in Africans with a French education, usually has a cultural and literary orientation, a "back to African origins" emphasis, but it also involves in many cases a belief in the superiority of black over white. The new African nationalism frequently shows racial overtones, and the reports of the rioting in the Congo, Angola, and elsewhere indicate that generalized anti-white attitudes often play a significant role. A cult of black superiority has developed among the so-called Black Muslims in the United States, the Rastafarians in Jamaica, and similar groups in other areas.

It is difficult to know with certainty how effective these movements have been, or how widespread is their influence, but they are certainly causing concern to whites and Negroes alike. One occasionally hears a defense of "racialism in reverse" on the ground that it is after all only a reaction to preceding white racialism and that it supplies a feeling of dignity and self-esteem to people who for so long have been burdened with a sense of inferiority. The present author can only express his own opinion that any philosophy which results in judging an individual by the color of his skin, whether that skin is "white" or "black" or "brown" or "yellow," is inappropriate and unrealistic. White racialism appears to be on the decline, slowly but unmistakably, and it would be tragic to see it revivified or supplemented or replaced by other forms of the same disease. Here again we are handicapped by not knowing enough of the nature and scope, either in Africa or America, of this new and disturbing phenomenon.

The Role of Leadership

This symposium is concerned, at least in part, with the role of leadership, an aspect of our problem which is implicit throughout this chapter, but in connection with which a few additional comments may not be out of place. Individuals in key positions, whether of an official or unofficial nature, are important in all, or nearly all, the topics we have reviewed. For example, much criticism has been directed against ex-President Eisenhower for not using the prestige of his office as well as his own charismatic leadership qualities to obtain a fuller compliance with the Supreme Court decision regarding school desegregation, and in that way, among other things, to enhance the position of the United States as the leader of the democratic world. The present administration appears to be assuming a more active leadership role in this connection, but it is too early to determine what the consequences will be.

There has been much discussion of the nature of Negro leadership in this country, and argument as to what techniques will be most effective in improving the Negro's position. The choice of personnel for overseas service involves a decision as to who shall be placed in a leadership position in the representation of the United States abroad; the changes taking place in the white South, both with regard to desegregation and to isolationism, depend to a considerable degree on people in key positions in Congress, in state government, in the press, in the church, and in private life; the phenomenon of racialism in reverse requires an understanding of the character of the leaders of such movements; the nature of the interrelationship between nationalism and racialism in the new African states will depend to a large extent on the kind of leadership exercised by the heads of governments in such states. Social psychologists know, however, that leaders can never be far removed from their followers, and the study of leadership must therefore always go hand in hand with an understanding of the nature of the groups whose willingness to be led is crucial to the nature and extent of change.

The problems we have reviewed are complex, and more questions have been raised than the present author is capable of answering. They appear to be sufficiently important, however, to deserve our continuing attention, and the application of the best research techniques of which we are capable.

References

Adorno, T. W., et al., 1950. *The authoritarian personality.* New York, Harper.

Davis, J. A. *Foreign reactions to civil rights and race relations in America.* Unpublished manuscript.

Hero, A. Personal communication.

Isaacs, H., 1961. Back to Africa. *The New Yorker,* 37, No. 13, May 13, p. 105.

MacIver, R. M. (ed.), 1949. *Discrimination and national welfare.* New York, Harper.

Sherif, M., et al., 1961. *Intergroup conflict and cooperation. The Robbers Cave experiment.* Norman, Okla., University of Oklahoma Book Exchange.

Strausz-Hupé, R., A. J. Cottrell, and J. E. Dougherty (eds.), 1956. *American-Asian tensions.* New York, Praeger.

8

THE VARIED and complex variables affecting decisions and actions within and between groups, even small groups, are documented in different instances in the chapters of this book. Most pale in comparison to the scope of variables involved in relations between modern nations. The political scientist cannot reject the task of studying international affairs because of the magnitude of the problems, for these are included in the daily fare of his discipline.

In keeping with contemporary trends in political science, Robert C. North approaches significant issues of internation relationships through investigation of policy making and decision making. Like several other chapters of this book, North's represents a glimpse into a research program initiated by its author. His program is addressed especially to the study of conditions in which intersystem conflicts may be productive of new integrative trends and institutions. Noting that even estimates of relative material capacity are shaped by more than sheer counting of men, materiel, and machines, North suggests a working model in which the perceptions of policy and decision makers are, successively, dependent variables shaped by incoming information, and then independent variables when, translated into decisions and actions, they affect other nations.

North seeks to avoid the error of reducing internation process to the subjectivity of its leading participants through suggestions for scaled measures of the "hard facts" of material economy coordinated with interaction processes in policy councils.

The scheme is employed in summarizing research by North and his associates into the policies and decisions culminating in World War I. The data are chiefly historical and state documents; the method a scaled form of content analysis. In his discussion following North's chapter, James A. Robinson suggests some limitations in the data and comments on the working model.

EDITOR

189

8 INTERNATIONAL CONFLICT AND INTEGRATION: PROBLEMS OF RESEARCH
by Robert C. North

States, like smaller organizations and groups, are frequently in conflict, and the assumption is not uncommon, indeed, that "peace within and conflict without" are essential characteristics of the national system. Closer investigation suggests, however, that conflicts exist within the various components of the state itself—within even the most cohesive and durable—and that to some considerable degree, at least, the integrative aspects of the national system are a function not only of the "outside threat" but also of the "conflicts within." Viewed this way, many customs, laws and a variety of "integrative" institutions appear to derive from pre-existing conflicts and largely justify themselves currently as moderators or "resolvers" of ongoing conflicts within the state.

If these assumptions are sound, then it seems reasonable to study world politics and the relations among states in terms of *international* conflict and integration—in terms, that is, of the disruptive and associative or cohesive processes among them. Under what circumstances, for example, do international conflicts result in the destruction or disruption of all or certain of the "peaceful" and perhaps even "unifying" bonds between states? And, conversely, under what conditions, if any, will conflict—either internal or external to the state unit—produce a stronger bond between parties than existed before? Is it justifiable, in short, to view international conflict as a potential catalyst for international integration?

From these basic questions it is not difficult to derive a series of hypotheses, nor is it difficult to identify significant variables.

The great challenge, on the contrary, is to devise units of analysis so that trends and degrees of conflict and integration can be measured and replicated, to find a way for dealing effectively with problems pertinent to the national and international—rather than the individual or face-to-face—spheres of human activity (Sherif and Koslin, 1960, p. 5).

Until now, the temptation has been to emphasize "hard" variables: to count GNP (Gross National Product) or troops or planes or ships or megatons and assume that all states accept the "objective" value assigned to these "capabilities" by the investigator. With a number of such quantities, a kind of economy is then set up with the various participants trading (or "gaming") back and forth on a supposedly "rational" basis. In such terms it is "logical" to predict that an aggressive State A will be deterred by the "objectively" ascertainable superior capability of State B. This procedure lends a sense of great "rationality" to the interstate transactions, and endows the investigator with the confidence of a hard "realist."

Actually, in making choices between various alternatives—in deciding between war and peace, for example—the "real" world and the "real" quantities are not the great "realities" at all. For even the hardest boiled decision maker has no touch with his environment at all except through two filters, so to speak: the filter of his senses (the color blind may not react "normally" to a red light); and the filter of his experience (including his education, his cultural conditioning, his psychological set, and so forth). In these terms, then, the "real" world of decision making is not necessarily what the "realist" accepts as ("obviously") "objective." The "real" world for the Prime Minister, the President, the Foreign Secretary—and for their counterparts in friendly and opposing states—is the *perceptual* world, and this means, then, that the crucial variables in a conflict situation are quite as likely to be "perceptual" as "hard and objective."

The great challenge is to develop techniques for the study of international conflict and integration which will draw perceptions, decisions, and "objective reality" into a viable analytic system. This is the problem to which the present chapter is addressed.

However difficult it might be to attack these questions in a small-group environment, the difficulty is compounded when attention is transferred to a nation-state universe. What is a state? How is one to determine what a state "perceives" and "decides"? How can we generalize about state behavior in psychological or sociological fashion without recourse to dangerous analogies drawn from individual or small-group behavior?

As a first step toward meeting this problem, the state has been defined as the sum total of those major decision makers who are empowered to make foreign policy decisions binding on the government. Monarchs and elective heads of state, prime ministers, foreign ministers, under secretaries of state, military chiefs of staff, and like officers are unmistakable candidates for inclusion, whereas ambassadors and other representatives abroad are necessarily excluded. These are the individuals who, as a small elite group, "perceive" for the state and "decide" for the state. At every step they are influenced, of course, by internal pressures from the various subsystems of the state, but as "perceivers" and "deciders" for that state they may be considered as receiving these pressures primarily as self-perceptions.

So defined, the state is viewed as a perceptual system in that it is sensitive to "certain types of physical energy, or information" and also "capable, when properly stimulated, of delivering messages that modify" its behavior (Dember, 1960, p. 6).

There are further difficulties. In studying the international activities of states we are forced to depend heavily for our information upon the messages exchanged among them—usually upon the "cleaned-up" printed texts (Osgood, 1959, p. 33). This is the kind of data most readily available in the various national archives and in the public records of relations between states.*
The intent will be to search these materials for clues about each state's perceptions of the changing environment, each state's purposes or goals, and each state's choices or pattern of decision making. Toward this end the search will be focused on three kinds of theme: *the policy condition; perceptions of policy conditions;* and a number of other designated *perceptions.* (The "theme" as a unit of content analysis is discussed by Berelson, 1952, p. 138.)

* As developing methodologies are improved, it should be possible in the long run—with protection and assistance from the states themselves and from international organizations—to supplement archival materials with on-the-spot investigations of on-going conflicts.

Policy conditions are normally considered as outbound messages. However, a state's perceptions of another state's policy conditions are treated as inbound messages—as are various other kinds of perceptions discussed further along. The research intent is to correlate various categories of inbound and outbound messages, to draw inferences about state behavior under various circumstances and, under given conditions, to make predictions about probable decisions in the future.

Policy conditions are statements—made by bona fide decision makers—of long or short range goal, aim, purpose, preference, choice, intent, or means toward a goal. All policy conditions fall explicitly or implicitly into a means-end chain, that is, more immediate goals are means toward more distant goals. By shifting perspective, therefore, one may view any policy condition either as an end in itself, or as a means toward some more distant objective. For a Communist Chinese artillery lieutenant, the firing of so many rounds of high explosives at Quemoy may appear as an end in itself, whereas a division commander may view the shooting as a means toward storming the island and seizing it. Ultimately, moreover, the Politburo member in Peking may perceive the whole Quemoy operation as a means toward the eventual seizure of Formosa.

Policy condition statements may express present, past, or future purposes, choices or goals, viz., "It is the policy of State A to shoot down foreign planes intruding illegally into its air space." Or, "State A will shoot down. . . ." Or, "It was the policy of State A to shoot down. . . ." Or, simply, "We [State A] shot down [intentionally]. . . ." A policy condition may also be expressed imperatively, as when a State A decision maker issues the order, "Shoot down all foreign planes intruding illegally. . . ."

We shall be concerned, of course, not only with statements of policy condition by bona fide decision makers, but also with the perceptions—recorded by such decision makers in one state—of the policy conditions held by decision makers in other states. Thus, "State B perceives that State A will shoot down [is shooting down, shot down] foreign planes intruding illegally into its territory."

It should be kept clearly in mind that policy conditions do

not necessarily coincide with objective "events" or "facts." Khrushchev, for example, may make the statement: "We shall shoot down foreign planes intruding illegally into Soviet air space." Actually, when the opportunity arises, he may or may not shoot down an intruding aircraft. If he does not, the investigator may then raise the question whether it really was not Khrushchev's policy to shoot down intruding planes, or whether he changed his mind, or whether he found himself incapable of carrying out the threat. Or Khrushchev may make the statement, "We shot down the U-2," whereas the investigator may keep open the possibility that the U-2 was *not* shot down, that it ran out of fuel, perhaps, or suffered some other malfunction. Or, Khrushchev may imply the opposite policy condition by asserting, "We shot down the U-2 accidentally." Again, the investigator does not know for a "fact" whether Khrushchev's "real" policy condition was not to shoot down the U-2 [the shooting was indeed an accident, as Khrushchev says] or whether it was to shoot the plane down and deny the intent.

In collecting policy conditions, therefore, the coders deal only with statements as they appear. Later, the analysis of contradictions, inconsistencies, the perceptions of other parties, the revelations of history and like evidence may suggest whether these statements are "real" or whether they are deceptions, or bluff, and what their significance was in association with other variables.

For the purposes of this study there are—in addition to perceptions of another state's policy conditions—five basic kinds of perception: (1) Power (Strength-Weakness); (2) Frustration-Satisfaction; (3) Hostility-Friendship; (4) Capability; and (5) Resolution of Conflict.

Policy conditions, perceptions of policy conditions, perceptions of capability, and perceptions of the resolution of conflict are taken to be essentially denotative and devoid of emotional content. Perceptions of power, frustration-satisfaction, and hostility-friendship, by contrast, are recognized by their affective content: their emotional "charging" or "loading" or "bloating."

The *perception of capability* is a passive, nonvolitional statistical statement. References to a possession of economic wealth, military weapons, or soldiers in uniform may be accepted as perceptions of capability, provided the decision maker considers such possession as a state resource which may be committed for the pursuit of a certain policy condition vis-à-vis another state. The category includes numerical estimates of state power and percentage changes in the military or economic machine. It is in terms of capability that most "gaming" and "deterrence" studies tend to be cast. There is a frequent tendency, however, to treat the capability perceptions of the investigator as if all states, including the "enemy" state, shared these perceptions. An assumption of this kind is likely to introduce a considerable—but frequently "hidden"—distortion into the findings.

Perceptions of hostility-friendship may be located on the following scale:

Antagonism   Protagonism
9 — — — — — — — — — — — — 0 — — — — — — — — — — — — 9

The spectrum may be broken down further into subdimensions of hostility-competition-friendship-cooperation-coalition. Some words typical of the antagonistic end of the scale would include: threatened, crushed, attacked, menaced, contriving, violating, and opposing. On the protagonistic sector we would find: sympathetic, cordial, sincere, favorable, approving, fraternal, loyal, and so forth.

It is possible to place *perceptions of frustration-satisfaction* along a similar scale between extremes of need-frustration and need-gratification. Subdimensions would be catastrophe-frustration-pacifism-satisfaction-elation. Clue words would include, on the one hand, tense, fearful, bitter, intolerable, urgent, disconcerting, insecure; and, on the other, satisfying, pleasing, relaxing, contented, reassuring, stabilized, and the like.

Perceptions of power (weakness-strength) should not be confused with the perception of capability category. The former is emotional, affective, "charged," and nonquantitative; the latter is denotative, statistical, and emotionally neutral. Perceptions of power may be located on a scale between power-deprivation at one extreme and power-manifestation at the other. Subdimensions would include collapse-decline-development-surpassing-predominance. Perceptions of power can be located through the presence of words like incapable, weak, dominated, declining, lagging, and limited at one end of the scale; and strong, powerful, consolidating, invincible, vigorous, and prevailing at the other.

A *perception of resolution of conflict* involves the view of a state in regard to the means by which the conflict is likely to be resolved.

Broken into their category units, these several kinds of data can be analyzed variously in terms of frequency, intensity, and contingency.

With material from the European crisis of 1914, for example, the following hypothesis was tested by frequency counts of perceptions of hostility, capability, and so forth, and also by contingency analysis:

A state will not go to war (i.e., commit aggression or allow itself to be drawn into an avoidable war) *if it perceives its power smaller than that of the enemy at the time when the decision to fight or not to fight must be made.*

Underlying this hypothesis is the assumption that states commit aggression, or allow themselves to be drawn into an avoidable war, only when they have assessed the consequences as being at least minimally favorable to themselves. Conversely, a confrontation of superior force, if perceived by the pertinent decision makers, will deter the weaker state from waging an avoidable war.

A test of this hypothesis by frequency counts required the formulation of the following alternative:

If a state's perception of injury to itself (or frustration, dissatisfaction, hostility, or threat) *is "sufficiently" great, this perception will offset perceptions of insufficient capability, making the perception of capability less important as a factor in a decision to go to war.*

In 1914, as a matter of fact, Germany entered the crisis situation with a clear perception of *inadequate* capability. Perceptions of hostility mounted during the development of the crisis, whereas remarkably little attention was focused on capability by the major decision makers. What capability they did assess continued to be generally negative for their own interests. In short, they were not deterred by perceptions of their own inadequate capability.

More recently certain of these units have been subjected to scaling for degrees of intensity. Results, up to now, have been partial and incomplete, but preliminary graphing has revealed close resemblance between frequency and intensity curves.

It is not difficult, in a conflict situation, to arrange the policy conditions of a country on a means-end chain—from the immediate "means" through "intermediate goals" and on to broader, more distant objectives. This conceptual arrangement is not unlike the Galanter-Miller-Pribram concept of the Plan (1960).

In 1914 Austria-Hungary put forward as a major, long-range policy condition "the preservation of the Dual Monarchy at all costs." Perceiving high levels of threat from the outside, however, the Vienna government proclaimed as an intermediate goal (as an indispensible prerequisite for "preserving the Dual Monarchy") the punishment of Serbia. In short-range context the more immediate Austro-Hungarian policy-conditions—the mobilization of troops, the inflexible ultimatum, the declaration of war—were highly consistent and "rational." It was not in this part of the Plan that the fatal Austro-Hungarian miscalculation lay.

The unfolding of history has revealed, of course, that the "punishment of Serbia," far from "preserving the Dual Monarchy," contributed to its early destruction. There is evidence to suggest, however, that states under perceptions of extremely high threat mix large amounts of "fancy" into their assessments of the environment and find it difficult to foresee even some of the more probable consequences of the actions they feel compelled to take.

It is also possible to arrange the "inbound" perceptions and the "outbound" goals and decisions (policy conditions) of two or more states into the following reciprocal pattern:

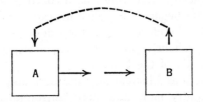

On this basis we can postulate that if State A (correctly or incorrectly) perceives a high level of threat to itself from State

B, there is high probability of subsequent hostile output on A's part. If State B then (correctly) perceives this hostility, it is likely that B, too, will produce policy conditions of high hostility content. This threatful behavior of State B will soon endow A's hostile perceptions with further "reality," and from that point forward the perceptual exchanges between the two parties will become more and more "affective" in their content.

With more than two states involved the interactions become rapidly more complicated. We have seen, for example, how the Austro-Hungarian Empire decided on a limited war in 1914 "to punish Serbia," a small Slavic state on its borders which Viennese leaders perceived as an outpost of Pan-Slavism and a dangerous threat. In striking out against this "threat," of course, the Austro-Hungarian decision makers set in motion a change of events that led to a precisely opposite consequence—the destruction of the Dual Monarchy. In a sense, the Empire brought about its own downfall.

What Austro-Hungarian decision makers failed sufficiently to take into account was the Russian view of an attack on Serbia as "intolerable" to the Tsarist Empire. In an attempt to "deter" Austria-Hungary, St. Petersburg wavered between partial and general mobilization, but the activities, however indecisive, were sufficient to convince the Berlin government that Germany was threatened.

Rapidly, then, the "limited" conflict began to spread—though Germany, from the beginning of the crisis, had been determined to keep it "localized."

Wedged between France on the west and Russia on the east, Germany had long been apprehensive of a two-front war. To guard against this possibility, German military strategists had evolved the Schlieffen Plan which, in the circumstance of an attack from either quarter, could be invoked quickly and effectively. As Russia began to mobilize in response to the Austrian attack on Serbia, therefore, and as the leadership in Berlin grew increasingly apprehensive, some German decision makers urged an early invocation of the Plan.

German leaders, and increasingly the German populace, began to see their country more and more "surrounded" and "threatened." Indeed, Russian troops, because of their government's inability to post "deterrence" forces discriminately, were moving closer to German borders; so this circumstance opened a wider "circuit" of hostile perceptions, hostile decisions, and more hostile perceptions. Now many perceptions, originally false, began to be validated by events: Austria, perceiving itself (unduly) threatened, had taken hostile action against Serbia (and, by association, Russia); St. Petersburg, perceiving Serbia (and the Russian Empire) threatened by Austria, had taken retaliatory hostile action which was perceived (incorrectly) by Germany as directed toward itself.

Germany, therefore, proclaimed a "state of threatening danger of war" and dispatched a twelve-hour ultimatum demanding that Russia cease its war-like preparation—though St. Petersburg still insisted that its activities were directed solely against Austria and not against Germany.

In the face of this German ultimatum, Russia (correctly, now) perceived itself as threatened and began to take measures against Germany. Perceiving themselves (correctly) threatened by Russia, the leaders in Berlin prepared further hostile steps. The prophesies were now fulfilling themselves, the threat-hostile action-threat interchange was rapidly building itself up.

There are further possibilities for testing propositions about conflicts among states and their modes of resolution. Once hostility begins to feed into an interstate relationship, for example, it is probable that another mechanism will go to work: each party will tend to protect its own part of this hostility from change—from getting moderated or "watered down"—by facilitating, in one fashion or another, a breakdown in communications that might otherwise bring an alteration about (Thibaut and Coules, 1952). It should be possible to test this proposition by correlating policy conditions and perceptions from a variety of international conflict situations. Again, the analysis should be in terms of intensities and contingencies as well as frequencies.

The further question then arises: how can a "self-feeding" hostility interchange be broken? It seems probable that at high levels of hostility a nonhostile act which would pass unnoticed in friendly negotiations will assume a positive "conciliation value" many times its normal weight, *only provided that the initiator is able to communicate and to make it credible to the recipient.* Under these circumstances it becomes essential for the initiator to anticipate distrust on the part of the recipient, putting forward the proposal more than once and using various devices to enhance its credibility. If, on the other hand, the initiator is unprepared, he is likely to interpret the recipient's disbelief and distrust with a new burst of hostility, and then the hostility will start building again.

Studies in intergroup behavior suggest that conflicts between small groups are best reduced, in the long run, by the introduction of goals (policy conditions) which are strongly shared by members of both sides and which require, for their fulfillment, the cooperative efforts of all (Sherif, 1958). There is no reason to believe that a similar hypothesis would be inappropriate for relations between states.

The true integration of two policy conditions, in contrast to a compromise through which each side gains something and loses something, suggests "that a solution has been found in which both desires have found a place, that neither side has to sacrifice anything" (Metcalf and Urwick, 1940, p. 32). Generally, the original conflict is not so much abolished as subordinated to some over-riding agreement. A situation of this kind can be facilitated either by a change in the policy conditions of one or both sides or by a modification of the problem itself—through an alteration of the environment or through some other solution that transcends the original problem or provides a condition satisfactory to both parties.

Custom, law, institutions—to a considerable degree these phenomena have emerged from compacts (written or unwritten) whereby conflicts are not so much solved as adjusted or moderated by agreed-upon means. It can be argued, then, that it is precisely out of conflicts that most integrations and associations emerge.

This discussion so far has been limited to interactions among states. Using the same concepts and the same research techniques it is entirely possible—providing source material is available—to isolate the same variables at various "levels" within a state. Content analysis will reveal, for example, the degree to which parliaments or party leaderships or newspaper editors share the perceptions and policy conditions of the major decision makers. Similarly, a properly designed poll should reveal the similarities and dissimilarities between public opinion and national policy. For investigation of pertinent factors in totalistic states, on the other hand, a different and highly specialized model is required.

Another consideration is important. The perceptual categories are so abstract in nature that they do not, in themselves, differentiate specifically among political, economic, social, and other factors in a conflict situation. Whenever desirable, however, it is possible to look for the stimulus behind a perception of hostility, for example, or a perception of frustration or of power, and inquire whether this "stimulating" or "irritating" phenomenon is political, economic, social, or psychological in nature. Often, too, it is important to inquire whether the stimulus exists, has existed, or is foreseen by the perceiver as likely to exist sometime in the future.

The investigator, then, can move not only from the international sphere into any given domestic sphere, and up or down the "hierarchical levels" of the internal state, but also from activities (decisions) and goals to perceptions, and from perceptions to the stimuli behind them. The further question now arises: can the investigator move from perceptions to "hard" variables, such as the "objective" capabilities of states, as contrasted to the perceptions of these capabilities as harbored by decision makers in various capitals?

There seems to be no reason why the perceptual sphere and the "objective" sphere cannot be systematically related. It should be possible, for example, to devise a way for placing each policy condition (or perception of policy condition) on an anchored scale of magnitudes—a scale which might rise by multiples of ten somewhat as follows:

	Per Cent
1,000,000,000	100.00
100,000,000	10.00
10,000,000	1.00
1,000,000	0.10
100,000	0.01
10,000	0.001
1,000	0.0001
100	0.00001
10	0.000001

Certainly the expenditure of funds internationally, or the commitment of troops, or the firing of high explosives could be measured upon a scale of this sort. Here the underlying assumption would be, of course, that "important" policies, such as wars, vast aid programs and the like, involve high rather than low levels of magnitude. Small skirmishes, or lesser negotiations, may involve tens (or even hundreds) of men (or dollars or tons of explosives), but large, "earth-shaking" transactions (whether violent or nonviolent) almost always involve millions or even billions (of men, dollars, tons of explosives, and so forth).

In these terms it should be possible to postulate an "economy" of "hard" transactions between states. From this starting point the postulation could be "trimmed" or "adjusted" or "corrected" to the essentially perceptive realm in which states "actually" operate. More specifically, a "hard" model of American-Soviet-Chinese Communist relations could be constructed on an anchored scale in terms of the "objective" capabilities and the appropriate orders of magnitude of the transactions prior to the Korean War. Then by marshalling perceptive units against the same scale it should be possible to "correct" the model according, for example, to American, Soviet, and Chinese Communist *views* of the relationship as it appeared to them respectively at that time.

Surely, it was the perceptive—rather than the "objective"—system that precipitated the North Korean attack on South Korea, first of all, and the Chinese Communist offensive against United Nations forces after that (Whiting, 1960). Yet it seems safe to assume that in the calculation of future conflict probabilities it is frequently the "hard" but essentially "unreal" economy that is assessed, rather than the "softer" and more elusive but often more determining interaction of perception. To relate these separate kinds of phenomena is a basic requirement for research into the international behavior of states.

References

Berelson, B., 1952. *Content analysis in communication research.* Glencoe, Ill., Free Press.
Dember, W. H., 1960. *The psychology of perception.* New York, Holt.

Metcalf, H. C., and L. Urwick (eds.), 1940. *Dynamic administration.* New York, Harper.

Miller, G. A., E. Galanter, and K. H. Pribram, 1960. *Plans and the structure of behavior.* New York, Holt.

Osgood, C. E., 1959. The representational model and relevant research methods. In I. de Sola Pool (ed.), *Trends in content analysis.* Urbana, University of Illinois Press.

Sherif, M., 1958. Superordinate goals in the reduction of intergroup conflict. *Amer. Sociol.*, 63, 349–356.

Sherif, M., and B. L. Koslin, 1960. The "institutional" vs. "behavioral" controversy in social science with special reference to political science. Norman, Institute of Group Relations, The University of Oklahoma.

Thibaut, J. W., and J. Coules, 1952. The role of communication in the reduction of interpersonal hostility. *J. abnorm. soc. Psychol.*, 47, 770–777.

Whiting, A. S., 1960. *China crosses the Yalu.* New York, Macmillan.

FURTHER PROBLEMS OF RESEARCH ON INTERNATIONAL RELATIONS (WITH SPECIAL REFERENCE TO ROBERT C. NORTH'S CHAPTER)

by James A. Robinson

Research as imaginative and thorough as Professor North's stimulates many comments. Within the space limitations imposed by the covers of a book, I would like to make three brief points, incorporating some of the discussion following his oral presentations at the symposium in which the authors of this book participated.

The first concerns a problem in evaluating analysis based on documents available to the historian. Dr. North's study is probably the most detailed reconstruction of the events culminating in a decision that has ever been undertaken. The only comparable effort known to me is Glenn D. Paige's account (1959) of the activity of President Truman and his associates during the seven days following the outbreak of hostilities in Korea in 1950. However, Dr. Paige does for one country and seven days only part of what Dr. North and his colleagues are doing for several countries and six weeks. In spite of North's impressive discovery of previously untapped documentary sources, one is tempted to ask what kind of a sample of relevant behaviors is found reported in documents? What is missing? What is irrelevant? Like North, I look forward to the day when social scientists may conduct on-the-spot investigations of many different kinds of governmental decisions. In the meantime, would it not be possible to undertake "research on research" to learn more about the adequacy of documents as sources of data?

I have in mind a study such as the following: Select several governmental agencies known for maintaining extensive documentation. Establish several observers who may also interview decision makers during and after the decisions they observe. Decision makers might also read and comment on the first drafts of the reports of their decisions. Finished reports would be deposited with the National Archives or another suitable institution to remain unopened for a decade or so. Subsequently another team of social scientists, using the same theoretical or conceptual framework, would "re-do" the same studies with this difference: they would rely exclusively on documents ordinarily kept by the agencies. Upon completion of the second round of studies, the first reports would be opened and compared. This should give us useful information as to what is missed by documents and the conditions under which interpretations vary when there are nondocumentary sources of data. (For an elaboration of this proposal, see Snyder and Robinson, 1961.)

Such findings would help a researcher interested in Dr. North's questions in many ways. To give only one example, we might have more systematic knowledge about the conditions under which public documents reflect "private"opinions. The German Ambassador to St. Petersburg kept a remarkable diary which differed radically from his dispatches to Berlin; but in an age when diary keeping has declined, future historians may not be so lucky as students of World War I.

Second, Dr. North's discussion illustrates one of the most persistent issues in the study of intergroup relations, the choice between models of individual and models of organizational behavior. For the most part North refers to individual perceptions and individual acts, but his larger study also focuses on organizational structure and process. I would like to put in a word for models or theories which interrelate individual and organizational factors. Theories combining these two kinds of variables might provide some answers to one of the key questions Professor North raised in his extemporaneous remarks following his oral presentation at the symposium: "How can we predict the point at which a state decision-maker says, 'I see so much external threat, I'll not pay any further attention to our own internal weaknesses'?"

One set of answers following theories of individual personality might try to predict the point after knowing something about the types of individuals involved in stressful decisions. Another set of predictions might be based on theories of organizational performance under stress. My suggestion seems scandalously simple: we need experimental, field, and historical studies which identify both the types of individual characteristics of the decision makers and the types of organizational structures in which they operate. However obvious this appears, there is little research of this kind. We hope to initiate such experiments at Northwestern University, but as of now we have only hypotheses, not findings about the interrelations of individual and organizational variables (see Robinson and Snyder, 1961).

Third, Professor North shows once again the general applicability of Sherif's notion of superordinate goals and their relevance for research on conflict. The growing social science literature on conflict (e.g., as reviewed by Mack and Snyder, 1957) seems to me to be pertinent to the second major question North raised in his extemporaneous remarks: "By what mechanisms do state decision makers move up and down the scale from normal diplomacy to summit diplomacy?" It is not clear to me whether the emergence of superordinate goals uniformly activates new diplomatic channels or whether it reinforces established procedures. If the relation is not uniform, what are the conditions under which the relationship between suporordinate goals and diplomatic procedures vary? To compete with the superordinate goals hypothesis, one might form other hypotheses with two concepts familiar to the literature on conflict, the *number of parties* and the *number of conflict issues*. An hypothesis, which would require data of various kinds, might be as follows: *Bipolar conflicts over highly crucial issues are more likely to evoke demands for summitry than conflicts involving a larger number of parties.* The truth or falsity of this hypothesis is unimportant here; the point is that the number of parties to conflict, and also the number of conflict issues, may provide conditions under which certain diplomatic mechanisms are more or less appropriate, or are believed to be appropriate.

Another partial theory applicable to this question would be one which relates the individual decision maker's satisfaction with previous experience in different kinds of diplomatic or organizational processes. Harold Guetzkow's work (1955,

1957) on social-psychological factors underlying satisfaction with various levels of international interaction is of obvious relevance.

These three different types of comment are not meant as adverse criticism of North's exciting research, but rather as complementary interests which his work evokes.

References

Guetzkow, H., 1955. *Multiple loyalties: Theoretical approach to a problem in international organization.* Princeton, Center for Research on World Political Institutions.

——, 1957. Isolation and collaboration: A partial theory of inter-nation relations. *Conflict Resolution*, 1, 46–68.

Mack, R. W., and R. C. Snyder, 1957. The analysis of social conflict: Toward an overview and synthesis. *Conflict Resolution*, 1, 212–248.

Paige, G. D., 1959. *The United States decision to resist aggression in Korea.* Ph.D. Dissertation, Department of Political Science, Northwestern University.

Robinson, J. A., and R. C. Snyder, 1961. Decision-making behavior: A research program combining comparison of teaching techniques and inquiry into the inter-relations of individual and organizational variables. (Dittoed paper.) Northwestern University.

Snyder, R. C., and J. A. Robinson, 1961. National and international decision-making. New York, Institute for International Order (see Project 2).

III

SOME INTERGROUP PROBLEMS ASSOCIATED WITH SOCIAL CHANGE

9

I N PRECEDING chapters, social change has been reported or predicted as a result of intersystem impacts as well as of conditions external to an intergroup system. The chapters which follow are more specifically concerned with certain aspects of social change involving intergroup problems.

Every human group exists and functions in a locale—a territory—and when its means of livelihood rest upon exploitation of the natural resources of its locale, the control of these resources becomes a problem of great significance to the entire group. In this Chapter, Raymond E. Crist discusses different institutionalized schemes for control and use of the land—land tenure systems—in different periods of history and parts of the world.

Probably every system of land control and use has its "cohesive" as well as its "divisive" aspects for human groups. Through historical perspective, Crist traces the impacts of various traditional systems on social and political groups and on the development of new movements aimed at alteration of the traditional systems. His treatment emphasizes the constant interplay of material and nonmaterial aspects of cultural systems, while examining in detail those relationships arising from differential control and access to environmental resources.

By and large, contemporary investigations of intersystem relationships have been prone to take for granted the natural and technological resources of the groups involved. As Crist points out near the end of his chapter, these include many resources besides territory and other social relationships besides land tenure systems. In addition to representing in this volume the problems arising from relationships governing the use and control of material resources, problems of land tenure are important in themselves, as one of the earliest and still vital areas in which man seeks livelihood and well-being, as well as other goals distinctive to his cultural setting.

EDITOR

9 SOME ASPECTS OF LAND TENURE SYSTEMS AND INTERGROUP RELATIONS

by Raymond E. Crist

In preparing this paper on some of the influences of land tenure systems on diverse societies, I am reminded of the story about the farmer who, when asked if he had gotten the price he had expected to get for his hogs, replied "No, I sure didn't, but then I didn't expect to." I do not expect to prove that land tenure systems alone are the "prime movers" in societies around the world, but I do hope to show that an aspect of the land tenure system, or systems, is very frequently "the straw that breaks the camel's back." I propose to discuss in certain selected areas the influences of land tenure systems on bodies politic, social, and economic.

For one of the most important facts to know about any country is who owns or controls how much and what kind of land—that is, what class, what group, or what clique of private or government individuals is in effective *control* of the land base of society. In the discussion that follows I propose to point out some of the influences of land tenure systems on group solidarity and on tensions between groups, and hence on intranational and international relations. Many other factors besides land tenure systems are, to be sure, coacting in every society to produce the present cultural landscape; but a significant (often the leading) role in the orientation of a society is played by those individuals, those groups, or those classes that own or control the land.

Man is not the only animal that appropriates specific pieces of real estate to his own uses and defends them against all comers. Territoriality is a common, easily observed phenomenon, and territorial behavior has been studied in many kinds of animals. Individuals, pairs, or large social groups of animals defend their territory against intruders.

When it is a group—family or tribe—that occupies a particular territory or home range, the shared terrain clearly helps to give cohesiveness, "togetherness," to the group, and thus may be of considerable importance in social behavior. Any mammal is ill at ease outside its familiar range—if I may be anthropomorphic—and tends to stay at home unless pushed away by events inside the range or powerfully attracted by events outside. There is reason for this, since an animal outside its familiar range is much more exposed to its enemies, not knowing where to dodge or hide, and there is some evidence that animals outside their territories, or that are unable to establish territories, are most subject to predation (Bates, 1960, p. 203).

Two clans of howler monkeys, when they meet on their territorial borders, will howl at each other until one group retreats. In this way, gradually the rough boundary zones between the territories of the several clans are determined. Many primitive, food-gathering peoples today have a territory organization similar to that of monkeys, but they also have lethal weapons with which to enforce respect for boundaries. Survival and successful reproduction have depended on effective communication and cohesiveness within the group, as well as on the ability to make and use tools. The savage Motilone Indians who inhabit the boundary zone between Colombia and Venezuela are an illustration of this point. They have been able to maintain their territory inviolate up to the present day by the simple but efficacious process of killing any and all intruders whether they be Spanish Conquistadores, revolutionary bands, or oil company geologists. And in the fastnesses of the tropical forest lands of eastern Ecuador and Bolivia, savage Indians protecting their hunting grounds today still occasionally bag with primitive bow and arrow a kindly but heedless missionary.

For hundreds of thousands of years, human beings, organized in families, in groups, or in clans, have made outsiders respect their claims to certain specified areas or territories. As man gradually evolved from the hunting and gathering stage to that of being a breeder of domestic animals and a producer of food crops, he became more territorial minded; over the millennia he has evolved elaborate systems of land holding, or control, thus codifying his concepts of territoriality.

Cultural Crosscurrents in the Mediterranean Basin

By the dawn of written history in the Near East, city-states had come into being, and the land which supported them was under the control of the state, or the city god. But the ruler was the representative of the god, and as such enjoyed the possession and usufruct of the land. Grants of land were occasionally made to court favorites. But the greater part of the land under cultivation was crown land, cultivated by serfs, who paid rent in kind to their god, in the person of their ruler. This system of land tenure has continued in force in Egypt millennium after millennium. It has made the typical Egyptian a *fellah*, a peasant par excellence; it supported the thousands of serf laborers who worked for years on the building of the pyramids, and it was in full vigor under the New Empire when Joseph, adviser to the Pharaoh, was naively credited with being its author. The plight of the peasantry is well portrayed in the verses from Genesis, which read:

So Joseph bought all the land of Egypt for Pharaoh; for the Egyptians sold every man his field, because the famine was sore upon them: and the land became Pharaoh's. And as for the people, he removed them to the cities from one end of the border of Egypt even to the other end thereof. Only the land of the priests bought he not: for the priests had a portion from Pharaoh and did eat their portion which Pharaoh gave them: wherefore they sold not their land. Then Joseph said unto the people, "Behold, I have bought you this day and your land for Pharaoh: lo, here is seed for you, and you shall sow the land. And it shall come to pass at the ingatherings, that ye shall give a fifth unto Pharaoh, and four parts shall be your own, for seed of the field, and for your food, and for them of your households and for food for your little ones." And they said, "Thou hast saved our lives: let us find favor in the sight of my lord, and we will be Pharaoh's servants." And Joseph made it a statute concerning the land of Egypt unto this day, that Pharaoh should have the fifth: only the land of the priests alone became not Pharaoh's.

Genesis, 47:20–26

The priesthood was not slow to realize the advantages of temporal as well as spiritual power, in Egypt as elsewhere. On the fertile alluvium of the Tigris and Euphrates the priests issued coined money, trained the scribes, and dominated economic life. Their great estates waxed ever greater, and the possessions of their temples increased. The great estates were cultivated by serfs, who could not leave the land, and who paid probably a third of their income to their master.

Much of the land of the eastern Mediterranean is rough and mountainous, with a few pockets of rich soil, large enough to give a start to civilization, but insufficient to support a large population. The narrow coastal plain, and the small patches of thin soil in the isolated valleys, were ill-adapted to farming on a large scale. Here the emphasis was on the small farmer and intensive agriculture. The natural increase in the population—growing, too, with constant recruits from the desert—was a factor in driving the Phoenicians to the sea to act as the seamen and merchants for the ancient world.

By and large, the rougher country was still held by the free peasant, and the idea of family ownership was strong. The Assyrian general, Rabshakeh, was well aware that the people of the rough hill lands were used to the possession of land and to the peaceful enjoyment of the usufruct thereof; he appealed to the sentiments of those who are familiar with the holding of land in fee simple when, in trying to persuade the men of Jerusalem to lay down their arms, he said:

> Hearken not to Hezekiah: for thus saith the king of Assyria, "Make your peace with me, and come out to me; and eat ye every one of his vine, and every one of his fig tree, and drink ye every one the waters of his own cistern; until I come and take you away to a land like your own land, a land of grain and new wine, a land of bread and vineyards, a land of olive trees and of honey that ye may live, and not die."
>
> II Kings, 18:31–32.

The large estate was conspicuously absent from the hilly sector of the eastern Mediterranean, which for millennia continued to be worked by a free peasantry. There were slaves, but no serfs. The Hebrew peasants were united against the Philistines, at a price, for the king took their best fields, vineyards and olive orchards to give to his servants, and he further took their children to plow his ground and to reap his harvests.

However, as the Pax Romana was enforced in the Mediterranean world there was a general movement away from mixed farming to a regime of specialized agriculture for export, which technical advance was followed by a kind of "Golden Age" in most branches of the arts. The small peasant, unable to compete, migrated to the cities where he searched in vain for work, and where he was thrown a sop of bread and circuses. The next step was the increase in the scale of agricultural operations through the organization of mass production based on the labor of slaves brought in from newly conquered territories. This plantation slavery was much more serious than domestic slavery, for it was impersonal and on a large scale.

Wherever it established itself it notably increased the productivity of the land and the profits of the capitalist, but it reduced the land to social sterility; for wherever slave-plantations spread they displaced and pauperized the peasant yeoman as inexorably as bad money drives out good. . . . The plantation-slave system persisted until it collapsed spontaneously in consequence of the breakdown of the money economy on which it was dependent for its profits. This financial breakdown was part of the general social *debacle* of the third century after Christ; and the *debacle* was doubtless the outcome, in part, of the agrarian malady which had been eating away the tissues of the Roman body social during the previous four centuries. Thus this social cancer eventually extinguished itself by causing the death of the society upon which it had fastened (Toynbee, 1947, p. 196).

Upon the decadent East Roman and Persian empires in the eighth century, there erupted from Arabia desert hordes of Bedouins with a new message and a fresh weapon. The new message preached—within its own spiritual community—the demolition of the barriers of race and color. The fresh weapon was the superior mobility introduced into warfare: the Arabian camel. Khalid, "the Sword of Allah," crossed by forced camel marches the trackless desert from lower Iraq to Damascus, which fell after a six months' siege. Syria and Iraq went down like ninepins before the conquerors. The people welcomed a change of political regime and looked upon the conquerors as deliverers from an alien and hated people.

Once more in world history the shattering of an empire by a handful of conquerors can in truth be explained by the fact that the conquered received them with open arms. The tidal wave of the Arabs of the open steppes broke and spent itself at last on the Taurus Mountains to the north, which remained for centuries the frontier between Islam and the Christian world, and to this day acts as the boundary line between Turks and Arabs.

The Arab of tradition is first and foremost a nomad, and it is only natural that nomadic herdsmen and warriors would look with disdain upon the patient husbandman. But this cultural attitude was crystallized at the time of the Arab conquest and has not changed since. Since before the time of Mohammed, the Arab elite have imbibed with their mothers' milk the poetry of the Bedouin and its stereotyped themes. The method of instruction has not changed. The *Koran* still forms the foundation stone of all learning, lower as well as higher.

The Prophet himself, to whom the *Koran* was revealed, was a leader of caravans, both commercial and military. In his world of western Arabia, working the land was by definition the labor of slaves. It would have been unthinkable for him not to be imbued with the current and socially acceptable attitudes of his class. References to the satisfaction to be derived from life in the country, so common with the Roman poets and in the *New Testament*, are not to be found in the *Koran*. It is inconceivable in the Arabo-Islamic tradition that a Cincinnatus would be called from behind his plow to accept political leadership, or that an Emir or Sultan, like the Roman Emperor Diocletian, would retire in his old age to his estate where he would potter around a vegetable garden.

The Arabs at one time were able to unite under the banner of Islam, "surrender to Allah," and under that banner they conquered the empires, the religions, and the ideologies of the whole vast area over which they swept, from Spain to India and from the Caucasus to the Sudan. It is quite within the realm of possibility for them to unite again, given the feeling that they are the bearers of a new message. In the United Arab Republic, even as in non-Arab Iran, the Moslems are solidly united against what they conceive of as "Western Imperialism." It is precisely the underprivileged and disinherited masses (comprised largely of peasantry), forming as they do the vast majority of the population of the Near Eastern countries, that support the national leaders in their position—no matter how extreme or even how absurd that position may seem to us. And perhaps the intense emotionalism which the leaders arouse is in large measure, when analyzed, only a kind of deep-felt protest against

the crushing poverty and the extremely low standards of living
of practically everyone, and particularly of the landless peasants.

The problem is localized and brought up to date in Algeria,
where a million French-speaking colons form an enclave in a
country of some eight or nine million Arabic-speaking Moslems.
Most of the good productive land of the country is in the hands
of the French, who export surplus grain, olives, grapes, and
wine to metropolitan France. The dispossessed, disinherited
native population cannot look with equanimity at *their* lands in
the hands of a few foreigners, or at the usufruct of these same
lands returning to France with almost nothing in the form of
wages or other perquisites accruing to the natives. Granted
that the French colons have been responsible for making their
lands productive, the fact remains that if the local population
is to benefit almost not at all from productivity induced by outsiders, they can hardly be expected to be enthusiastic supporters
of the privileges which those same outsiders enjoy—privileges
that are all too readily demanded as "rights." Algerian public
opinion has been implacably crystallized against the French
colon, and metropolitan France must sooner or later bow to the
inevitable, and give independence to the Algerian Moslems.

Land Holding and Group Cleavages in Spain

The present system of land tenure in Spain dates largely from
the time when the industrious Moors were expelled. Their land
was confiscated and parcelled out in immense estates to the
Catholic Church, to noble families, and to army officers of high
rank. The estates were really feudal fiefs, and the people living
on them became serfs, attached to the estate. And as a result
of the law of primogeniture, many of these estates have remained almost intact even to the present day, after more than
four hundred years.

The English geographer, Mr. Dobby, in an article on "Agrarian
Problems in Spain" in the April, 1936, issue of the *Geographical
Review*, gives a graphic picture of the distress of the laborers
and the attitude of the landowners. I quote:

I recall an incident during a visit to an experimental pig farm in an
out-of-the-way part of Andalusia. From the darkness at one end of

the building came a red glow. I went along and found a laborer's family crouched on the floor round a twig fire with smoke so thick that breathing was difficult. The malodorous squalor contrasted with the carefully washed pig pens than I had been seeing. To my query an old woman mumbled: "Yes, we live here. Worse than the pigs." At which the owner beside me exclaimed indignantly: "You have a roof over your head. What more do you want?"

The consequences of the great landed estates have been: depopulation of the countryside, inefficient methods of farming, very low average wages, high rents, scarcity of livestock, and a generally precarious economic situation for about a third of the country. In whole regions, as a result of a too rainy or a too dry season, a windstorm, or a bumper crop with a consequent sharp drop in prices, the entire population may be reduced to the verge of starvation or economic deprivation. Small wonder then that the people of this vast rural slum of Andalusia have for over half a century been ready to follow any political party—anarchosyndicalist or socialist—that has promised speedy and sweeping agrarian reform.

One of the first acts of the new government, when the Republic was established in 1931, was to write the law of agrarian reform, and this was formulated in September, 1932. The law defined the properties liable to expropriation, established cooperative societies, and encouraged agricultural instruction. The breaking up of the estates was begun in 1932. Although the great landlords—only 25,000 in the entire country—were to be paid off gradually in the course of a generation, they at once became bitterly hostile to the new government. The church property, valued at $500,000,000, was nationalized in 1933. This act served to make the Catholic Church implacably hostile to the new regime.

The breaking up of the great landed estates and the nationalization of the property of the Roman Catholic Church made the two most powerful elements in Spain deeply hostile to a government duly elected by a huge majority. These two major factions backed a leader who would restore their lands and privileges, but this restoration did not increase production.

Although the division and subdivision of holdings is greatest in northwestern Spain, where the great density of agricultural population is related to *minifundia*, it is in the arid lands of the south where the highest rural unemployment is to be found, and there it is related to the great landed estates, or *latifundia*. The present government of Spain, hoping to diversify Spanish agriculture and thus cut down on the excess of rural population and the great numbers of seasonally unemployed, has embarked on an ambitious program of irrigation projects. The project to colonize new zones has a high propaganda value for the present government, with the result that the bigger problem of *latifundia* is sometimes neglected. The breakup or more intensive use of the *latifundia* and the more intensive use of the dry-farming, or *secano*, lands are other partial solutions to Spanish agrarian problems, which have perhaps not received the attention due them. Until this is done, there can be little hope of reducing the zones of friction between the hungry landless and the government that has fastened itself upon them. Mouths are not necessarily fed by the preservation of the status quo. As the Spanish proverb has it: *Barriga llena, corazon contento* (a full belly, a contented heart).

The concluding sentences of my review of Pascual Carrion's great work on *latifundios* in Spain (published in the April, 1936, issue of the *Geographical Review*) are still valid and applicable: "All other problems in Spain fade into insignificance beside this one of agrarian reform. According as it is or is not satisfactorily solved, millions of people either will achieve a standard of living to which human beings are justified in aspiring or will continue to vegetate in illiteracy, misery, and squalor."

The Fighting Irish

Toward the end of the twelfth century adventurers from England took sides in the quarrels of the chieftains of the Irish clans, and under Henry VIII the struggles between British adventurers and the local Irish became progressively bitter as religious differences became more marked. English and Scottish colonists gradually pre-empted the land of Ulster, and at the end of the wars of the seventeenth century, the English confiscated most of the land of the original Irish owners; only a sixth of the whole island, and that in the poorest parts, remained in the hands of the original inhabitants of the country. Conditions on the island became shocking as the dispossessed native Irish became either sharecroppers or landless laborers. Absentee landlords were interested in rents and not in good agricultural practices. The steadily increasing and ignorant population was ever at the mercy of a famine.

From the beginning of the nineteenth century there was a steady stream of emigration directed mainly towards the United States; it increased very much after the great famine of 1846, when the potato crop, the chief subsistence crop of the people, failed because of a blight. The dispossessed Irish in Ireland and the emigrants to the United States continued to be solidly and unanimously hostile to the English.* De Valera, born in the U.S. of an Italian father and an Irish mother, one of the ring leaders among Irish nationalists, was saved from the British firing squad in 1917 only because of his U.S. citizenship. National aspiration, heightened by religious antipathies and economic inequalities, resulted in the civil strife of 1919–1921, and finally in the accord of 1921, by which Ireland was granted Dominion status. Farms owned by the operator have increased in number, and rents to absentee English landlords, long a nightmare to the Irish, were abolished. Local political autonomy accompanied by the evolution of a land-owning and operating middle class, has tended to bring social and economic stability.

Peace by Revolution in Mexico

After centuries of misgovernment under the Spaniards and the Republican dictators, the great mass of the Mexican people, oppressed, landless, and wretched, were utterly apathetic and without hope. These semi-serfs finally realized that any change would be for the better, and the cry of the landless for *tierra y libertad* (land and liberty) became more and more insistent.

* The father of President Kennedy, grandson of an Irish immigrant who fled the harsh physical and political environment of England-dominated Ireland, was himself imbued with bitter, anti-English feelings, which, it is reported, he overcame only with the greatest difficulty when he was our Ambassador to Great Britain just before World War II.

Revolution broke out in 1910, and in the next eleven years more than a million and a half people moved from the great estates to the free villages; they fled from their landlords during the period of social and political upheaval in order to return to the free villages where they could till their small plots of land under the age-old system of communal tenure. The old landholding aristocracy thus lost some of its power to the village, to agricultural workers, and to the newly developed city proletariat.

Land Distribution

At first, land distribution proceeded slowly. In 1930, fifteen years after the inauguration of the agrarian reform, almost seven-tenths of the total economically active population engaged in agriculture still belonged to the disinherited landless masses dependent upon day wages or upon such meager earnings as may be derived from tenant farming or sharecropping. President Cardenas saw that the aims of the Revolution of 1910 had not been completely fulfilled largely because there was no middle class to carry them through. Hence, he speeded up the program of land distribution. In the first twenty months of his administration he awarded some 3,000 villages nearly four and one-half million hectares (about 10,000,000 acres) of land—over half as much land as had been distributed by all his predecessors together.

By 1945, 30,619,321 hectares (77,000,000 acres) had been distributed to 1,732,062 recipients. About one-fourth of this land was cropland; while three-fourths was pasture, woodland, mountains, and waste. The average recipient has received only about 10 acres of cropland, and only a very small part of this was irrigated land. Agrarian communities have been organized into *ejidos* with the result that, according to the census of 1940, there were 1,601,392 *ejidatarios*. The population living on *ejidos* in 1940 numbered 4,992,058 inhabitants, or one-fourth the inhabitants of Mexico (Whetten, 1948, p. 592). The *ejidatarios* now have possession of about half of the cropland in the nation. In addition, there were 928,583 small private landholders in 1940 having plots of twelve acres, or less, in size. It is estimated that at least 40 per cent of the total population of Mexico either lives on *ejidos* or on small, privately owned holdings having 12 acres or less. Some of the expected benefits of the reforms have been absorbed in supporting the rapidly increasing population. The Rockefeller Foundation, working in close cooperation with the Mexican Government on its Mexican Agricultural Program, is trying to increase productivity of land by sponsoring: (1) fundamental research, and (2) a training program for selected Mexican scientists.

The social revolution in Mexico has largely destroyed the feudal environment. Much of the land has now been redistributed to the people who work it, in response to the government's goal of "land for the landless." Much has been done to achieve the "emancipation and incorporation of the Indian masses": educational facilities are rapidly being extended and transportation systems developed; minimum wages and working conditions have been established; social welfare legislation has been enacted.

In spite of these basic reforms, the levels of living among the masses of the population are still very low; but they have been raised. Millions of people who formerly had next to nothing now have next to something—which involves a fundamental change in living and in outlook. Mass despair has given way to hope in the hearts of millions, the channels of social mobility have opened, and the hewers of wood and the drawers of water have a chance of rising to middle-class status. It is hoped that the redistribution of land will be more and more carefully planned, for the social and political advantages of breaking up large holdings tend to be ephemeral and illusory unless farmers are in a position to make a good livelihood from their new holdings and to set aside capital for improvement. As ex-President Cardenas said long ago, "We want fewer Indians and more Mexicans!" People who have a stake in the land of their country—whether that land be devoted to agriculture, to industry, or to commerce—are more readily integrated into the body politic and culture than are a horde of landless, hungry floaters who feel rejected in the land of their birth.

The Rustic Versus the City Dweller

A great deal of the bitter feeling between the townsman and the farmer, between the sophisticated city dweller and the ignorant, routined country man has been engendered by the practice on the part of the urban dweller of coming into control of the land—the very foundation of existence of the country dweller —often by methods far from ethical. Hence farmers, generally illiterate or barely able to sign their names, have been victimized so long that they are very suspicious of the motives of any outsider.

Their usual attitude was well expressed by a man near Merida, whose little plot of ground was being made the subject of an intensive study in land utilization. Pictures were duly taken of the tiny fields, the yoke of oxen, the house, and the family. After this was done the wife asked timidly if she might have a picture, and was told that one would be sent her husband from Caracas, where the films were to be developed. But when the head of the house was asked to give his name, he stubbornly refused, saying, *"dar la firma es una cosa seria"* (it's a serious thing to give one's signature). Only after it was carefully explained that what was wanted was his name, given orally and not in writing, did he reluctantly give it, and then only when urged by his wife and children. Such an attitude is the product of several centuries of dealings with shysters of all kinds: lawyers, quack doctors, usurers, and high-handed storekeeper-landlords.

"Good Fences Make Good Neighbors"

The vagueness of property lines in many sectors of the world— particularly in Latin America—is an aspect of land tenure with wide ramifications. The patch agriculturalist is certain that if he produces very much more than what he and his family consume, or can carry away with them, someone will show up who says that he owns the land, someone who can enforce his claims with police action if necessary. Hence, the small nomadic farmer pushes farther and farther into the forest or the brush, where he can rotate plots or fields rather than crops. If a cultivator is apt to be evicted at any time, there is no reason for him to think in terms of improvements in techniques, in fertilization, or in the selection of better seeds, for instance.

A great mass of the rural population is forced to live the life of floaters, with no chance of putting down permanent roots. Indeed these uprooted and disinherited people acquire a kind of floater psychosis, a "what's-the-use" philosophy. These are the ones who, dreaming of a modern El Dorado, are increasingly floating into the mushrooming cities of Latin America, where they are creating some massive slum problems. They have no skills, they are illiterate, many of them, undernourished and disease-ridden, and are woefully inefficient. Furthermore, having deep-seated feelings that they have been and still are victims of unjust treatment, they are ideal bait for demagogues.

Castro and the Cubans

Time and again conquerors or dictators have been welcomed by the conquered because the latter looked upon the new overlords as deliverers. Time after time the aspirations of the people have not been fulfilled, with the result that they were willing to topple the original superimposed regime or its successor. The most recent and widely remarked case in time and in proximity to the United States is Cuba, which fell to the United States as a result of the successful war against Spain in 1898.

There was for generations a great reservoir of good will and friendliness of the entire Cuban people vis-à-vis the United States, to which I can testify from personal experience over more than thirty years of living, traveling and working in Cuba. Most of this good will has been dissipated in two short years. A little background material is highly revealing: by 1956 the United States controlled 80 per cent of Cuban public utilities, 90 per cent of the mines and cattle ranches and, with the British, nearly all the oil industry and 40 per cent of the sugar industry. This investment was accompanied by the usual succession of blood-thirsty (it is believed that Batista killed at least 20,000

Cubans in "restoring order") and plunder-minded dictators who were tolerated as long as they did not interfere with U.S. business.

Behind the glittering façade of gorgeous Havana, the City of Light, adapted to soft pleasures and hard business, the poor lived on the edge of subsistence. A quarter of the entire Cuban population was permanently unemployed, and at least a third was illiterate. Vast and fertile estates went uncultivated, with the attendant evils of absentee landlordism, the company store, scrip payment, and sharecropping. To support these institutions, an idle and brutal soldiery was established like an occupying power in forts all over the island—forts now, in many instances, transformed into schools, it may be remarked in passing.

Furthermore, there was a supposedly beneficent law on the books in Cuba, to the effect that anyone living a certain number of years as a squatter on any property had a right to the land his hut occupied as well as to the plot of ground he had been using for the growing of his foodstuffs. To prevent anyone from invoking this law, the landlords (Cubans and foreigners alike) saw to it (by force if necessary) that squatters never lived very long in one place. Nomadism was forced upon them. The result is that there were vast numbers of ribbon settlements in Cuba, of houses built dangerously close to the highway, for here the home owner could put down roots; this was definitely public land, and here the poor could at last find sanctuary, a place to call their very own. Small wonder that this great mass of people, treated little better than pariahs for decades, lend unqualified support to a leader who expropriates lands, which, he tells them in hours-long TV appearances, is *theirs* and for *them*.

Woe unto them that join house to house, that lay field to field, till there be no place.

A quotation is appropriate from a volume by Professor Schultz, a keen student of classic agricultural economics:

The revolutionary implications of land reform in countries where most of the property consists of land, where this property is held not by cultivators but mainly by a small group of families who do not farm and where most of the political power and social privileges are vested in those who own land, are, for a person living in a technically advanced community, virtually impossible to grasp (Schultz, 1953, pp. 126–127).

I trust that I have succeeded in bringing the subject of de jure landholding out of the law books into the de facto light of day of our everyday lives. I quote the contents of two recent newspaper clippings, cut out at random:

Indians Go on Warpath

Two thousand Indians armed with clubs ambushed a police patrol recently near Columbe in Chimborazo province.

The Interior Ministry said an officer and two patrolmen were seriously injured. Troops were ordered into the area to put down the uprising and several tribal chieftains were arrested.

Interior Minister Carlos Cornejo said the Indians ostensibly went on the warpath because a rancher in the area owed some of them a year's back pay.

Brazilian State Plans Program of Land Reform

Rio de Janeiro, Feb. 9—Sao Paulo, Brazil's richest state, has made a start toward solving one of Latin America's most explosive problems —the need for land reform.

The Sao Paulo plan calls for the sale of 125-acre tracts to landless persons, who will work them and pay for them over ten years. The program also schedules progressively higher taxes on unworked and unforested lands.

The Sao Paulo program comes at a time when squatters are reported to be resisting state militia who are attempting to expel them from lands in the neighboring state of Parana. In the northeastern state of Pernambuco, members of the so-called Peasant League led by Deputy Francisco Juliao have occupied sugar mills and plantations.

The coffee planters' association said plots of 125 acres were too small to be economical. They contended that such farms did not justify the use of tractors and other equipment—although coffee planters themselves use little modern equipment. Most of all, they complained about the progressively higher taxes on unused lands.

Eighty per cent of the farm population does not own any land. Two per cent of the landowners hold 50 per cent of the land.

One could go on ad infinitum with analyses of regional, national, or international situations under subheadings such as, "Land Tenure the Basis of Mau Mau Murders in Kenya," or "Armies of Landless Peasants Overwhelm Chiang Kai-shek," or "Uprooted Landless Tribesmen on Warpath in Congo," and so on.

I strongly feel that the landless peasant can be upgraded, incorporated into the great world society by being given access to

land and know-how. Then there will be less "agrarian unrest"
and fewer revolutions. But people cannot cast off their cultural
patterns like a dirty garment. Peasants who have been living
in virtual serfdom are no exception to this rule. The distribution of land to peasants does not automatically induce democracy,
or solve the problem of increasing production. If the peasant
does get land, and the capital and know-how to give it value,
he needs a ready market; and if he does find a market, it should
not be, as it all too often is, one in which prices for his produce
are ridiculously low and costs of his necessities are exorbitantly
high. Furthermore, an improved diet would greatly increase the
productive capacity of any rural population, but it is as necessary to have people *want* to eat the productive foods—meat, eggs,
dairy products, fruits and vegetables—as it is to be able to produce them.

In a recent report, George Hoffman of the Ford Foundation
wrote: "The yearnings of one billion people in substandard areas
for a better life can bring a better world or, if their yearnings
are ignored, a world of mounting tensions and explosive unrest."
Although land reform will in many underdeveloped areas go a
long way toward fulfilling these yearnings, changes cannot be
effected overnight. The new findings in science and technology
can be incorporated only very slowly into the culture of the so-
called "backward" areas: these modern findings cannot be applied to nontechnical peoples like a bandage to a bruised arm;
they must instead be widely diffused in order to become gradually part of the cultural blood stream of the peoples who are to
benefit from them.

Conclusion

To conclude, I trust that I have shown some aspects of the
fundamental and universal nature of the problems of land tenure: much of the unrest of the world is caused by the tensions
engendered between the "haves" and the "have-nots," between
the landed and the landless, and between those simple, often
gullible, country folk and the shrewd operators from the city
who oftimes prey on them. Furthermore, there are those who
farm small plots as a kind of protective coloring, a defense

mechanism, against predatory landholders who would skim off any surplus should the small farmer increase his productive capacity.

But the world does move! It is not enough to cut land up into small parcels to be thrown to the land hungry. In this day of mechanization, high-speed transport, widespread access to education, and so on, profits are greater on large mechanized farms than on tiny, owner-operated farms—the United States has fewer farmers now than a century ago, yet these modern farmers produce infinitely more than their predecessors did in 1860. In this age of rapid change, security of tenure in land may not be as important as job security or as social security, but many sectors of the world, considered underdeveloped, will not emerge full grown from the brow of modern technology. The process will take generations. During the period of evolution from the pre-industrial to the industrial era it may be advantageous for many newly created nations to anchor a large well-fed population on the land. Unless some mechanism is evolved whereby national income can be increasingly prorated on a fair percentage basis between the rural and the urban population, it may still hold true that

> Ill fares the land, to hastening ills a prey,
> Where wealth accumulates, and men decay.
> Princes and lords may flourish, or may fade;
> A breath can make them, as a breath has made:
> But a bold peasantry, their country's pride,
> When once destroyed, can never be supplied.

References

Bates, M., 1960. *The forest and the sea.* New York, Random House.

Schultz, T. W., 1953. *The economic organization of agriculture.* New York, McGraw-Hill.

Toynbee, A. J., 1947. *A study of history.* (Abridgement of Vols. I–VI), New York, London, Oxford University Press.

Whetten, N., 1948. *Rural Mexico.* Chicago, University of Chicago Press.

10

O NE OF the functions of cultural traditions in a group is to define for its members a range of choice and the "fitting," "proper," and "desirable" alternatives for behavior within this range. Especially when a striking change in the environment or in relationships with other groups is presented, there are frequently no clear and traditionally acceptable alternatives. Or, new alternatives may be posed alongside the old, thus increasing the range of choice. The resulting dilemmas are not infrequent in the modern world as the technology and values of industrial societies encounter those of less industrialized groups. In such situations, new alignments develop, cutting across traditional groupings within the society. These new alignments—which may be temporary agglomerations or may develop into well-organized groups or social movements, depending upon a variety of circumstances—have been dealt with by some anthropologists as phenomena of "factionalism."

In this chapter, David H. French surveys varying approaches and conceptualizations of factionalism, considering factionalism as distinct from intrasystem conflicts for which traditional modes of solution are available. "Ambiguity"—the existence of numerous or poorly defined alternatives—is seen as a condition conducive to the development of factionalism and of several related phenomena. For example, numerous and diverse alternatives pose the possibility that factions may take positions which, though conflicting, are not polar opposites, but directed at choices on entirely different continua.

The "irrelevance" of the two positions may be related to the frequent charges by each faction that the other is not acting "legitimately." But the charges and countercharges of evil intent also seem to be characteristic of all sharp intergroup conflict, as indicated in other chapters.

Interest in factionalism can be linked with problems in groups with less developed technologies when they face industrialized and often colonial powers, and with the development of social movements embodying indigenous and exogenous solutions. Thus the study of factionalism may well contribute to a rounded picture of the rise of nationalisms, protest and counterprotest trends of varying kinds.

EDITOR

10 AMBIGUITY AND IRRELEVANCY IN FACTIONAL CONFLICT *

by David H. French

Factionalism has been a particularly puzzling form of conflict. It was discussed in classical times and represented a problem to English and American political philosophers during the eighteenth century. It has been of interest in relation to political behavior in modern national states. Anthropologists have long known that factional conflicts are widely distributed among the peoples of the world. Until relatively recently, however, documentation of these phenomena consisted principally of brief passages in publications primarily concerned with other matters (e.g., see the references to Pueblo Indian factionalism cited in French, 1948, pp. v–vi). Contemporary anthropologists have available to them new modalities of interpretation for the study of factionalism (e.g., Siegel and Beals, 1960a, 1960b) and of conflict in general (e.g., LeVine, 1961). In addition, the number and adequacy of field research studies on factionalism has increased markedly (e.g., see the bibliography in Siegel and Beals, 1960a, and the papers accompanying LeVine, 1961).

No attempt will be made here to survey this growing anthropological literature on factional conflict or to offer fundamental criticisms of the interpretations that have been employed. Instead, attention will be directed to some special problems in the area of such conflict. Data, largely limited to American Indian populations, will be used to exemplify features of conflict which are worth fresh attention. The relationship between factionalism and ambiguity will receive special scrutiny. It will then be argued that the positions of participants in factional splits

* The author wishes to acknowledge the assistance of Suzanne Hanchett, George Roth, Professor John Pock, and Dr. Kathrine French.

are not necessarily relevant to each other. It will also be noted that factional contenders frequently charge each other with having illegimate means or ends.

In discussions of such phenomena as factionalism, the frame of reference of many observers predisposes them to see these phenomena in terms of ideological differences. In this paper a distinction will sometimes be made between ideological and non-ideological behavior, and this distinction will be made pertinent to the aspects of factionalism mentioned above.

Factionalism as Intrasystem Conflict

Excellent discussions of factionalism on a general level are those of Siegel and Beals (1960a, 1960b), which differentiate factionalism from intergroup conflict, party conflict, and the application of overt social sanctions. These authors define factionalism as "overt, unregulated (unresolved) conflict which interferes with the achievement of the goals of the group" (1960a, p. 108). They divide factionalism into two types: schismatic ("conflict between well-defined and cohesive sub-groups within the larger group"), and pervasive ("conflict which occurs not only between larger sub-units of the group, but also within the sub-units") (1960a, pp. 108–109; see also 1960b).

Siegel and Beals regard factionalism as only one type of "unrealistic" solution to group problems; others are dissolution of the group, individualistic solutions, and fantasy solutions. They discuss the combinations of variables which can bring about factionalism. Basically, there must be a change in the relations between a group and its external situation; the external "stresses" affect the group in a manner determined by the "strains," or potential lines of cleavage, within it (1960a, pp. 109–116). More specifically, they suggest that: "the situation most likely to lead to the development of factionalism is one in which a dominant external society selectively influences the group in a manner which is covert and which tends to accentuate existing cleavages within the group" (1960a, p. 112). The reader is encouraged to examine Siegel and Beals' paper for discussions which are generally consistent with the position taken here but which differ in facets of interpretation. Many of the problems they discuss, such as that of the determinants of factionalism, will not now be considered. Neither will there be any discussion of their assumption that factionalism is dysfunctional nor of the opposite assumption (see LeVine, 1961, pp. 3–4, 8–10, for analyses of their position and that of Gluckman and others).

The definition of factionalism employed in this paper is a simpler one than that of Siegel and Beals. Factionalism refers here to *those forms of conflict which occur within a system* (e.g., a group) *and which cannot be settled by traditional means.* The conflict must persist long enough for there to have been opportunity for the employment of traditional means.

Factional disputes should clearly be regarded as forms of conflict, but not all instances of conflict are most usefully classed as factional. On the basis of our definition there are several criteria for identifying nonfactional conflict. When a dispute occurs between systems, rather than within a system, some other term, such as "war" or "party conflict," is preferable. Similarly, if a dispute is of brief duration, or is capable of being settled by traditional mechanisms, then it is best not called factionalism.

In his useful discussion of factionalism among American Indians, Fenton (1954–1956, pp. 330–332) does not make precisely the distinction between factionalism and other forms of conflict that is being favored here. With respect to true political parties, he does differentiate between factionalism and disagreements; he says, "faction is reserved for partisan groups which are as yet unorganized and do not have their claims validated by a constitutional appeal to a free democratic election" (1954–1956, p. 332). Consistent with this, he includes as examples of factionalism—explicitly or implicitly—various institutionalized forms of dual organization, the segmentary structure of certain African societies, and the normal differentiation into contending positions of various American Indian peoples. In the present article these conflicts would be excluded because of the existence of mechanisms for settling them.

Factionalism has been defined as a form of intrasystem conflict. There is, of course, a problem as to what constitutes a system and a subsystem. In one frame of reference, a group of students and their teacher for a particular course represent a system. From another standpoint, such a group is simply a part of the school, which in turn can be seen as included in an educational system or some other higher-level form of organization. In discussing the anthropological study of conflict, whether factional or not, LeVine stresses the importance of specifying the "structural levels of conflict" which are under discussion. He offers a classification of such levels which is potentially useful in analyses of conflict (1961, pp. 4–5).

With regard to systems and subsystems, it should be clear that to discuss factionalism as intragroup conflict, one has no alternative but to view the data on the level of a system, with the factional participants constituting subsystems, rather than separate systems. It is both convenient and consistent with the existing literature to focus most of one's efforts on those disputes which those involved define as being intragroup or intrasystemic. The possibility that an observer might sometimes wish to view an instance of conflict as intrasystemic which the actors regard as intersystemic is beyond the scope of this paper.

Factionalism and Conflict among Traditional Subsystems

When a population—for example, a tribe—is segmented into stable, overtly defined groups, well recognized by all the participants in the system, an obvious structural basis is thereby provided for intragroup conflict. Subsystems of the larger system already exist to allocate persons differentially in relation to issues. The sociocultural boundaries around groups (French, ms; cf. French, 1961, pp. 421–424), which have functioned for other ends, may become boundaries of the contending factions.

It is less easy to understand the development of factional opposition within systems which lack stable, overtly defined, "bounded" groups. Many American Indian populations in the western United States lack such bounded groups, yet some have experienced factionalism. Even among such peoples as the Pueblo Indians, who have a variety of bounded subsystems, the factional disputes have not necessarily been structured in terms of these. For example, Taos (Fenton, 1954–1956, 1957; Siegel and Beals, 1960b) and other Pueblo villages during certain periods (cf. French, 1948, pp. 15–23) have experienced disputes between younger, "progressive," and older, "conservative" factions. Membership criteria other than age and orientation toward acculturation were involved, but the crucial fact is that the factions did not divide neatly along lines determined by earlier group boundaries.

One Indian population that has conspicuously displayed factional conflict is that of the Klamath Reservation in Oregon (Fenton, 1954–1956, p. 333, pp. 336–337; Clifton and Levine, 1961, p. 7). None of the Klamath, Modoc, and Paiute "tribes"— i.e., linguistic groupings—who became the reservation residents, had ever been organized into overtly bounded subsystems. The linguistic groupings did not become bounded groups. There have, in short, never been organized tribes, bands, sodalities, clans, or lineages. Nash (quoted in Fenton, 1954–1956, p. 333) is convinced that certain kinds of conflict were prevalent in aboriginal times. He refers to the ever-shifting groups as "factions," but in terms of the definition employed here, the success of traditional mechanisms for the settlement of such disputes would suggest that some other name should be applied to them. Under any circumstance, the structuring of both aboriginal and modern conflict groups among the Klamath Reservation Indians differs markedly from the neatly bounded subgroups that sometimes come into conflict in other parts of the world.

A fundamental question can be raised at this point: should we not expect the "truest" factional splits to divide systems along lines other than those traditionally functioning to subdivide the systems? The point is that conflict between stable subsystems of a system may easily be recurrent, and there may be traditional means for resolution of such conflicts. In fact, the generation and resolution of such subsystem conflicts has been said to be "eufunctional" for the operation of the system as a whole (cf. LeVine, 1961, p. 3). In contrast to the conflicts which occur at traditional subsystem boundaries, it is precisely those which create new subsystems which have a low probability of being settled by traditional means. This would hold true whether or not the larger system is currently subdivided into firmly bounded subsystems (e.g., lineages or sodalities).

It has been asserted that: "the faction arises in the struggle for power and represents a division on details of application and not on principles" (Lasswell, 1931, p. 49). The idea that principles are not at stake does not necessarily follow from Lasswell's definition: "The term faction is commonly used to designate any constituent group of a larger unit which works for the advancement of particular persons or policies" (Lasswell, 1931, p. 49). Rather, it relates principally to the fact that at that period he chose to limit his discussion to conflict within explicitly defined groups, as opposed to more general sociocultural systems. It should become clear in the discussion that follows that "principles," as well as "applications," can become involved in intrasystemic, factional conflict.

It has also been suggested (Siegel and Beals, 1960a, p. 109) that the opponents in a factional dispute are agreed on the worth of preserving the system in which they are participating. When they cite the American Civil War, however, as an example of factional conflict (pp. 108–109), they are evidently involved in a contradiction. The Confederate States surely had a certain commitment to the dissolution of the United States as it had existed. Similarly, in factional disputes among American Indians, one common position is that of increased participation in non-Indian American life. To cite an example, the principal issue dividing the Klamath Reservation population was the question of dissolving the reservation; from the actors' point of view, this was precisely the question of destruction of a formal group or system.

Factions and Reference Groups

The fact that factionalism can occur within systems that are not groups in any obvious sense can be illustrated by further reference to the Klamath Reservation Indians. The lack of firm boundaries around or within the reservation population has already been mentioned. It should also be noted that a great many Indians affiliated with the reservation have not been living there but yet have preserved a legal and sociopsychological relationship with reservation activities (cf. Clifton and Levine, 1961, pp. 5–6). Part of the motivation here has been the claims on monies available to enrolled Indians. These financial resources have functioned as a point of reference for people of

Indian ancestry who might otherwise have preferred not to define themselves as "Klamaths," or as Indians in any sense. They have thus been participants in a system and intermittently active members of factions.

There is no way to understand the behavior of Klamath Reservation Indians in terms of certain traditional ideas of group membership. The idea of reference groups (see, e.g., Sherif, 1953; Merton, 1957, pp. 225–386) provides a model adaptable to the problem at hand. Whether they participate in Indian "groups" or not, orientation toward a system called "Klamath" has significance for these people of Klamath ancestry. They have a point of reference, and they have participated in a system which has exhibited intrasystemic factional conflict. In partial contrast, the Wasco Indians on another Oregon reservation, Warm Springs, have learned how to act like whites but nevertheless have continued in certain situations to act like Indians. They can be understood as doing so not only because they orient themselves toward their Wasco ancestors but also because in certain situations they are positively oriented in relation to a larger and more obviously Indian grouping, the Sahaptin-speaking Indians on the same reservation (French, 1961).

Ambiguity as a Condition Conducive to Factionalism

Some of the problems of understanding factionalism may be clarified by considering the ambiguity which so frequently is associated with it. Ambiguity refers here to a lack of clarity with regard to appropriate behavior. If ambiguity is phrased in terms of means-ends relationships, either means or ends, or both, may be in some sense unclear.

From an observer's point of view, a certain amount of ambiguity characterizes all of behavior, even though the participants may not be aware of this. From moment to moment, perceptual activity consists of assimilating phenomena to a particular set of percepts, in preference to other possible sets. In the flow of speech, ambiguity is constantly being faced (so to speak) as the individual sorts out the phenomena he is discussing and handles these in terms of one word or sentence rather than another.

When we move to another level, we find that communities are constantly facing the fact that new events are not identical with past events. Despite the differences, the new events are almost always handled in terms of their similarity to other phenomena for which there are standardized responses. For example, if money as an exchange medium is introduced to a people who are using cowrie shells as tokens of value in trade, the metal currency may well be assimilated easily to the existing cowrie shell pattern. The fact that such assimilation of the new to the familiar does not always occur smoothly suggests that ambiguity can potentially become involved in group problems.

On the Klamath Reservation, the ambiguity during recent years has been centered on the worth of remaining affiliated with a loosely structured Indian reservation community, as against the effect of formal disengagement from that community. An orientation toward Indian culture cannot automatically align a person with the continuation of the reservation, since Indian activities of symbolic importance no longer occur in any overt sense. Yet, any lingering identification with Indian life has been consistent with preserving the reservation. Undoubtedly many Klamath Reservation Indians have regarded it as safer to perpetuate the status quo. In contrast, the short-term economic gains derivable from the distribution of the assets of the reservation have a conspicuous desirability. For a good many Indians, decisions of this kind have not been easy to make because the situation is ambiguous and the alternatives are not comparable.

There are also ambiguities in the situation facing the mixed population living on the Warm Springs Reservation. The possibility of economic advantage and increased participation in non-Indian life could also be seen as furthered through reservation termination. Many residents are aware of this possibility, but factionalism has not appeared (cf. French and French, 1955).

It is clearly not being asserted that ambiguity itself is a determinant of factional conflict in any significant sense. In fact, Leach (1954, pp. 105–106) argues convincingly that particular kinds of ambiguity function to keep systems operating. Perhaps it can be asserted that when internal and external conditions are appropriate, the existence of an ambiguity can precipitate the outbreak of overt conflict.* It can be affirmed more confidently that ambiguity in the actors' views of means-ends relations will precede and accompany factional schisms. Furthermore, there is high probability that the ambiguity will be reflected in differences in the explicit ideologies of the contenders. Characteristically, but not invariably, the arguments of the factions are based on different premises or follow different lines of reasoning. They are "beside the point" in relation to each other.

Incongruence and Charges of Illegitimacy

At times, the form of participation in the nonideological sociocultural activities of each of the conflicting parties is not in fact congruent with that of the other or others (cf. Pock, 1961, for noncongruent positions in a pseudo-conflict). Examples of this would be those instances in which one faction is removing itself from the system while another is working to achieve some specific end through participation of the entire group. Thus, the "structural positions" or "organizational positions" of the factions are mutually beside the point. The positions are not true opposites. A further example would be the factional splits among Pueblo Indians in which some participants are acting in relation to a traditional theocratic structure and others in terms of economic advantage. (Yet both are involved in the same system.) In such cases, the ideologies are likely to be irrelevant to each other, as well, even though they may not mirror precisely the nature of the irrelevance in the rest of the sociocultural structuring. In passing, it might be noted that it happens to be easier in the present state of anthropological methodology and theory to detect and describe incongruities in the ideologies than in the nonideological behavior.

Discordant ideologies may be based on differing stances toward precisely the same ambiguous situation. In other words,

* Ambiguity bears some relationship to the dimension of covertness, and possibly also to that of complexity, postulated by Siegel and Beals in their discussion of determinants of factionalism (1960a, pp. 110, 112).

factions may be participating differently (and this can include having differing ideologies) with regard to a system which all have in common and which all understand equally well. Another possibility is that conceptual, as opposed to structural, ambiguity can be related to ignorance. Adams (1957, p. 225) writes:

At the time of my study in the Egyptian Delta (1952–1954), many of the villagers did not fully understand the philosophy and aims of the revolution. In the village which I studied most intensively, the men had formed two distinct factions and several cliques within each of these in response to the startling events that were occurring.

Actually, the residents of this village differed not only in regard to information and understanding, but also in regard to wealth, power, and prestige.

When factions—as opposed say, to political parties—are in conflict, there is a high probability not only that ambiguity and irrelevance will be present but also that charges of illegitimacy regarding the actions of opponents will occur. In America today Republicans and Democrats accuse each other of being mistaken, but they do not often seriously charge their opponents with having illegitimate means or ends. These accusations are made against foreign states who are defined as enemies of America, but such conflict, while not easily settled by traditional means, is defined by the actors as intersystemic, hence not factional and beyond the scope of a paper on factionalism. Potentially relevant here would be the charges that factions within the Republican party make against each other.

Factions among nonliterate peoples accuse their opponents of cheating or of deviating from traditional methods. When Siegel and Beals (1960b, p. 399) refer to the belief of members of factions that their opponents do not "conduct themselves properly," this suggests the kind of illegitimacy being discussed here. In the 1941–1942 factional dispute in Isleta Pueblo, New Mexico, each major group accused the other of monetary speculations and sorcery. They also questioned the legitimacy of elections, and one faction charged that a member of the other belonged to the wrong ceremonial group to act as *cacique* (village priest) and to make nominations for office in the traditional manner (French, 1948).

Factionalism and Sociocultural Change

Anthropologists have been inclined to assume that populations undergoing rapid sociocultural change are most likely to experience factionalism; the best known examples of rapid change involve acculturation and assimilation. Certain kinds of factionalism may be present in systems which have not experienced such new types of outside influence. Nevertheless, factional disputes are frequent enough among those people experiencing acculturation and assimilation that some kind of determining relationship is easy to postulate. It follows almost by definition that intragroup problems which cannot be solved by traditional means are likely to appear when outside influences are operative. Obviously, the very newness of outside influences provides a basis for ambiguity and for subsequent charges of illegitimacy in the behavior of contending parties. It is unlikely that it would be useful, however, to regard factional conflict as peculiar to systems undergoing rapid change. They simply provide us with our most convenient arenas for study.

This discussion has explored some of the phenomena of conflict within groups and other systems. Differences in forms of organization among sociocultural systems create problems in the understanding of factional divisions. Consequently, some of these organizational differences were delimited. It became necessary at times to differentiate between ideological and non-ideological behavior. The place of ambiguity and of charges of illegitimacy was discussed, especially in relation to ideology. At the same time, it was suggested that below the ideological level there often is "structural or organizational irrelevancy" in factional conflict.

References

Adams, John B., 1957. Culture and conflict in an Egyptian village. *Amer. Anthropologist,* 59, 225–235.

Clifton, James A., and David Levine, 1961. *Klamath personalities: ten Rorschach case studies.* Eugene, University of Oregon, Department of Anthropology.

Fenton, William N., 1954–1956. Factionalism in American Indian society. *Actes du IVᵉ Congrès International des Sciences Anthropologiques et Ethnologiques, Vienne 1952*, Tome II, 330–340.

——, 1957. *Factionalism at Taos Pueblo, New Mexico*. Bureau of American Ethnology, Bulletin 164, Anthropological Paper No. 56, 297–344.

French, David H., 1948. *Factionalism in Isleta Pueblo*. Monographs of the American Ethnological Society, No. 14.

——, 1961. Wasco-Wishram. In Edward H. Spicer (ed.), *Perspectives in American Indian culture change*. Chicago, University of Chicago Press, 337–430.

French, Kathrine, and David French, 1955. The Warm Springs Indian community. *Amer. Indian*, 7, 3–17.

Lasswell, Harold D., 1931. Faction. *Encyclopedia of the social sciences*, Vol. 6, 49–51.

Leach, E. R., 1954. *Political systems of highland Burma: a study of Kachin social structure*. Cambridge, Harvard University Press.

LeVine, Robert A., 1961. Anthropology and the study of conflict: an introduction. *J. Conflict Resolution*, 5, 4–15.

Merton, Robert K., 1957. *Social theory and social structure*. Revised and enlarged edition. Glencoe, Ill., Free Press.

Pock, John C., 1961. The problem of organizational integration: a study of medical and paramedical services in a state mental hospital. Paper read at the annual meeting of the American Sociological Association, St. Louis, Missouri, August, 1961, 26 pp., dittoed.

Sherif, Muzafer, 1953. The concept of reference groups in human relations. In Muzafer Sherif and M. O. Wilson (eds.), *Group relations at the crossroads*. New York, Harper and Brothers, 203–231.

Siegel, Bernard J., and Alan R. Beals, 1960a. Conflict and factionalist dispute. *J. Royal anthropol. Inst.*, 90, 107–117.

——, 1960b. Pervasive factionalism. *Amer. Anthropologist*, 62, 394–417.

11

THE FORMATION of human groups, as well as the development of harmonious or conflicting relationships among them, takes time. The implications of this necessarily historical nature of intergroup relations are realized neither by those who restrict their study of group processes to the "here and now" nor by those who, for convenience, take contemporary arrangements within and between groups as "givens" in research. In earlier chapters, especially those by Killian, Klineberg, North, and Crist, we have seen historical processes on broad canvas. Aspects of the natural and technological resources, the social relationships developed for their utilization and for other aspects of living, and related systems of values were combined in broad strokes. Broad pictures summarizing historical process and their import for contemporary intergroup and intragroup relations are essential.

However, there are advantages to research conducted over periods of time in social units small enough so that their membership and interactions can be studied directly and in detail. The chief advantage lies in the opportunity to specify the significant variables and to obtain evidence of their interrelationships. When this study continues over periods in which significant changes occur, one may begin to assess the relative contributions of different conditions to behavioral and sociocultural outcomes.

From this perspective, Alan R. Beals' study in the next chapter of one village in modern India—combining an investigation of traditional means of livelihood, social organization, and values with direct observation in the village—tells us some things with a precision not easily acquired through other means. The effects of innovations by a colonial power—innovations which may have been "planned" from the colonial point of view but which were not planned with respect to their diverse ramifications for village life—and influences from modern urban centers are seen as productive of the "pervasive" factionalism which Beals found in 1952–1953. Factionalism of this kind, as he describes it, is a fluid process, relatively devoid of clear ideological differences (using French's terms in the preceding chapter).

Yet, as Norman A. Chance emphasizes in his discussion, the description of pervasive factionalism here seems to indicate choosing sides, albeit in transitory and even fickle fashion, relative to systems

245

of control and discordant systems of value (which are themselves conflicting). Against the background of near breakdown in village customs and morals accompanied by bickering and choosing of sides, the changes between 1953 and 1960 reported by Beals as stemming from industrial and commercial innovations are striking indeed.

EDITOR

11 PERVASIVE FACTIONALISM IN A SOUTH INDIAN VILLAGE

by Alan R. Beals

Although conflict occurs from time to time in most human groups, it does not necessarily lead to marked change. The need to solve pressing group problems and to achieve goals which can be reached only through cooperation is correlated to the presence of devices which regulate and control conflict, thereby preventing disruptive escalation of existing conflicts. Nor is human conflict necessarily irrational. It often contributes to the stability or functional integration of the group; it is often associated with the attainment of goals or policy conditions (North et al., 1960; Gluckman, 1955).

When attention is given to a particular group or organization, instances of conflict which interfere with the attainment of policy conditions and sometimes lead to fission or disintegration can be observed. If the term "factionalism" is used in a general sense to describe conflict within an organization, "disruptive factionalism" may be used to describe internal conflicts which tend to disrupt the normal or traditional activities of the group and to interfere with the achievement of policy conditions.

Within the area covered by the term "disruptive factionalism," a distinction, although not always a clear-cut distinction, can be made between "schismatic factionalism," in which conflict occurs between well-organized subgroups, and "pervasive factionalism," in which conflict tends to occur both within and between subgroups of the organization (Siegel and Beals, 1960a, 1960b). Although disruptive factionalism might lead to an abandonment of organizational goals and of the organization itself, it appears probable that the motive for factional conflict is preservation of the organization under circumstances requiring rapid change.

This paper represents an exploratory attempt to find an explanation for the fact that some organizations respond to crises by engaging in apparently pointless internal bickering, while other organizations dissolve, organize religious movements, or make prudent or imprudent attacks upon the source of the crisis.

Theoretical Background to the Study

The hypothesis is that the development of alternative ways of reacting to changing situations is the product of an interaction between internal strains, or tendencies toward conflict, and new external stresses or problems. The internal aspect of an organization may be defined as the tradition or pattern of shared understandings transmitted among its successive members. External to an organization are the biological and constitutional characteristics of its members and the physical, social, and biological environments within which the organization functions. Collectively these forces can be described as the milieu across which a tradition operates as an organization is formed and maintained. The fact that traditions set up, or are used to set up, particular patterns of behavior within organizations is inconsistent neither with the idea that human beings form traditions both deliberately and accidentally nor with the idea that human beings and other forces modify traditions.

Although a tradition is not wholly an adaptive or predictive device, traditions must maintain a capacity to solve most of the major problems encountered by the organization which bear them. Presumably, modification of traditions occurs largely in response to incompatibilities developing between the tradition and the milieu of sufficient magnitude to require problem solving alteration of either the tradition or the milieu. It can be noted that all known traditions are primitive, in the sense that they reflect imperfect and unrealistic adaptations to the milieu. Traditions are characterized by a tendency to deny the presence of incompatibilities with the milieu. In fact, the man-made or artificial character of the tradition itself often is denied. As a result, at any one time, the members of an organization control neither the tradition nor the milieu but only parts of them.

Such faulty control of tradition and milieu leads repeatedly to situations in which culturally induced expectations run directly counter to actual happenings in the milieu. The resulting cognitive dissonance, tension, frustration, negative reinforcement, or psychological conflict leads to the development of real and potential conflicts between individuals and subgroups. Conflicts of this type are defined as *strain*. They are considered to be the direct result of complete or partial failure to resolve *incompatibilities between the milieu and the tradition*, or of failure to prevent the development of *inconsistencies within the tradition*.

Turning now to the village of Namhalli in Southern India, an attempt will be made to indicate a connection between recurrent stresses or unsolved problems within the milieu, and the development of strains within Namhalli's traditional culture. Field study of the village was carried out between May, 1952, and August, 1953, and again during February, 1960, under a grant from the Social Science Research Council. The name of the village, "Namhalli," is a pseudonym.

Recurrent Sources of Stress in the Village's History

Traditionally, the major agricultural pattern in Namhalli has been the growing of a millet crop requiring rainfall for its success. Depending upon the distribution of thundershowers in time and space, it is possible for one village to experience crop failure while a neighboring village has good crops. Within the village, it is also possible for one farmer to achieve good crops while another fails. This condition is independent of the skill of the farmer or of the value of the land which he holds. The recurrent stress of uneven rainfall is met within the cultural tradition with the explanation that those who experience crop failure have sinned, perhaps in previous existences, while those who succeed have not sinned. Although this solution of the rainfall problem appears unrealistic, it is a parsimonious explanation of the facts known to the people of Namhalli.

Another recurrent stress in agricultural activities lies in the fact that the crops grown in the fields require differing quantities of attention at different seasons. The man who operates a five-acre field is able to work steadily over most of the year.

Those who assist him with such operations as weeding and harvesting work for a relatively brief period. Within the cultural tradition, there appears to be no obvious solution for the problem posed by the fact that farmers work nearly all year long, whereas laborers work only part of the year. Both laborers and farmers must receive minimum subsistence if agriculture is to be carried on. Traditionally, the farmer has received the larger portion of the harvested crop and the laborer has received the smaller portion. The laborer usually received a higher rate of return, per man hour invested in agriculture, than does the farmer. Despite the absence of significant biological differences between farmers as a class and laborers as a class, the realities of botany and land distribution have forced the cultural tradition to develop a pattern which is inconsistent with the realities of human biology. In addition, until after 1946, it was a major problem to obtain a supply of labor and cattle adequate to farm the village lands.

Other recurrent stresses included famine, such epidemic diseases as cholera, plague, and smallpox, and threat of attack. Namhalli and neighboring villages were continually threatened and frequently attacked by armed marauders. The village remained fortified until 1910. Of course, the village also shared with other human groups and cultures the usual problems of birth and death, of fertility and infertility, and of the transmission and perpetuation of the cultural tradition.

Traditional Ways of Dealing with Stress

Namhalli's well-defined and still largely extant traditional culture offers a set of techniques, together with appropriate values and beliefs, for dealing with the major recurrent stresses outlined above. The basis for interpreting reality lies in the belief that the universe is perfect, and that everything that occurs is perfectly predictable and orderly. Although the universe is perfectly harmonious, certain portions of the universe are considered to be dominated by an *illusion* of disharmony. These portions constitute the world as it is perceived by the six senses. Complete freedom and identification with God, who represents the harmonious and "real" universe, is achieved through developing the ability to blot out sense impressions. Because the ordinary man is unable to blot out sense impressions, it follows that the ordinary man is incapable of perceiving the underlying perfection of the universe.

Although ideal behavior consists of withdrawal from the world of sense impressions, the man who lacks sufficient spiritual development to be capable of ignoring his sense impressions is told that he may achieve spiritual progress by conforming to the rules of behavior appropriate to his station in life. As illustrated later in this chapter, these two strategies, of withdrawal from the world of the senses and active participation in the world of the senses, are attached to particular social roles where they have the function of preventing the outbreak of conflict or signaling its existence.

The notion that individuals proceed toward ultimate recognition of transcendent reality through a series of rebirths permits a solution to the problem of social inequalities posed by the agricultural way of life, and provides a justification for the caste system characteristic of India's villages. Poverty, misfortune, and low social status represent punishment for sinful behavior in previous lives. Wealth and high social status are the rewards of virtue. The everyday observation that persons of low status sometimes conduct themselves virtuously, while persons of high status conduct themselves sinfully, is met by the fact that role reversal, in terms of status, often occurs in the future life.

The caste system, supported by this and related beliefs, is consistent with several of the recurrent stresses affecting the village. Practices which reduced the availability of cattle and land for the lowest ranking Madiga caste helped provide a pool of agricultural laborers. Despite the opportunities provided by sizable acreages of virgin land, this caste had a religious obligation to remain agricultural laborers. Ranked above the Madigas in the caste system were a string of specialized castes— barbers, washermen, blacksmiths, potters, carpenters—who provided essential services to the farmer. These specialists were paid in grain immediately after harvest. Members of specialized castes worked for a traditionally fixed return in terms of measures of grain. During years of good crop production when labor needs were higher than normal, specialists found it economically rewarding to serve as agricultural laborers. Madigas and other agricultural laborers were paid at the time their work was performed and throughout the year through various forms of charity. The differences in economic and social status provide, among other things, a means of determining who shall survive a famine and who shall not survive. The farmer, who could refuse to hire laborers and refuse to compensate specialists following the harvest, probably had a relatively good chance of surviving.

Incompatibilities and Inconsistencies as Sources of Strain

Although the caste system and its ideological rationale provides a solution to the recurrent stresses posed by agriculture, it is not realistically based upon true or demonstrable biological differences between human beings. For this reason, it can be considered to represent a major strain within the traditional culture.

Because caste groups do not intermarry and the preferred form of marriage is for men to marry women from other villages, women from Namhalli are scattered over a wide region. Women who marry men in Namhalli have close relatives scattered over an equally wide region. This range of kinship obligations helps to facilitate temporary and permanent emigration for economic reasons. This again contributes to a solution of the problems of famine and labor shortage. The pattern of castes and intervillage marriages serves to produce coalitions between villages and offers a means of developing protection against bandits and political oppression.

On the other hand, the need to develop external relationships in order to meet recurrent stresses leads to the emergence of a class of outsiders, mostly wives, within the village and to the development of a segmental type of organization which can serve as a basis for conflict. Here again, solution of one set of problems has led to the development of internal strains.

Use of the hereditary principle in assigning social roles extends far beyond the caste system. The preferred marriage partner for a man is a cross-cousin or his father's sister's daughter; the head of a household is the older of a set of brothers; the head of the village is the son or brother of a former head of the village; the head of the caste is the son or brother of a former head of the caste; and the priest in the temple is the son or brother of the former priest of the temple. Although the hereditary principle and the religious explanation of the hereditary principle provide a basis for the social inequality necessary to a division of labor under traditional circumstances, they tend to run counter to biological facts, particularly those related to chance variations in the ability and character of individual men. As a result of this and other inconsistencies, the most crucial authority relationships carry a high load of strain.

To balance the many real-life situations in which the system of ascribed social statuses leads to deprivation or apparent unfairness, the cultural tradition contains a number of devices which have the effect of rationalizing and supporting the traditional authority system. The desirability of unquestioning support of authority figures is partially supported by the belief that the father, husband or older brother who serves as an authority figure is thereby sacrificing the opportunity to seek personal spiritual salvation. The authority figure, charged with feeding and clothing his subordinates, must concern himself primarily with the world of illusion. He must consider every action in terms of its economic and other effects upon the social unit of which he is the head. On the other hand, the subordinate, having no major responsibilities, is free to pursue salvation in his own way; he is free to be honorable, idealistic, and generous.

However, the major motive for unquestioning support of authority has lain in the presence of grave external threats to security. Internal harmony has been an essential requirement for the protection of the village from bandits, from failure of rainfall, and from disease. Internal harmony is a requirement at every stage of the social, economic, and religious life of the village. The New Year's ceremony, for example, requires that every house be whitewashed and that everyone wear new clothing. Failure to perform such ceremonies results directly in divine displeasure, manifested in crop failure and other misfortunes.

Strict definition of the limits of authority and the require-

· ment that every man contribute to the harmonious functioning of the village provide wide areas within which a spirit of self-respect, freedom and equality can be maintained. Authority and inequality are viewed in some ways as merely temporary expedients. They have been accepted in much the same way that one accepts a role in a drama. Outside of well-defined authoritarian contexts, there has been a strong emphasis on equality. Any man can achieve salvation; any god by sinning can become a man. Relationships between castes are regarded as familial. The Village Headman and Accountant are referred to as the mother and father of the village, in the sense that they must give equal love to all of the castes just as parents give equal love to all of their children. Marriage between castes is forbidden, not because castes are unequal, but because castes are fraternally related and intermarriage is incestuous.

Decision making within the village is vested in a council which includes the head of each of the castes and which must make all decisions unanimously. All households in the village must contribute equally to any project. Fellow villagers are addressed as father, brother, mother, and sister. Although husband and wife are unequal, mother's brother and father's sister's husband are equal—kinship is traced bilaterally. A family which receives a bride in one generation must return a bride in the next generation. Although brothers are unequal, they share property equally. The ideal Pandava brothers in the epic literature of Hinduism shared the same wife. Master and servant are unequal, but a servant is not expected to work in the fields unless his master works beside him. Persons who take food at feasts are unequal; but they must all receive equal portions of food, and they must all accept the proffered food.

Traditional Means of Regulating Internal Conflicts

Maintenance of the idea of equality in a situation of inequality leads back to the basic inconsistency in the belief system—the presence of disharmony in a harmonious universe. The need to preserve unity in the face of outside threats has lead to the development of beliefs and patterns of behavior designed to prevent the emergence of any kind of overt conflict. Children, constantly supervised, are rarely permitted to initiate conflicts with other children and never permitted to continue conflicts once initiated. Adults are sensitized to conflict. Even minor quarrels between husband and wife are distressing and require immediate remedial action.

Subordinates are trained to express dissatisfaction subtly by withdrawing from participation. At the caste level, the most common practice is to boycott an offending individual or caste. The barber refuses to cut his client's hair; the blacksmith refuses to repair the farmer's plow. The dispute is settled by nonparticipants, not by direct negotiation. At the family level, refusal of food and shirking are the commonest forms of withdrawal. Judicial action, by outside authorities, is taken when the subordinate is observed to be starving or is seen leaning on the brink of a well, obviously contemplating suicide. Ordinarily, punishment of a subordinate, no matter how severe, becomes a judicial matter only when the subordinate initiates conflict. Once a conflict has been initiated, judicial action seeks the best means of resolving the conflict. There is little concern with the abstract principles of justice that are characteristic of western judicial procedures. Proper behavior is strictly specified. Once improper behavior has occurred, the principal concern is not punishment of the offender, but restoration of proper conduct.

Differences in economic status lead to a situation in which only a few families, who usually belong to the higher ranking castes, are wealthy enough to store sufficient grain for the next year's planting. These families loan seed grain annually to other families, and are in a position to control behavior through the application of economic sanctions. In many villages, this factor alone has proven sufficient to maintain many aspects of traditional culture.

Judicial mechanisms and a host of economic, religious, and social sanctions did not prevent the appearance of conflict in Namhalli in former times. However, they do appear to have regulated and controlled conflict, and to have permitted continuation of those forms of economic, religious, and social cooperation which were considered vital. It should be noted that emphasis was placed almost entirely upon the presumption that unprecedented or unresolvable conflicts would not occur. Within the tradition, few allowances are made for dealing with a situation in which unanimous decision might become impossible. There is a presumption that everyone shares the same belief and value systems, and that agreement can always be gained through discussion and the use of influence. Of critical importance is the fact that the cost of conflict and disagreement under traditional circumstances was always greater than the cost of harmony and agreement.

Generalizations from the Study of Village Tradition

The cultural tradition offers solutions to major recurrent stresses. These solutions are, for the most part, logical and esthetically pleasing, but the unrealistic nature of some of these solutions is not readily apparent. The tradition is linked to a particular technology which has remained relatively unchanged for several thousand years. It has been linked to an external political system of marked instability. Many of the recurrent stresses to which the cultural tradition is accommodated are recurrent not because they are intrinsically insolvable, but because technological and social change is required to solve them.

To generalize, it can be suggested that cultural traditions develop as they accumulate solutions to problems which arise during interaction between the cultural tradition and the milieu. When the problems are temporarily or permanently insolvable in character, the solutions or explanations of them are imperfect. These imperfect explanations lead to inadequate predictions concerning the results of human behavior—that is, to situations within which the individual is punished when he expects to be rewarded and rewarded when he expects to be punished. Such imperfect reinforcement of the cultural tradition leads, in turn, to tendencies toward deviations from cultural norms. The resulting tendencies toward conflict are controlled through the ritualization of existing patterns of conflict, and through the development of religious and social sanctions which reinforce the traditional way of doing things.

When a new stress appears, the resulting change within the cultural tradition is dependent upon the kind of influence which the new stress exerts upon existing stresses and strains. The same new stress applied to two different cultural traditions may have radically different effects. When a single basic cultural tradition is replicated over a wide area, as is the case of villages functioning within a larger civilization, the same stress may have different effects upon different villages due to the fact that the cultural tradition is not equally well replicated in all of the villages. In the region within which Namhalli is located, many villages possess a single large caste which is economically and politically dominant. In such villages, order and conformity can be maintained by force of numbers and through the use of economic power. Namhalli's economic system was originally based upon a single rain-fed crop, a far more insecure economic base than those of neighboring villages possessing irrigated land.

Modern Sources of Stress

The major new stress or new set of stresses to which Namhalli has been subjected in recent years stems from the development of British and urban influences upon the village and its milieu. These influences, which might be described as "modern" influences, began to be felt in strength in the years following 1877. The new stress had certain major characteristics which can be summarized.

First, modern influences were relatively covert. Instead of taking the form of a problem to be solved, they often took the form of relief from the pressure of established and recurrent stresses. Bandits disappeared, the region was pacified, and many of the more serious epidemic diseases were controlled. Changes were made in the traditional systems of land tenure and taxation, and the effects of these changes were felt long after the changes had been made. Other changes, such as the building of roads, railroads, and irrigation works, are not likely to be considered stressful.

Second, the new stress was relatively random in character. Its nature varied with changes in the world economic picture and with changes in the political situation in England. From the point of view of Namhalli, there was little possibility of preparing for changes or predicting their effects.

Third, the new stress was complicated. Any general solution

of the stress required the solution of its innumerable and separate aspects.

Fourth, the new stress had a curtailing effect upon the range of behaviors which might have led to its solution. The introduction of a western type of legal system ruled out such traditional ways of acting as outcasting offenders, applying severe physical punishment, or taking away land or cattle. Increases in population density ruled out emigration from the village for most of the population. Government concern with direct administration of village affairs led to the virtual excision of traditional patterns of authority and social control. For example, the government's persistent attempts to "revive" the village council led to the development of a "government council" which had virtually no powers.

Fifth, and perhaps most important in terms of the development of conflict, the new stress had selective effects upon different subgroups within the village. Legal restrictions were placed upon the village Headman, and several headmen were thrown in jail. Weavers were ruined economically by competition from mill-made fabrics; blacksmiths and carpenters became wealthy by manufacturing carts for use on newly constructed roads. Government policies involved deliberate economic discrimination against persons of high caste and favored treatment for persons in the lower ranking castes. The new stress was persistent and continuous, and could not be wished away even by a change in government.

In discussing strain within Namhalli, it was suggested that the traditional culture relied heavily upon a strong system of authority and social control, and upon the presence of such external threats as epidemics, crop failure, bandits, and political instability. The new stress removed or weakened all of these. Simultaneously, modern influences added a wide range of urban-based reference groups which provided several new systems of value and belief. Reference groups formed by missionaries, English officials, educated urban Indians, urban laborers, and urban reformers shared one common characteristic; namely, that membership in the various groups was not readily accessible to people in Namhalli. Thus, although competing reference groups weakened attachments to traditional values and beliefs, they did not provide any organizational background within which new values and beliefs could be activated. Together with the traditional values and beliefs, the "modern" values and beliefs provided a basis for justifying almost any form of behavior (Sherif and Sherif, 1953, pp. 160–161).

In 1953, the contribution of the new reference groups to the *social organization* of the village was almost entirely negative. Attempts to mobilize social sanctions through appeals to the urban legal system, for example, produced dangerous and unpredictable results. Even such simple matters as reporting murders, suicides, or riots often led to police or legal decisions which ran directly counter to the villagers' perceptions of the event. Attempts to enforce order through appeal to urban law courts ran afoul of new laws permitting the inheritance of land by widows, forbidding the practice of outcasting, and sharply restricting many other traditional practices. Under such circumstances, Namhalli's leaders feared to exercise their traditional authority and hesitated to appeal to outside authority. The result was a lack of any clear pattern for the enforcement of behavioral norms.

By 1953, the only clearly positive contribution of modern influences to Namhalli's social structure was the presence of a public school and of a volleyball team. These two innovations provided some basis for the development of cohesive relationships among the "educated class" in the village, but they did not provide any basis for the development of village-wide cooperative activities.

Disappearance of the wartime prosperity of the 1940's had the effect of curtailing Namhalli's participation in the urban economy and, at the same time, of bringing attention to the fact that the village was overpopulated. Excessive use of available lands was resulting in decreased yield. Pasture lands were overgrazed; profitable gardening had been abandoned because theft could not be controlled. Large extended families, which had contributed to capital formation in more traditional times, had been broken up by modern influences and the weakening of traditional authority patterns. The economic pie was becoming smaller, and the number of people desiring to consume it was increasing. Furthermore, wartime prosperity had altered the definition of poverty. People were no longer satisfied with adequate food and clothing; most had come to desire wrist watches, fountain pens, trips to the motion pictures, and stylish clothing.

The Rise of Factionalism

In terms of the traditional culture, the explanation for the failure of the village to meet the crisis resulting from the loss of wartime prosperity was to be found in the breakdown of harmonious relationships within the village. To most people, the unhappy state of affairs was due, not to external threats, but to a rise in immorality, disobedience, and selfishness within the village. The effective strategy for dealing with the crisis seemed to be one of banding together to enforce conformity to the proper moral code, but there was no agreement as to what the nature of an appropriate moral code might be.

Nor were there clear-cut lines of cleavage which might have provided a basis for an organized division between "right-thinking" persons and "wrong-thinking" persons. All had been heavily exposed to modern influences of various kinds. Even the aged had strongly ambivalent attitudes toward traditional values and ways of behaving. Had the only point in question been the relative position of the farmer and the agricultural laborer, development of organized conflict along class lines might have been expected. Similarly, had it been possible to express conflict in terms of two different castes, or in terms of a division within a single dominant caste, conflict might have followed clear lines of organization.

In fact, the main sources of conflict involved traditionally defined authority relationships. All of these relationships centered around the family head, and they were justified and supported by the same system of traditional belief. Therefore, the focus of possible conflict lay, not in relationships between subgroups, but in the relationships of husband and wife, older brother and younger brother, master and servant, and borrower and lender. When the individual in Namhalli looked about him in search of suitable persons to join him in the punishment of offenders, he found himself in opposition to the very persons whose support he counted upon. As a result, even though Namhalli was divided into two opposed factions, conflict within the factions was as frequent and as disruptive as conflict between the two factions. As a result, membership in the factions was subject to change.

Between July, 1952, and July, 1953, there were in Namhalli approximately six hundred persons, of whom about two hundred and fifty were too young or too old to participate actively in conflict. Within the group of active adults, there was persistent conflict. Field notes record serious new disputes between parents and older children in eight families; new disputes between adult brothers occurred in four families; and new disputes between husband and wife occurred in twenty families. Some of them were resolved through the use of traditional methods of arbitration, but the disputes resulted in seven cases of family division, eight cases of divorce, and one case of suicide. In addition, field notes record six public quarrels over land or property; eighteen public disputes between borrowers and lenders; and four disputes between master and servant. At least half of these disputes were unresolved, in the sense that they led to permanent enmity between the parties concerned. During the harvest season, minor thefts of grain, fruit, and agricultural equipment were an almost daily occurrence.

Beginning in July, 1952, there was a series of disputes between the two factions which continued intermittently through to August, 1953. Village-wide cooperation was observed upon three occasions: once when most of the able-bodied men in the village carried out a search for some thieves, who were not found; once when a man accused of attempted rape was publicly punished; and once when a group of men banded together to threaten the Bharati bus conductor, who was accused of stealing a package. All three cases of cooperation appear to have been stimulated by visible, outside threats to the safety and well-being of the village which could be dealt with immediately and violently. Village-wide ceremonies, formal adjudication of disputes, arrangements for fair distribution of irrigation water, and construction and repair of the drainage canals, cart roads and irrigation works were not carried out. Funds collected to build curbs along the main street of the village were stolen. Fruit trees were cut up for firewood by members of rival factions. The village deities were stolen and not replaced.

When an old man committed suicide in the well used for drinking water, no one would cooperate to clean it. (The well was constructed in 1941 through cooperative labor.) Uniformly, household heads explained their failure to cooperate by saying that any money collected would be stolen, and that others could not be counted upon to do their part because they were either too modern or too old-fashioned and hence immoral.

The two principal factions consisted of loose alliances of small groups of people, each assembled under the leadership of a particular influential individual. Sometimes the subgroups were nuclear or extended families; sometimes they were congeries of families held together by ties of caste, neighborhood, occupation, or education. The stability of the subgroups *within* the factions appeared to depend largely upon the success with which a particular leader could control and direct those who were tied to him by economic and kinship bonds.

The village Headman, one of the leaders of Faction A, had followers consisting of most of the members of his caste and family (fifty-five persons); only one important relative of the Headman was identified with Faction B. The Lingayat caste of agriculturalists (one hundred members) was divided into four or five subgroupings representing families with associated servants and friends. One of these families provided leadership for a major subgroup (perhaps fifty persons), consisting of a number of families from different castes. In the Spring of 1952, the leader of this major subgroup dropped a pending court case against the Headman, and joined with the Headman to form Faction A. Another small, but wealthy Lingayat family was originally linked with the major subgroup in Lingayat caste described above. In July, it joined Faction B, and then returned to Faction A in August. Other Lingayat families appeared to be distributed more or less equally between the two factions.

The Smith caste (forty-eight members) was identified with Faction B, although one member of the caste divorced his wife and joined Faction A. The Oil Merchants (fifteen members) had two families headed by brothers, one brother in each faction. Two sons of the brother belonging to Faction A joined Faction B after locking their father out of the house and threatening to cut off his head.

Almost all of the members of the conservative but relatively wealthy Shepherd caste, numbering over one hundred, belonged to Faction B. Two small families, said to contain the illegitimate children of the Lingayat leader of Faction A, were identified with Faction A. The Weavers and the Madiga laborers (one hundred and fifty persons) were economically handicapped and did not reveal their membership in factions; it appears likely that they were divided equally between the two factions. The fifty Muslims, all relatives, tended to assist Faction B. Other castes in the village were not of political or numerical importance. There were a fair number of neutrals or apparent neutrals among the Shepherds, Weavers, Madigas, and smaller castes; but there were no neutrals who were politically influential in the village.

A group of younger men from all of the castes listed above formed a group referred to as the "educated class." The nucleus of this group lay in Faction B, but at least five of its thirty members were in Faction A. There was also some connection between faction membership and neighborhood groupings, but this probably reflects the tendency of relatives to live close together. When relatives belonged to opposing factions, the neighborhood tended to harbor vigorous enmities.

The shifting and rather indeterminate nature of faction membership is consistent with the character of the major focii of factional disputes. Such disputes centered around the holding of a particular ceremony, decisions as to the order in which castes should participate in a particular ceremony, the cutting of a tree branch, or determining which individual should confiscate a thief's cart. Neither the nature of faction membership, nor the nature of factional dispute indicate any strongly felt desire to achieve any larger end. Engaging in conflict with the opposing faction to win power seemed an end in itself. Factional conflict was unproductive of clear victories or defeats. It generally resulted in substantial economic losses to both factions.

In July, 1953, toward the end of the first field trip to Namhalli, there seemed little likelihood of a cessation of existing conflicts. It appeared probable that factionalism would lead further down the road of community disorganization, perhaps toward a kind of spiritless anomie or perhaps toward participation in an emergent political or religious revitalization move-

ment. Without sweeping change there appeared to be no likelihood that the village would solve its economic problems, and
little likelihood that members of the village organization could
develop a workable system of authority or establish a consistent
relationship to the value systems of the various reference groups
influencing the village.

Effects of Changed Economic Conditions

A revisit to Namhalli in February, 1960, provided an opportunity to verify the predictions about the effects and course of
pervasive factionalism which had been observed in 1953. It
was immediately obvious that the economic condition of the
village had changed radically for the better. Houses were whitewashed, the approach road to the village had been improved,
and people in the village street wore an air of quiet self-satis-
faction. These changes could be attributed largely to the fact
that factories, which were on the drawing boards in 1953, and
which I had privately believed would never be built, had been
built. In 1953, only one man in the village was employed in a
factory; over fifteen men were employed in factories in 1960.
In fact, in 1960, very nearly one member of every nuclear family
was engaged in some kind of salaried employment.

In the field of social organization, factory workers had introduced a new device, the "chit fund" which made indirect cooperation possible. To form a chit fund, a sum of money is
collected from any source. This sum is auctioned monthly to
whoever is willing to pay the highest rate of interest. Return
of the auctioned funds is guaranteed by compelling the borrower to sign a promissory note. Although some chit funds are
merely profit-making affairs for which shares are sold, five of
the chit funds in operation during February, 1960, were for
cooperative projects. There were two funds for the rebuilding
of temples and the replacement of stolen gods. There was one
fund for the holding of a village ceremony; one fund for a
group pilgrimage; and one fund to take the school children on
a motorbus tour of neighboring Madras State. The importance
of these funds is that they introduce bookkeeping, voting, and

other urban organizational devices into the village, and make possible cooperative effort without unanimous agreement.

Capital made available by salaried employment and by chit funds has enabled Namhalli's agriculturalists to invest in increasing amounts of chemical fertilizer and in expensive orchard and garden crops. One man has invested over five hundred dollars to prepare a one-acre grape orchard; in four years he expects to make an *annual* profit of over five hundred dollars. These are enormous sums in a region where a day's supply of food costs less than fifteen cents.

The impact of salaried employment upon the value systems of Namhalli was to shift the individual from ambivalent identification with ill-defined urban reference groups toward actual participation in government offices and factories. In particular, the factory laborer commuting daily to work in a modern motorbus provided by the government had become a person of political and economic importance. Even Head Constables in the police force spoke respectfully to the factory laborer. One of the first remarks made to the field worker when he returned to the village in 1960 was, "We know now that it is dark in your country when the sun is shining here because our factory manager telephones to New York." In other words, "we accept your urban belief system." While the village contained five persons who had attended high school in 1953, every child was in school in 1960; and a high school education, essential to factory employment, was an accepted goal for all.

Namhalli's rapid acceptance of a wide range of urban beliefs, values, and practices can be explained in part by the fact that urban values have been available for a considerable period of time, and by the basic traditional belief that success is a reward of virtue. Although it cannot be said with certainty that factionalism no longer exists in Namhalli, it is clear that cooperation is now taking place with increased frequency, and that a measure of agreement has been reached concerning acceptable values and practices. What was evidently required to reverse the tendency toward conflict within the village was the introduction of new superordinate goals *and* of a practical means of reaching the new goals. The basic change which took place between 1953 and 1960 was the presentation of a practical means of solving the economic difficulties of the village.

Concluding Remarks

In this discussion of factionalism in Namhalli and of the aftermath of factionalism, the movement of a village through several periods of its history has been considered. The cultural tradition of Namhalli has been described as a system established within a particular milieu. A correlation has been suggested between certain recurrent stresses existing within the milieu and patterns of strain and conflict within the social organization of Namhalli. It was also indicated that there is evidence that the traditional culture of Namhalli was free of unregulated or escalating conflicts of sufficient severity to disrupt normal patterns of cooperative activity.

The development of disruptive and unregulated conflict within Namhalli has been traced to the interaction between a particular configuration of "modern influences" and the pattern of strain characteristic of Namhalli. One of the effects of the new stress was to weaken traditional mechanisms for resolving conflict and developing cooperative activity. Observations carried out in 1960 support the idea that conflict in the village stemmed from the insolvability of the new stress and from the weakening of traditional mechanisms of social organization. Reduction of the previously observed conflict appears to have been connected with economic prosperity and the introduction of new forms of social organization centering around the chit fund.

References

Gluckman, M., 1955. *Custom and conflict in Africa.* London, Oxford University Press.

North, R. C., H. E. Koch, Jr., and Dina A. Zinnes, 1960. The integrative functions of conflict. *Conflict Resolution,* 4, 355–374.

Sherif, M., and Carolyn W. Sherif, 1953. *Groups in harmony and tension.* New York, Harper.

Siegel, B. J., and A. R. Beals, 1960a. Pervasive factionalism. *Amer. Anthropologist,* 62, 394–417.

——, 1960b. Conflict and factionalist dispute. *J. Royal anthropol. Inst.,* 90, 107–117.

FACTIONALISM AS A PROCESS
OF SOCIAL AND CULTURAL CHANGE
(WITH SPECIAL REFERENCE
TO ALAN R. BEALS' CHAPTER)

by Norman A. Chance

One of the key theoretical problems facing many social scientists today is that of reconciling the structural-functional approach of sociologists and social anthropologists with the cultural process approach held by many ethnologists and historians. While the former conceptual frame of reference has provided a wealth of testable hypotheses, the theoretical model has usually been limited to an essentially "flat" time scale. The great dilemma of the structural-functionalists has been the time dimension. For the cultural historian, on the other hand, time has not been the problem, but an adequate theoretical interpretation. Although a number of unilateral theories have been suggested to explain the process of change, including those of the biological, geographical, economic, political, social, and cultural determinists, none of these theories in themselves has been completely adequate to account for the many similarities and divergencies in human growth and development. If, however, a multi-variable approach is taken, in which the process of any given change is seen as dependent on a series of intervening factors, much of the weakness of the earlier theories can be resolved.

But how can we combine the structure and process approaches? If we accept the premise that "the only thing constant is change itself," we are also bound to accept the corollary that any sociocultural system is constantly changing. The rate may be minimal, due perhaps to cultural "drift"; or it may be maximal, as when the members of one society are completely assimilated by the members of another; but it is never static. What we often call "social structures" within this context, would actually be *recurring processes* which take place with a relatively high degree of regularity. *Directional processes*, on the other hand, would be those which bring about an accumulative change in the social and cultural system.* The latter has been the traditional area of interest for many ethnologists and historians. By finding a common denominator for structure and process in recurring and directional processes, it is possible to make a theoretical analysis which capitalizes on the insights of both approaches.

Let us apply this conceptual frame of reference to Alan Beals' stimulating chapter, "Pervasive Factionalism in a South Indian Village." Beals' study is particularly helpful in this regard, in that he provides us with an essentially structural account of an Indian village over a long period of time.

In this analysis I would like to focus major attention on three sets of variables: (1) *technology and environment;* (2) *the social structure;* and (3) *the cultural-value system* (including religious values). Implied in this choice is the assumption that these are the three most significant sets of factors influencing both recurring and directional processes of change in the South Indian village of Namhalli.

We may begin a discussion of the traditional village profile by first noting that the village was continually faced with a series of essentially unresolvable problems or "stresses," including those of crop failure, labor problems in obtaining seasonal laborers and bullocks, poor health due to a number of severe epidemics and poor nutrition, underpopulation combined with a good deal of unworked land, and external attacks by hostile outsiders. As Beals clearly pointed out, many of these recurring stresses could have been resolved, given an increased amount of technological knowledge and resources. But due to the limited technology and control over the environment, solutions and "explanations" for these continuing problems could only be provided by the *social* and *cultural* system (including in the latter, religious and other values). The cultural traditions did

---

* For further amplification of this concept, see: Evon Z. Vogt, 1960. On the concepts of structure and process in cultural anthropology, *Amer. Anthropologist*, 62, 18–33.

not provide completely adequate solutions, however, and also presented a number of "strains" and inconsistencies, such as:

1. An inconsistent belief system whereby an individual was asked to withdraw from the world of illusion (i.e., sense impressions) and at the same time participate in it.

2. A rigid caste system which limited an individual's creative potential.

3. A preferred marriage pattern which was inconsistent with caste requirements.

4. Dominant-submissive conflicts in patterns of authority and marriage.

5. Segmental type of village organization and potential conflict between castes.

6. A class of outsiders (wives) living in the village.

While these conflicts or "strains" could not be prevented, the culturally approved judicial, social, and religious sanctions did appear adequate to control them. Furthermore, the value placed on village harmony and unity (brought about through fear of famine, hostile outside attack, etc.) effectively limited overt manifestations of conflict.

In essence, the social structure and cultural-belief system together provided a generally effective—though imperfect—solution to a series of problems which could not be resolved by available technological resources. Here, then, the relatively adequate integration of the *technological, social,* and *cultural* systems in providing solutions to problems of village life, help to explain the dominance of "recurring" processes of change.

Then, with the influx of English and urban Indian technology and thought, a number of dramatic changes took place. These new changes were predominantly "directional" processes in that they brought about an accumulative change in the community. Some of the most immediate and obvious changes occurred in the technological-environmental sphere:

1. Many serious epidemics were controlled by new medicines, thereby affecting the illness and death rate.

2. Roads and irrigation works were constructed.

3. Crops were favorably affected by new irrigation systems.

4. More land was made available for agricultural purposes.

In other words, many of the traditionally unresolved technological and environmental problems were removed, which in
turn disrupted the previous balance between the technological,
social, and cultural systems. Given this new imbalance, a number of other changes were generated—suggesting that one of
the more common internal sources of directional change in any
society is found in the unevenness between its various segments.
Beals' study has shown, for example, that many of the sanctions
supporting traditional village life in Namhalli were based on a
need for community unity due to the ever-present threat of
famine, outside threats, and so on. Once these earlier unresolved problems disappeared, the traditional sanctions lost
much of their effectiveness. This fact, combined with the continuation of "strains" in the social and cultural sphere no doubt
set the stage for more *overt* conflict irrespective of the change
in patterns of authority.

However, predispositions to directional processes of change
were also encouraged by major changes in the social structure.
Examples include the new land tenure and taxation systems that
were introduced, the introduction of a western type of judicial
system with the resultant loss of traditional patterns of local
authority and social control, the new government policies which
favored some caste groups at the expense of others, and the new
modern public school.

Given these technological and social structural changes, and
the fact that the village possessed no single dominant caste or
well-established source of income, it is hardly surprising that
factions developed. But to complete the analysis, we must also
take into account the value system. It appears from the study
of Namhalli that changes in the value system lagged behind
those in the technological and social sphere. This cultural lag
is evident in the following examples:

1. The rejection of outside judicial authority and external
police control.

2. Continuation of the belief that widows should not inherit
their husband's property.

3. The view that much of the village crisis was related to the
breakdown of harmonious relationships due to a rise in immorality, disobedience, and selfishness.

These and other examples suggest that there was an important discrepancy between the speed and extent of technological, social, and cultural (i.e., value) change, and furthermore, that this very discrepancy played a major role in encouraging the type of "pervasive factionalism" described by Beals in his study. Also to be noted is the fact that most of the technological and social structural changes were externally introduced. Cultural values, on the other hand, are an internal matter and can seldom be changed by means of external coercion.

Given these factors we may ask: Under what conditions are we most likely to find a reduction of village factionalism? It would be possible, of course, for Namhalli values to remain relatively stable and the technological and social structural aspects of community life to revert back to their previous pattern. However, since these changes were for the most part externally introduced and reflected a major innovation occurring throughout much of India, this is highly unlikely.

A second alternative, and one which the villagers themselves could bring about, would be to change their value system in such a way as to make it more compatible with the technological and social structural changes noted above. In this manner, the gap between the three sets of variables would be narrowed.

This choice, however, has its attendant problems. Since values are ideas involving preferential interest, they usually relate to some particular goal. If, for example, the goal is unattainable, the resulting frustrations may be more disruptive than if the values had remained unchanged. And this, of course, is exactly what happened. With the increased village prosperity fostered by World War II, came higher aspirations for material goods and services—a partial change in the value system. It was not a complete change, however, since the response to the loss of income following the war was couched in traditional value terms. As Beals stated in his chapter: ". . . the explanation for the failure of the village to meet the crisis from the loss of wartime prosperity was to be found in the breakdown of harmonious relationships within the village. To most people, the unhappy state of affairs was due, not to external threats, but to a rise in immorality, disobedience, and selfishness within the village."

In numerous studies of cultural change, anthropologists and other social scientists have shown that when the aspirations of a group of people change *without* a corresponding culturally approved means of attainment, various forms of deviant behavior and factionalism tend to arise. This fact certainly influenced the amount of factionalism in Namhalli. But the problem was compounded by using traditional cultural beliefs to explain events which occurred following the initial rise in level of aspirations. In this instance, then, we not only have an example of incompatibility between the social and cultural spheres, but within the cultural system itself. It is hardly surprising, therefore, that when Beals completed his initial study in 1953, he foresaw little hope for any reduction in pervasive factionalism in Namhalli. Where values did change, the accompanying goals were not attained. Where they did not change, they remained incompatible with the new technological and social structural systems.

The fact that Beals returned to Namhalli in 1960 and found factionalism no longer immediately apparent in the village—that, in fact, village cooperation was steadily increasing—offers the clearest possible example of why we need more long-term studies of cultural process and change. It also supports the hypothesis that increased compatibility between the technological, social, and cultural systems in any given community will increase the degree of community cooperation and integration. For in a period of seven years, there appears to have been a major shift in Namhalli value orientations, toward increased identification with modern urban Indian culture. Behavioral examples of this new identification include the tremendous new interest in formal school education, participation in the new economic opportunities made available by the construction of local factories, village contribution of funds to send school children on a bus tour of the neighboring state of Madras, and expressions of interest in the outside world.

In summary, these and other examples given in Beals' chapter suggest that the present value system is becoming much more closely integrated with the new social structural system; that the increased cultural identification with urban India has diminished the conflict brought about by the previous introduction of land tenure, taxation, external judicial authority, and other social innovations. While the recent increases in economic opportunities available to the local villagers has provided them with an opportunity to participate in this new world, the actual decisions to participate necessitated an important change in the value system.

It should also be mentioned that given a serious conflict in the internal structure of a social system, such as the breakdown of traditional patterns of authority in Namhalli, factionalism can have a creative influence in that it can provide an important avenue for new leaders to emerge; it can provide an opportunity for more opinions and sentiments to be openly expressed; and it can provide more flexibility in the search for solutions to the new problems. But these insights are seldom attained from a short term study. If we are to have anywhere near complete understanding of factionalism or any other type of intergroup phenomena, we must study not only the structure but also the process of change in these phenomena.

NAME INDEX

SUBJECT INDEX

279